Billions

Fortunes Made and Lost

J.F. Hughes

Copyright and Legal Disclaimer

Copyright Notice

Legal Disclaimer and Important Notices

General Disclaimer

This book is designed to provide information and analysis about the lives and fortunes of notable billionaires throughout history. It is sold with the understanding that the publisher and author are not engaged in rendering legal, accounting, investment, tax, or other professional services. If professional advice or other expert assistance is required, the services of a competent professional should be sought.

The author and publisher specifically disclaim any responsibility for any liability, loss, or risk, personal or otherwise, which is incurred as a consequence, directly or indirectly, of the use and application of any of the contents of this book.

Accuracy of Information

Every effort has been made to ensure the accuracy of the information presented in this book. The author has conducted extensive research using publicly available sources, including but not limited to: published biographies, financial records, court documents, news reports, academic studies, and historical archives.

However, information about wealth, particularly historical wealth comparisons, involves estimates and approximations. Net worth figures, especially those adjusted for inflation or expressed as percentages of historical GDP, should be understood as approximate rather than precise calculations. Different methodologies can produce different results.

The publisher and author make no representations or warranties with respect to the accuracy or completeness of the contents of this work and specifically disclaim all warranties, including without limitation warranties of fitness for a particular purpose. The information contained in this book is accurate to the best of the author's knowledge as of the publication date but may be subject to change.

Investment Disclaimer

THIS BOOK IS NOT INVESTMENT ADVICE. Nothing in this book should be construed as a recommendation to buy, sell, or hold any security, investment, or asset. The analysis of how billionaires built their fortunes is provided for educational and informational purposes only.

Past performance of investments or business strategies discussed in this book is not indicative of future results. The fact that certain individuals achieved extraordinary wealth through particular strategies does not mean those strategies will work for others or will continue to work in the future.

Readers should consult with qualified financial advisors, accountants, and legal professionals before making any investment or business decisions. The author and publisher are not responsible for any financial losses incurred by readers who attempt to replicate strategies discussed in this book.

No Endorsement

The inclusion of any individual, company, product, or organization in this book does not constitute an endorsement by the author or publisher. Similarly, analysis or criticism of individuals, companies, or practices does not constitute legal accusations or determinations of wrongdoing beyond those already established by courts of law.

References to living individuals are based on publicly available information and should not be construed as personal attacks or defamatory statements. The author has made good-faith efforts to present balanced, factual accounts based on available evidence.

Historical and Factual Analysis

This book presents historical and contemporary analysis of wealth creation and destruction. The interpretation of events, the drawing of connections between patterns, and the analysis of causes and effects represent the author's perspective based on research and should be understood as analytical interpretation rather than absolute fact.

Where individuals have been convicted of crimes in courts of law, this book presents those convictions as established facts. Where individuals have not been convicted but have faced allegations or criticism, this book attempts to present multiple perspectives and allow readers to draw their own conclusions.

Fair Use and Attribution

This book contains quotations from and references to various published sources, all used in accordance with fair use provisions of copyright law for purposes of criticism, comment, news reporting, teaching, scholarship, and research.

All efforts have been made to properly attribute sources and provide citations where appropriate. Any omissions or errors in attribution are unintentional, and the publisher will correct them in subsequent editions upon notification.

Privacy and Public Figures

The individuals discussed in this book are public figures whose lives and business activities have been extensively documented in public records, media coverage, court documents, and other publicly available sources. The information presented about them is drawn from these public sources.

The author respects privacy rights and has focused on publicly available information relevant to understanding wealth creation and business activities. Personal information not relevant to the book's themes has been omitted.

Case Studies and Examples

Where this book discusses business strategies, innovations, or practices, these are presented as historical examples and analysis, not as recommendations or instructions. Business, legal, and regulatory environments change over time. What was legal or effective in one era may not be in another.

Liability Limitation

To the maximum extent permitted by applicable law, the author and publisher shall not be liable for any direct, indirect, incidental, special, consequential, or punitive damages arising out of or relating to the use of or inability to use the information contained in this book.

Research Limitations

While extensive research has been conducted for this book, certain limitations exist:

- Some historical records are incomplete or contradictory
- Private financial information is not publicly available for many individuals
- Wealth estimates, particularly historical ones, involve assumptions and approximations
- Information about living individuals continues to evolve after publication
- Access to certain archives, documents, or sources may have been limited

Readers should understand these limitations when evaluating the information presented.

Updates and Corrections

Information about living individuals and current economic conditions continues to evolve. While this book is accurate as of its publication date, subsequent events may change or contradict information presented here.

Educational Purpose

This book is intended for educational and informational purposes. It is designed to provide insight into economic history, business strategy, and the dynamics of wealth creation, not to provide specific guidance for individual financial, legal, or business decisions.

By reading this book, you acknowledge that you have read, understood, and agree to be bound by this disclaimer.

Table of Contents

Introduction

In 1324, Mansa Musa, emperor of Mali, set out on a pilgrimage to Mecca with an entourage so lavish it defied comprehension. Sixty thousand men accompanied him. Eighty camels carried two tons of gold each. He distributed so much wealth along the route that he crashed the economy of Cairo for a decade, causing inflation that took years to correct. Historians estimate his personal wealth at over $400 billion in today's money, making him arguably the richest person who has ever lived.

Seven hundred years later, in November 2022, Sam Bankman-Fried watched his $26 billion fortune evaporate in seventy-two hours. The cryptocurrency exchange he'd built, FTX, collapsed after revelations that he'd been using customer deposits to fund risky bets. Within months, he went from being featured on magazine covers as the future of finance to being sentenced to twenty-five years in federal prison for fraud. The rise took three years; the fall took three days.

Between these two extremes, Mansa Musa's golden caravans crossing the Sahara and SBF's crypto empire collapsing in real-time on Twitter lies the entire spectrum of human ambition, innovation, luck, hubris, and catastrophe that defines the story of extraordinary wealth. This book is about the people who have accumulated fortunes so vast they seem to transcend normal human scale, and about what those fortunes reveal about capitalism, human nature, and the societies that produce such extreme inequality.

Why Billionaires Matter

The study of billionaires is not simply celebrity gossip or aspirational fantasy. Understanding how extreme fortunes are built and lost teaches us fundamental lessons about economics, technology, psychology, and power. Billionaires are not just rich people, they are individuals who have accumulated wealth sufficient to shape markets, influence governments, fund scientific research, build institutions, and affect the lives of millions or even billions of people.

When John D. Rockefeller controlled 90 percent of America's oil refining capacity, his business decisions determined whether factories ran, whether homes were heated, whether transportation systems functioned. When Bill Gates achieved near-monopoly in computer operating systems, he shaped how billions of people would interact with technology. When Jeff Bezos built Amazon into a dominant retail and cloud computing platform, he transformed how goods move through the economy and how digital infrastructure operates. These individuals wielded power comparable to nation-states, yet they were accountable primarily to their shareholders rather than to voters.

The concentration of wealth in individual hands also reveals deeper truths about economic systems. In theory, competitive capitalism should prevent anyone from accumulating truly extreme wealth, competition should drive profits toward zero, and value should be broadly distributed among many participants. The existence of billionaires, particularly on the scale we see today, suggests that markets are not as competitive as economic theory predicts. Monopolistic tendencies, network effects, regulatory capture, and winner-take-all dynamics create conditions where a few individuals capture outsized shares of economic value.

Moreover, billionaires serve as case studies in human psychology under extreme conditions. What happens to ambition, relationships, and sense of purpose when money ceases to be a constraint? What does unlimited wealth reveal about character, both its virtues and its flaws? The lives of billionaires are natural experiments in what human beings become when normal limitations are removed.

The Arc of This Book

The twenty-five chapters that follow trace the history of extraordinary wealth from medieval merchant princes to modern tech titans, examining both spectacular successes and catastrophic failures. The structure is roughly chronological, divided into six parts that correspond to different eras and patterns of wealth creation.

Part I: The Early Titans explores wealth creation from ancient times through the nineteenth century. Here we meet Mansa Musa with his legendary gold, the Rothschild banking dynasty that financed European governments, and the American robber barons, Rockefeller, Carnegie and Vanderbilt who built industrial empires through methods both innovative and ruthless. These chapters establish foundational patterns, the importance of monopolistic control, the role of technological change in creating opportunities, and the complex relationship between wealth accumulation and philanthropy.

Part II: The Industrial Age Moguls examines billionaires from 1900 through the 1970s. Henry Ford revolutionized manufacturing with the assembly line while harboring troubling political views. J. Paul Getty became the richest man in the world while installing pay phones for guests and refusing to pay ransom for his kidnapped grandson. Howard Hughes built aircraft and bought casinos before descending into paranoia and isolation. Sam Walton created the world's largest retailer while driving a pickup truck and living modestly. These stories reveal how personality, brilliance and dysfunction alike shapes the trajectory of fortunes.

Part III: The Tech Revolution covers the explosion of wealth created by personal computing, software, and the internet from the 1980s through the 2000s. Bill Gates built Microsoft into a monopoly before transforming into a philanthropist. Steve Jobs revolutionized multiple industries before dying too young to see his full legacy. The Google founders organized the world's information and struggled with the tension between idealism and power. These chapters explore how technology created unprecedented wealth concentration through network effects and winner-take-all dynamics.

Part IV: The Modern Titans examines today's wealthiest individuals. Jeff Bezos built Amazon from an online bookstore into an "everything store" and saw his marriage end in the largest divorce settlement in history. Elon Musk bet everything on electric cars and reusable rockets, nearly went bankrupt, and emerged as the world's richest person before his volatility tanked his wealth again. Mark Zuckerberg connected billions through Facebook while grappling with the unintended consequences of social media. Warren Buffett became the oracle of value investing while living in the same modest house for decades. These stories show how modern billionaires navigate celebrity, responsibility, and the challenges of operating at global scale.

Part V: The Cautionary Tales shifts focus to fortunes lost through fraud, hubris, and catastrophic judgment. Elizabeth Holmes's Theranos promised revolutionary blood testing but delivered only lies. Bernie Madoff ran a $65 billion Ponzi scheme for decades before being caught and dying in prison. Sam Bankman-Fried built a cryptocurrency empire in three years and destroyed it in three days. These chapters remind us that not all billionaires earned their fortunes legitimately, and that even legitimate fortunes can vanish through miscalculation or malfeasance.

Part VI: Patterns, Principles, and Perspectives synthesizes lessons from all the previous chapters. What are the common threads across centuries of wealth creation? What can money actually buy, and what remains forever beyond its reach? What does the future hold for billionaires as we face questions about artificial intelligence, wealth inequality, and social stability? These final chapters move from specific stories to broader analysis, asking not just how billionaires are made but whether they should exist at all.

What This Book Is Not

Before going further, it's worth establishing what this book does not attempt to do.

This is not a how-to guide for becoming a billionaire. While the patterns we identify might be instructive for entrepreneurs and investors, the primary goal is understanding rather than replication. Moreover, the honest truth is that becoming a billionaire requires not just strategy and execution but also extraordinary luck, timing, and circumstances that cannot be engineered.

This is not hagiography. While some billionaires have made genuine contributions to society through innovation, job creation, and philanthropy, others have caused enormous harm through fraud, exploitation, and monopolistic practices. We examine both the achievements and the failures, the brilliance and the moral compromises, without either demonizing or lionizing our subjects.

This is not economic theory. While we draw on concepts from economics, sociology, and psychology, this is fundamentally a work of narrative nonfiction. The goal is to tell compelling human stories that illustrate broader principles rather than to construct formal theoretical arguments.

This is not a screed against capitalism or wealth. While we critically examine how extreme fortunes are built and the social consequences of wealth concentration, we also acknowledge the innovations, efficiencies, and genuine value creation that have accompanied many of these fortunes. The relationship between capitalism, innovation, and inequality is complex, and this book attempts to honor that complexity rather than reduce it to simple condemnation or celebration.

The Questions That Drive This Exploration

Throughout these pages, several fundamental questions recur:

What role does individual genius play versus historical timing and luck? Were these people extraordinary, or were they simply in the right place at the right time? Could John D. Rockefeller have become a billionaire if he'd been born fifty years earlier or later? Would Bill Gates have achieved his success without his mother's connection to IBM?

How do personality traits both build and destroy fortunes? What made these individuals willing to take enormous risks when others played it safe? How did obsessiveness, ruthlessness, charm, or paranoia shape their trajectories? Why do some billionaires die alone and unhappy despite their wealth while others find meaning and purpose?

What is the relationship between private enrichment and public good? When Andrew Carnegie built libraries, was he giving back to society or laundering a reputation built on exploitation? When Bill Gates fights malaria, does it justify Microsoft's monopolistic practices? Can extreme wealth concentration and broadly shared prosperity coexist, or are they fundamentally in tension?

What does extreme wealth reveal about human nature? Do people change when money ceases to be a constraint, or does wealth simply reveal character that was always there? Why do some billionaires remain humble while others become megalomaniacs? What psychological needs drive people to continue accumulating wealth long after they have more than they could ever spend?

How should societies respond to extreme wealth concentration? Should billionaires exist at all? If so, what obligations come with great wealth? What combination of taxation, regulation, philanthropy, and social norms produces the best outcomes for society?

These questions don't have simple answers. Different chapters will suggest different perspectives. Some billionaires seem to validate capitalism's promise of rewarding innovation and risk-taking. Others reveal its capacity for exploitation and monopolistic abuse. Some used their fortunes to improve the world. Others squandered them or destroyed lives in accumulating them.

A Note on Numbers and Comparisons

Comparing wealth across centuries presents methodological challenges. How do you compare Mansa Musa's gold in 1324 to Jeff Bezos's Amazon stock in 2024? We've made efforts to present wealth figures in inflation-adjusted terms or as percentages of contemporary GDP where meaningful comparisons are possible. But readers should understand that these comparisons are approximate rather than precise.

Similarly, the line between "millionaire," "multi-millionaire," and "billionaire" has shifted dramatically over time. In John D. Rockefeller's era, being worth a billion dollars (roughly $25 billion today) was almost unimaginable wealth. Today, there are over 2,500 billionaires globally, and the richest individuals are worth more than $100 billion. The scale has changed even as the dynamics of wealth creation show remarkable continuity.

We've generally focused on individuals who reached or exceeded roughly $1 billion in net worth adjusted for their era, though some chapters examine people who were merely very rich rather than ultra-rich because their stories illuminate important patterns.

The Promise and Peril of This Moment

We live in an extraordinary time for both wealth creation and wealth concentration. The richest individuals today are wealthier in absolute and relative terms than at almost any point in history. Technology has created opportunities for fortune-building at speed and scale that previous generations couldn't imagine. A company can go from startup to global dominance in years rather than decades. A single product can reach billions of users. The potential rewards for success have never been higher.

At the same time, this extreme concentration has created social, political, and economic tensions that threaten stability. Wealth inequality in many countries exceeds levels seen during the Gilded Age. Trust in institutions has declined. Political polarization has increased. The sense that the system is rigged in favor of the wealthy has moved from fringe complaint to mainstream concern.

We stand at a potential inflection point. The forces that have created today's billionaires, technological change, globalization, network effects and financialization continue to accelerate. But political movements questioning whether such extreme concentration should be allowed are also growing. The question of whether we'll see the first trillionaire competes with the question of whether democratic societies will tolerate billionaires at all.

Understanding how we got here, how these extraordinary fortunes were built, what they reveal about economic systems and human nature, what they've contributed to society and what damage they've caused is essential for deciding where we go next.

An Invitation to Think Differently About Wealth

This book is ultimately an invitation to think more deeply and critically about wealth, power, and what we value as a society. The lives chronicled here are exceptional in their outcomes but reveal universal human dynamics: ambition and greed, innovation and exploitation, generosity and selfishness, brilliance and delusion.

By understanding these extreme cases, we better understand ourselves. Most of us will never face the choices that confront billionaires, but we face analogous choices at different scales: How do we balance personal enrichment with social responsibility? How do we handle success without losing our humanity? How do we use whatever resources we have, time, money and influence to create meaning and contribute to something larger than ourselves?

The billionaires in these pages made different choices and reached different conclusions. Some died alone despite their wealth. Others found purpose in giving it away. Some created genuine innovation that improved lives. Others committed fraud that destroyed lives. Some maintained their humanity; others lost it. Their stories are not just about money, they're about what it means to be human when normal constraints are removed and fundamental questions about purpose, meaning, and responsibility can no longer be avoided.

The fortunes made and lost in these pages are measures not just of wealth but of human ambition, creativity, folly, and consequence. They are mirrors that reflect both the promise and the peril of the economic systems we've built and the choices we face about what kind of society we want to become.

Welcome to the world of billionaires. These are their stories and ours.

PART I: THE EARLY TITANS (Ancient Times - 19th Century)

Chapter 1

Mansa Musa - The Golden King

In 1324, a caravan departed from the West African empire of Mali that would fundamentally alter the global economy. Stretching for miles across the Saharan sands, this was no ordinary merchant expedition. It consisted of 60,000 men, including 12,000 slaves dressed in Persian silk, military escorts, advisors, entertainers, and officials from the royal court. Five hundred slaves walked ahead of the procession, each carrying a golden staff weighing approximately four pounds. Eighty camels followed, each bearing between 50 and 300 pounds of pure gold dust.

At the center of this extraordinary display was Mansa Musa, the emperor of Mali, on his way to fulfill the religious obligation of hajj, the pilgrimage to Mecca that every able Muslim is called to make once in their lifetime. But this would be no simple act of devotion. By the time his journey concluded, Musa would have spent or given away so much gold that he would destabilize the economies of every region he passed through, causing a gold market depression that would last more than a decade.

Economists and historians, when adjusting for inflation and attempting to compare wealth across vastly different economic systems, estimate Mansa Musa's fortune at somewhere between $400 billion and $600 billion in today's currency. Some argue the number could be even higher, perhaps incalculable making him not just a billionaire, but arguably the wealthiest individual in human history. His story reveals how geography, resources, timing, and strategic control of trade routes could create wealth on a scale that even modern tech titans struggle to match.

The Source of Unimaginable Wealth

To understand how one man accumulated such staggering wealth in the 14th century, we must first understand the geography and economics of medieval West Africa. Mali was blessed or cursed, depending on one's perspective with natural resources that the rest of the world desperately craved.

Gold was the foundation of Musa's empire. The empire of Mali controlled approximately half of the world's known gold supply during the 14th century. Massive gold deposits lay beneath the soil of regions like Bambuk and Bure, territories firmly within Malian control. But Musa didn't simply dig gold from the ground and sell it. His true genius lay in his monopolistic control of the gold trade network.

In medieval Africa, gold was extracted through sophisticated mining operations that contradicted European assumptions about African "primitiveness." Miners would dig deep shafts into the earth, using complex ventilation systems to work underground. Surface mining along riverbeds supplemented the deeper operations. The gold was then transported along carefully guarded trade routes to markets in North Africa, where it fed into trade networks stretching to Europe, the Middle East, and beyond.

Musa's control was absolute. He didn't need to mine every ounce of gold himself; he simply controlled access to it. Any gold that left Mali did so with his permission and, more importantly, with his profit. This was horizontal integration in its medieval form, control not through owning every mine, but through political and military power that made alternative trade routes impossible.

But gold was only half the equation. Mali's other great resource was salt, specifically the massive salt deposits of Taghaza in the northern reaches of the empire. In the scorching climate of West Africa, salt was not a luxury but a biological necessity. It preserved food, maintained health, and served as currency in many transactions. The slabs of salt mined at Taghaza were so valuable that they were literally worth their weight in gold in some markets.

Musa controlled both ends of this equation, the gold-producing regions in the south and the salt mines in the north. This allowed him to dominate the most lucrative trade dynamic in West Africa, exchanging salt from the north for gold from the south, and profiting magnificently on both ends. Some historians have noted that in certain markets, the exchange rate could reach 1:1, one pound of salt for one pound of gold, a testament to just how valuable salt was in the right market.

This dual monopoly on gold and salt created a self-reinforcing cycle of wealth. Gold brought international traders to Mali, who needed salt to survive their journeys and to trade in West African markets. Musa's empire provided both, extracting maximum value at every transaction. It was an economic position so dominant that it would be comparable to a single entity today controlling both the world's oil reserves and its fresh water supply.

The Empire of Mali: More Than Gold

Mansa Musa inherited an already powerful empire when he took the throne around 1312, but he would expand it significantly during his 25-year reign. Mali at its height under Musa stretched from the Atlantic coast to the interior of West Africa, encompassing territory that today includes parts of Mali, Mauritania, Senegal, Gambia, Guinea, Burkina Faso, Niger, Nigeria, and Chad. Governing this vast territory required more than military might; it demanded administrative sophistication.

The empire was organized into provinces, each governed by appointed officials who reported to the mansa (emperor). A complex system of laws maintained order, with the Malian empire following Islamic legal traditions while also incorporating local customs. Property rights were respected, contracts enforced, and a degree of security maintained that made trade possible across vast distances, no small feat in an era when banditry could destroy commercial networks.

Musa inherited this system from his predecessor, Abu-Bakr II, in unusual circumstances. According to the account of the Syrian historian Al-Umari, who interviewed Malian officials decades later, Abu-Bakr II became obsessed with exploring the Atlantic Ocean. He outfitted a fleet of 200 boats filled with men, women, food, and gold, sending them west to discover what lay beyond the ocean. Only one boat returned, reporting that the ships had been swept away by a powerful current.

Undeterred, Abu-Bakr II commissioned an even larger fleet of 2,000 vessels and set out himself, leaving Musa as his deputy. Abu-Bakr II never returned. Whether this account is entirely true remains debated, some historians view it as legend, others as evidence of pre-Columbian African exploration of the Americas. Regardless, Musa found himself emperor of the wealthiest kingdom in Africa.

Under Musa's rule, Mali became not just an economic powerhouse but a center of learning and culture. The emperor himself was educated and literate in Arabic, unusual for a monarch of his era even in the Islamic world. He understood that lasting power required more than gold, it required legitimacy, education, and cultural achievement.

The Journey That Changed History

The hajj of 1324 was Musa's opportunity to announce Mali's and his own significance to the wider Islamic world. Medieval Mali was peripheral to the major Islamic centers of Cairo, Damascus, Baghdad, and Mecca. It was known for gold, but viewed as a distant frontier. Musa intended to change that perception forever.

The numbers associated with his pilgrimage are staggering even by contemporary standards. Historical sources vary, but most agree on the core elements: approximately 60,000 people in the caravan, 12,000 of whom were personal slaves of the emperor, each dressed in silk and carrying golden staffs. Eighty to 100 camels, each loaded with 300 pounds of gold dust. Herald riders went ahead of the procession, announcing the emperor's approach and distributing gold to the poor.

The journey from Mali to Mecca covered approximately 2,700 miles and took over a year, following ancient trade routes across the Sahara Desert to Cairo, then across the Sinai Peninsula to Arabia. Every Friday the Muslim holy day Musa would commission the construction of a mosque in whatever location the caravan found itself. By some accounts, he built a mosque for every Friday of his journey, creating a trail of architectural monuments across North Africa.

But it was in Cairo where Musa made his most memorable and economically devastating impression. Egypt in 1324 was ruled by the Mamluk Sultanate, a powerful military regime that controlled one of the wealthiest regions in the Islamic world. Cairo was a sophisticated city of hundreds of thousands, a center of trade and learning that dwarfed anything in West Africa. Musa arrived with the intention of demonstrating that Mali was Egypt's equal, if not its superior.

The emperor stayed in Cairo for three months, and during that time, he spent and gave away gold with abandon that shocked even the wealthy merchants of Egypt. He made gifts to the poor, to religious scholars, to Mamluk officials, and to anyone who approached him with a request. He purchased goods at inflated prices, paying in gold dust without haggling. His entourage, following their emperor's example, spent lavishly on souvenirs, supplies, and luxuries.

Al-Umari, writing twelve years after Musa's visit, recorded interviews with Cairenes who still remembered the emperor's stay. One noted that Musa had brought so much gold that "the people of Egypt earned incalculable sums." Another observed that the emperor was "a young man with a brown complexion, a pleasant face, and good figure," who was "generous and virtuous."

But generosity has economic consequences. By flooding Cairo's markets with gold, Musa inadvertently triggered severe inflation followed by deflation. The value of gold in Cairo plummeted by approximately 10-25% depending on the source, and it would take more than a decade for the market to recover. This might be the only recorded instance of a single individual, through acts of generosity rather than malice, single-handedly destabilizing a major economy.

The irony was not lost on Musa himself. On his return journey from Mecca, he passed through Cairo again and found himself in an unusual position for the world's richest man: he was running low on gold. The lavish spending, combined with the need to maintain his entourage for the months-long return journey, had depleted even his vast reserves. In a remarkable reversal, Musa borrowed gold from Egyptian merchants at high interest rates, since gold was now scarce and valuable again partly due to his own earlier generosity.

Some historians see this loan as evidence that Musa's wealth, while vast, was not infinite. Others interpret it as evidence of his economic sophistication, he could have sent for more gold from Mali, but borrowing was faster and allowed him to maintain the pace of his journey. That he could secure such loans despite having just crashed the gold market speaks to his reputation; the merchants of Cairo believed Mali's wealth was sufficient to repay any sum.

The Pilgrimage's Purpose: Religion and Realpolitik

Why did Musa undertake such an extravagant pilgrimage? The simple answer is religious obligation, but the fuller answer reveals a sophisticated understanding of medieval geopolitics and the value of reputation.

In the 14th century, a ruler's legitimacy in the Islamic world was enhanced by fulfilling hajj. It demonstrated piety, commitment to Islamic principles, and connection to the wider Muslim community. For Mali, a kingdom on the periphery of the Islamic world, this was particularly important. By making the pilgrimage, Musa established himself as a proper Muslim ruler rather than merely a wealthy pagan king who happened to control gold-producing regions.

But Musa went far beyond the minimum requirements. Every aspect of his journey was calculated to create a lasting impression. The golden staffs, the silk garments, the construction of mosques, the lavish gifts all of these sent a clear message, Mali was not a backward frontier kingdom but a sophisticated empire worthy of respect.

This had practical implications for trade. Merchants from Cairo, Damascus, and other commercial centers would be more willing to establish long-distance trade relationships with an empire whose ruler had demonstrated such wealth and sophistication. The pilgrimage was, in effect, an extremely expensive marketing campaign, one that positioned Mali at the center of trans-Saharan trade networks for generations.

Musa also used the pilgrimage to recruit talent. In Mecca and Cairo, he encountered scholars, architects, and poets. He convinced many to return with him to Mali, offering generous salaries and the opportunity to work at a court that, while distant, was clearly wealthy enough to support their work. Among these recruits was Abu Ishaq al-Sahili, a Granada-born poet and architect who would design several buildings in Mali, including the famous Djinguereber Mosque in Timbuktu.

Timbuktu: Building a Legacy Beyond Gold

If Musa's pilgrimage was about announcing Mali's arrival on the world stage, his development of Timbuktu was about creating a lasting legacy that transcended mere wealth. Under Musa's patronage, Timbuktu transformed from a seasonal settlement into one of the great centers of Islamic learning in Africa.

The Djinguereber Mosque, designed by al-Sahili and built around 1327, became the architectural symbol of this transformation. Constructed from mud brick and wood in a distinctive Sudano-Sahelian style, it could accommodate thousands of worshippers. But more importantly, it became the center of an educational complex that attracted scholars from across the Islamic world.

Musa established the Sankore University, which functioned more like the medieval Islamic madrasas than modern universities but served a similar purpose: advanced education in theology, law, mathematics, astronomy, and other sciences. At its height, Sankore hosted up to 25,000 students and possessed one of the largest libraries in the world, with collections numbering in the hundreds of thousands of manuscripts.

The emperor understood something that many wealthy individuals throughout history have failed to grasp: gold could buy buildings, but only knowledge and culture could create a civilization worth remembering. He reportedly established a stipend system for scholars, ensuring that intellectuals could pursue learning without worrying about material survival. This early form of academic patronage helped establish Timbuktu's reputation as "the City of 333 Saints," a center of Islamic scholarship that would endure for centuries.

The books and manuscripts of Timbuktu covered subjects from astronomy and mathematics to poetry and law. They represented the accumulated knowledge of Islamic civilization, preserved and studied in a city that Europeans of the time believed to be shrouded in mystery or nonexistent. These collections challenge persistent narratives about African intellectual history, demonstrating sophisticated literary and scientific traditions that contemporary Europeans were largely unaware existed.

Musa's investment in Timbuktu had economic benefits as well. A center of learning attracted not just scholars but also students, who needed housing, food, and books. It attracted merchants who traded in luxury goods that educated people desired. The city became a node in trans-Saharan trade networks, famous for both its gold and its books, sometimes of equivalent value.

The Economics of Medieval Wealth: Why Musa's Fortune Was Incalculable

Modern economists attempting to calculate Musa's wealth face a fundamental challenge: how do you compare wealth across economic systems so different that they barely share common metrics? Medieval Mali operated on fundamentally different economic principles than contemporary capitalism.

First, there's the question of what Musa actually owned. In a sense, he owned everything. Mali was an absolute monarchy where the emperor's authority was theoretically unlimited. All gold mined in his territories belonged to him; he graciously permitted others to mine it in exchange for tribute. But in another sense, his wealth was inseparable from the empire itself. He couldn't liquidate his assets and retire to a private island because his assets were the territorial control that made him emperor.

This differs fundamentally from modern billionaires whose wealth is largely held in corporate shares that could theoretically be sold. Jeff Bezos's wealth is primarily Amazon stock, which has a market price determined daily by thousands of transactions. Musa's wealth was land, resource rights, trade monopolies, and tribute systems none of which had a market price because markets for such things didn't exist in the same way.

Second, there's the question of purchasing power. Musa controlled gold at a time when gold was the primary store of value and medium of exchange for large transactions across much of the Afro-Eurasian world. This is roughly equivalent to controlling the printing press for the world's reserve currency. But the medieval economy was also much smaller than today's global economy, meaning there were fewer goods and services to purchase with that wealth.

When economists estimate Musa's wealth at $400-600 billion, they're typically trying to calculate how much of the world's total wealth he controlled and then comparing that proportion to today's global economy. If Musa controlled 1% of global economic output (a conservative estimate), and global GDP today is approximately $100 trillion, that would put his wealth at $1 trillion. Other methodologies yield different results, but all converge on the same conclusion: by any reasonable metric, Musa ranks among the wealthiest individuals in human history.

What makes this wealth particularly remarkable is its source. Unlike modern billionaires who created new technologies or business models, Musa's wealth came from controlling access to natural resources that people already desperately wanted. He didn't invent gold or discover new applications for it; he simply controlled where it came from. This is a pattern we'll see repeated throughout history, from Rockefeller's oil to Getty's petroleum to modern mining magnates but rarely with such complete monopolistic control.

The Paradox of Golden Generosity

Perhaps the most intriguing aspect of Musa's story is what he did with his wealth. By all accounts, his generosity during the pilgrimage was genuine, not merely strategic. Islamic tradition emphasizes charity as a religious obligation, particularly for the wealthy. Musa seems to have taken this obligation seriously, distributing gold to the poor wherever he traveled.

This creates an interesting paradox. Musa's generosity in Cairo caused significant economic disruption, hurting many of the same people he intended to help. The inflation triggered by his gold distribution eroded the savings of ordinary Egyptians. The subsequent deflation, when Musa borrowed gold back, further destabilized the economy. His good intentions produced harmful consequences, illustrating a timeless principle: in complex economic systems, good intentions don't guarantee good outcomes.

Modern parallels exist. When wealthy philanthropists inject massive resources into a community or sector without considering systemic effects, they can inadvertently cause harm. Food aid can undermine local agricultural markets. Large donations can distort nonprofit priorities toward whatever wealthy donors prefer to fund. The "resource curse" that afflicts many resource-rich developing nations has parallels to Cairo's gold glut; abundance of a valuable resource can create economic dysfunction.

Yet Musa's legacy in the Islamic world was overwhelmingly positive. Chronicles written decades after his reign remember him as a just, pious, and generous ruler. The mosques he built along his pilgrimage route stood for centuries as monuments to his devotion. Timbuktu's transformation into a center of learning created intellectual traditions that persisted long after his death. Perhaps the lesson is that strategic generosity that builds institutions and infrastructure creates more lasting positive impact than spontaneous charity, however generous.

The Mysterious End and Uncertain Legacy

Musa died in 1337, approximately thirteen years after his famous pilgrimage. The circumstances of his death are not well documented, a common problem with medieval African history, where sources are scarce compared to contemporary European or Middle Eastern records. He was succeeded by his son Mansa Maghan, who proved to be a far less capable ruler.

The empire Musa built declined gradually over the following century. His successors lacked his administrative abilities and vision. Regional governors asserted greater independence. Trade routes shifted as political conditions changed. By the mid-15th century, the Mali Empire had fragmented, though successor states continued to control gold-producing regions.

Some historians argue that Musa's lavish spending, particularly on the pilgrimage, weakened the empire's finances. The gold he distributed represented a significant outflow of wealth that wasn't replaced by equivalent productive investment. Others counter that the pilgrimage enhanced Mali's international reputation and trade relationships, generating returns that exceeded the initial cost.

The truth likely lies somewhere between these extremes. Musa's spending was enormous but not crippling for an empire with Mali's resource base. The empire's decline had more to do with succession crises, military challenges, and shifting economic conditions than with Musa's generosity. Nevertheless, his pilgrimage represents a fascinating case study in how even the wealthiest individual cannot spend unlimited amounts without eventual consequences.

Lessons from the Golden Throne

Mansa Musa's story offers several insights that echo through the subsequent history of wealth accumulation and expenditure. First, he illustrates the power of natural resource monopolies. Controlling access to resources that others desperately need remains one of the most reliable paths to extraordinary wealth. The Rockefellers, the Gettys, and modern oil sheikhs follow a pattern Musa established in the 14th century.

Second, Musa demonstrates that wealth alone doesn't create lasting legacy, strategic investment does. The gold he distributed in Cairo is long forgotten except as an economic curiosity. The libraries and universities he established in Timbuktu preserved knowledge for centuries and influenced generations of scholars. Modern billionaires wrestling with how to deploy their wealth for maximum positive impact might study Musa's mixed record: spontaneous generosity can backfire; institutional investment endures.

Third, his story reveals how wealth operates differently in different economic and political systems. Musa's wealth was inseparable from political power in ways that modern wealth, though certainly influential politically, is not. Today's billionaires are constrained by laws, markets, and democratic institutions (imperfectly, but meaningfully). Musa faced fewer constraints, which gave him more immediate power but also meant his empire's fate depended heavily on his personal capabilities and those of his successors.

Finally, Musa reminds us that extraordinary wealth has existed throughout human history, not just in the modern era. The specific mechanisms for accumulating wealth change, gold monopolies give way to oil, which gives way to software and data but the fundamental dynamics remain surprisingly consistent. Someone finds a way to control access to something many people desperately want. They leverage that control to accumulate resources on a vast scale. They face choices about what to do with those resources. And history judges them, often harshly, on those choices.

As we journey through the stories of history's billionaires, from the Golden King of Mali to the tech titans of Silicon Valley, Musa's pilgrimage serves as a useful touchstone. It reminds us that wealth on an almost unimaginable scale has always existed, that humans have always struggled with how to use such wealth wisely, and that the consequences of these choices ripple through generations, sometimes in unexpected ways. The staff-bearing slaves and gold-laden camels have long since turned to dust, but the questions Mansa Musa's life raises about wealth, power, generosity, and legacy remain as relevant today as they were in 1324.

Chapter 2

The Rothschild Dynasty - Banking Empire Builders

On a narrow, crowded street in Frankfurt's Jewish ghetto, behind a door marked with a red shield, "Roth Schild" in German a coin dealer named Mayer Amschel Rothschild contemplated an audacious plan that would transform his family from modest merchants into the architects of international finance. The year was 1764, and Rothschild was just twenty years old, recently returned from an apprenticeship in Hanover where he'd learned not just the money-changing trade but something more valuable, the art of cultivating relationships with nobility.

The Rothschild story is fundamentally different from Mansa Musa's tale of resource monopoly. Where Musa controlled gold from the ground, the Rothschilds would control something more abstract and ultimately more powerful: the flow of money itself across borders, the credit that funded wars and governments, and the information networks that made all of this possible. They would become for nearly a century the closest thing the world had ever seen to a central bank, except this bank was a family business answering to no government, bound by no constitution, constrained only by market forces and their own strategic judgment.

At their peak in the mid-19th century, the Rothschild family controlled a fortune estimated at over $5 trillion in today's currency, more wealth than the GDP of most nations. They financed the British purchase of the Suez Canal, supported the defeat of Napoleon, funded the development of railways across Europe, and influenced the political decisions of monarchs and prime ministers. Yet they remain shrouded in mystery, conspiracy theories, and deliberate obfuscation, making their true story both more interesting and more consequential than the myths that surround them.

The Five Sons Strategy: Conquering Europe Through Finance

Mayer Amschel's breakthrough came through his connection with Crown Prince Wilhelm of Hesse, one of the wealthiest royals in Europe. Wilhelm had accumulated a vast fortune by, among other things, renting Hessian soldiers to other nations, most infamously to Britain during the American Revolutionary War. Managing Wilhelm's coin collection gave Mayer Amschel access to the crown prince, and access led to trust. When Wilhelm needed someone to handle financial transactions discreetly, he turned to the reliable Jewish merchant from the Frankfurt ghetto.

But Mayer Amschel's true genius wasn't in winning Wilhelm's trust, it was in how he structured his family business for multigenerational dominance. He had five sons, Amschel, Salomon, Nathan, Carl, and James. Rather than keeping them all in Frankfurt where they would compete for the same opportunities and clients, he deployed them strategically across the financial capitals of Europe.

Amschel remained in Frankfurt, maintaining the family's original base. Salomon went to Vienna, the seat of the Habsburg Empire. Nathan, the most brilliant of the brothers, established himself in London, then becoming the financial capital of the world. Carl took Naples, a major Mediterranean trading hub. James, the youngest, went to Paris, the continental rival to London's financial dominance.

This geographical distribution created something unprecedented, a multinational financial network with trusted family members at each node, speaking the local language, understanding local customs, but ultimately loyal to family interests above national ones. At a time when communication was slow and unreliable, when moving money across borders was complicated by different currencies, regulations, and political instability, the Rothschilds had agents in every major capital who could coordinate transactions with speed and efficiency that no competitor could match.

The strategy also provided crucial diversification. When one nation faced an economic crisis or political upheaval, the family's interests in other countries could absorb the shock. When war broke out between nations, as it frequently did in 19th century Europe the Rothschilds could finance both sides, ensuring that regardless of the outcome, the family would maintain influence with the victor.

This raises uncomfortable questions about loyalty and ethics that would follow the family for generations. Were the Rothschilds really Jewish, or were they primarily Rothschilds, with national and religious identities subordinate to family and financial interests? When they financed both sides of conflicts, were they simply being prudent businessmen, or were they profiting from human suffering in ways that transcended normal business ethics? The family's defenders point out that they operated in an era of constant warfare and had to navigate between hostile powers to survive. Critics argue that their neutrality enabled conflicts to continue longer than they might have otherwise.

The Waterloo Fortune: Myth and Reality

No Rothschild story is more famous or more misunderstood than the legend of Nathan Rothschild and the Battle of Waterloo. According to the popular version, Nathan learned of Napoleon's defeat at Waterloo on June 18, 1815, before anyone else in London, thanks to the family's private courier network. He then manipulated the stock market by selling British government bonds, creating a panic that suggested Britain had lost. When prices crashed, he secretly bought vast quantities at bargain prices. When news of Wellington's victory finally arrived, bond prices soared, and Nathan made a fortune estimated at over £1 million, tens of billions in today's currency in a single day.

It's a great story. It's also largely false, or at least significantly exaggerated.

Here's what actually happened, as best historians can reconstruct from archives and contemporary accounts. Nathan Rothschild did have superior intelligence networks, this part is true. His courier did likely bring him news of Waterloo's outcome before the official messengers reached London. The Rothschild family archives suggest Nathan learned of the victory on the evening of June 19th, a full day before the government's official dispatch arrived.

But the stock market manipulation story appears to be largely fabricated, popularized by an anti-Semitic French pamphlet published decades later. Contemporary accounts show that Nathan was indeed positioned heavily in British government securities, but he'd been accumulating these positions for months as part of a longer-term strategy of supporting the British war effort (for which he was being well compensated).

The real Waterloo fortune came not from market manipulation but from something more mundane yet equally impressive, logistics and information arbitrage. The Rothschilds had spent years developing the capability to move gold and payments between Britain and the Continent despite the war and blockades. They had contracts to pay British subsidies to allied armies, to supply Wellington's forces with gold, and to facilitate countless other financial transactions that kept the anti-Napoleon coalition functioning.

When Wellington won at Waterloo, it validated Nathan's long position in British securities and secured payment for the many services the Rothschilds had provided. The profits were enormous, but they came from being on the right side of history through calculated support of the likely winner, not through a single day of devious trading.

Yet the myth persists, and understanding why reveals something important about the Rothschilds and how they've been perceived. The true story, patient positioning, superior information networks, logistical excellence, and strategic betting on the British Empire is actually more impressive than the mythical version. But the myth serves narrative purposes, particularly for those who want to paint the Rothschilds as puppet masters manipulating events from the shadows.

This pattern would repeat throughout the family's history. Real achievements that demonstrated genuine financial innovation and skill would be exaggerated into conspiracy theories about world domination. The family's actual influence, which was considerable but constrained by market forces and political realities, would be inflated into fantasies of unlimited power.

Building the International Banking System

The Rothschilds' post-Waterloo dominance rested on several key innovations that would fundamentally shape modern finance. First was their system for moving money across borders. In an era before electronic transfers or even reliable banking correspondent networks, moving large sums between countries was extraordinarily difficult. Currency had to be physically transported, with all the risks of robbery and loss that entailed. Different nations had different currencies, coinage standards, and regulations.

The Rothschilds solved this through a simple but revolutionary approach: they didn't move money at all. Instead, they used their branches in different cities as clearing houses. If a client in London needed to pay someone in Vienna, the Rothschilds would simply record a debt in London and a credit in Vienna within their internal accounting system. No gold had to physically travel. This reduced risk, increased speed, and lowered costs dramatically.

This system required something crucial, trust. All five branches had to trust that the others would honor their commitments. This is where family ties proved invaluable. Blood was thicker than water, and the brothers had been raised with the understanding that family loyalty superseded everything else. They communicated constantly; the Rothschild archives contain thousands of letters between the brothers, discussing markets, politics, opportunities, and personal matters in equal measure.

The second innovation was in government finance. Before the Rothschilds, governments typically borrowed money through a chaotic system involving local bankers, merchant companies, and wealthy individuals, often under terms that were opaque and disadvantageous to the borrowing government. The Rothschilds professionalized this process.

When a government needed to raise funds, the Rothschilds would underwrite bonds, essentially agreeing to buy the entire issue at a set price and then reselling the bonds to investors. This provided governments with immediate capital and certainty, while the Rothschilds profited from the spread between their purchase price and the resale price. It required enormous capital to underwrite major government bond issues, but it also gave the Rothschilds tremendous influence. Governments became dependent on their services, and the Rothschilds could (and did) refuse to underwrite loans for governments whose policies they opposed.

This raises a profound question about private power versus democratic governance. When an unelected banking family could effectively veto a government's fiscal policy by refusing to underwrite its bonds, where did sovereignty actually lie? The Rothschilds would argue they simply imposed market discipline, governments that pursued reckless policies should pay higher borrowing costs or be denied credit entirely. Critics argued that a family business, however capable, should not wield such power over elected governments.

The third innovation was information. The Rothschilds invested heavily in private courier networks, carrier pigeons, and later telegraph lines. They knew market-moving information before competitors, and sometimes before governments. This information advantage was carefully guarded and ruthlessly exploited. It gave them the ability to anticipate market movements, position themselves advantageously, and advise their clients with superior insight.

The Golden Age: Mid-19th Century Dominance

By the 1850s, the Rothschilds were arguably the most powerful financial institution in the world. They financed the British purchase of the Suez Canal in 1875, Prime Minister Benjamin Disraeli approached Lionel de Rothschild for £4 million, received it overnight, and secured British control of this crucial waterway. They financed railroad development across Europe and America. They funded mining operations in Africa and South America. They held positions in countless industrial companies, banks, and trading firms.

Contemporaries struggled to comprehend the scale of Rothschild wealth and influence. The family was notoriously secretive about their finances, a tradition that continues to this day but estimates suggest their combined wealth exceeded that of any other family or institution. Some historians argue that for several decades in the mid-1800s, the Rothschilds controlled roughly 50% of the world's wealth, a level of economic concentration that had never existed before and has never been matched since.

Yet they remained, in many ways, outsiders. Despite their wealth, European aristocracy looked down on them as Jewish parvenus. Anti-Semitism was pervasive, and the Rothschilds faced constant suspicion and hostility. Some governments refused to allow them full civil rights despite their financial power. In Britain, it took until 1858 for Lionel de Rothschild to take his seat in Parliament, having been elected four times but blocked from serving because he wouldn't swear the Christian oath.

The family responded by buying their way into respectability through philanthropy, art collecting, and eventually intermarriage with aristocracy (though always maintaining Jewish identity). They built magnificent estates, Waddesdon Manor, Château de Ferrières and Villa Ephrussi that rivaled royal palaces. They amassed art collections that would eventually stock major museums. They supported universities, hospitals, and Jewish communities across Europe.

This strategy was partially successful. By the late 19th century, the Rothschilds had achieved a degree of social acceptance that would have been unimaginable a century earlier. But acceptance was always conditional, always fragile, and the family never fully escaped the suspicion that attended Jewish success in Christian Europe.

The Seeds of Decline: Changing Financial Systems

The Rothschilds' dominance began to erode in the late 19th and early 20th centuries, though they remained immensely wealthy and influential. Several factors contributed to this decline, offering lessons about how even the most dominant business models eventually face disruption.

First, the financial system evolved beyond what the family structure could efficiently manage. Joint-stock banks, corporations with many shareholders rather than family partnerships had advantages in scale and capital-raising that family banks couldn't match. J.P. Morgan in America, Deutsche Bank in Germany, and others could raise capital through stock offerings and bond issuances in ways that family partnerships couldn't without diluting family control.

The Rothschilds faced a classic business dilemma, grow by incorporating outside capital and losing family control, or maintain control and accept slower growth and eventual relative decline. They chose control, a decision that preserved family unity but ensured they would be overtaken by more aggressively expanding competitors.

Second, technology disrupted their information advantage. The telegraph, telephone, and eventually radio democratized information. What once required private couriers and carrier pigeons could now be transmitted instantly by anyone with access to telecommunications infrastructure. The Rothschilds' information edge, so crucial to their success, diminished dramatically.

Third, the world wars devastated their European operations. World War I severed communication between the different branches, the British Rothschilds and the Austrian/German Rothschilds suddenly found themselves on opposite sides of a catastrophic conflict. The family's traditional neutrality and international cooperation became impossible. World War II was even worse, with the Nazis seizing Austrian and French Rothschild properties and forcing family members to flee.

Fourth, the rise of central banks and government regulation of finance reduced the space for private banking dynasties to operate. When governments took control of money supply, interest rates, and international finance, private bankers, even ones as powerful as the Rothschilds became less central to the system.

Finally, the family simply didn't produce another generation of financial geniuses comparable to the founding brothers. Subsequent generations were competent, cultured, and wealthy, but they lacked the hunger, risk tolerance, and strategic vision of their ancestors. This is a common pattern in dynastic wealth, the first generation builds, the second generation maintains, and the third generation often squanders. The Rothschilds never quite squandered their wealth, but they also never recaptured their former dominance.

Conspiracy Theories: Confronting the Myths

Any discussion of the Rothschilds must address the conspiracy theories that have surrounded the family for two centuries. These theories range from the merely exaggerated to the virulently anti-Semitic, but they share common themes: the Rothschilds secretly control world events, they manipulate wars and economies for profit, they are part of a shadowy cabal seeking world domination.

The factual basis for these theories is thin to nonexistent. Yes, the Rothschilds were extremely wealthy and influential. Yes, they had connections to governments and sometimes influenced policy. Yes, they operated with secrecy that fueled speculation. But the leap from "wealthy and influential banking family" to "secret controllers of world events" requires abandoning evidence-based reasoning.

The persistence of these theories tells us more about anti-Semitism than about the Rothschilds. The tropes are familiar: Jews as manipulators, as having dual loyalties, as being part of conspiracies against Christian civilization. The Rothschilds became a focal point for these ancient prejudices precisely because their success was so visible and undeniable.

Modern research into Rothschild archives reveals a different picture. The family was indeed strategically brilliant and extraordinarily successful. They did finance governments and influence policy. But they were also constrained by market forces, made mistakes, faced setbacks, and operated in an environment where their power, while significant, was far from absolute. They couldn't prevent wars, indeed wars often disrupted their business and put family members on opposite sides of conflicts. They couldn't manipulate gold prices indefinitely, market forces always eventually reasserted themselves. They couldn't prevent the rise of competitors or the regulatory changes that diminished private banking's role.

Paradoxically, debunking the conspiracy theories doesn't diminish the Rothschilds' historical significance. Their real achievements, pioneering international finance, developing mechanisms for moving capital across borders, professionalizing government bond markets and building information networks were genuinely revolutionary and shaped the modern financial system. The myths obscure these real accomplishments while substituting a cartoonish villainy that serves no analytical purpose.

The Modern Rothschilds: Wealth Without Dominance

Today, the Rothschild family remains wealthy, estimates suggest combined family wealth in the tens of billions but they are no longer the dominant force they once were. The family bank, now called Rothschild & Co, is a respected but mid-sized investment banking firm. Family members are involved in finance, wine-making (the French Rothschilds own several prestigious vineyards), philanthropy, and various business ventures.

The family's decline from the absolute pinnacle of financial power offers several lessons. First, no competitive advantage lasts forever. The Rothschilds' edges, superior information, family cohesion and an international network were eventually replicated or rendered obsolete by technological and institutional change. Second, maintaining dynastic business control often comes at the cost of maximum growth. Had the Rothschilds been willing to incorporate and bring in outside shareholders, they might have maintained greater market share, but they would have ceased being a family business. Third, even the wealthiest families are subject to historical forces beyond their control, wars, regulatory changes and technological disruption that can erode power and wealth.

Yet the family's legacy in shaping modern finance is undeniable. The mechanisms they pioneered for international banking, the professionalization of government bond markets, the use of family networks for international business, all of these became standard practice.

When J.P. Morgan built his banking empire, he was following a playbook the Rothschilds had written. When modern investment banks underwrite government bonds, they're using methods the Rothschilds developed. The international correspondent banking system has roots in Rothschild practices.

The Rothschilds also demonstrated that in finance, reputation and trust can be as valuable as capital. Their name alone was worth millions, governments and businesses wanted to work with the Rothschilds because association with the family signaled creditworthiness and reliability. Building that reputation took generations; maintaining it required careful attention to risk management and client relations. This remains true in modern finance, where firms like Goldman Sachs or J.P. Morgan trade on reputations built over decades.

Lessons from the Red Shield

The Rothschild story illuminates several enduring themes in the accumulation and preservation of extraordinary wealth. First is the power of network effects. The five-sons strategy created a network where each node made every other node more valuable. This is a pattern we'll see repeatedly in subsequent chapters, from Rockefeller's integration strategies to modern tech platforms where controlling the network becomes more valuable than owning the individual components.

Second is the tension between family control and business growth. The Rothschilds chose family control, which preserved unity but limited scale. Other families made different choices, the Walton family allowed Walmart to become a public company while maintaining control through share structure, tech founders like Zuckerberg use dual-class shares to maintain control while accessing public capital markets. There's no obviously correct answer, but the tradeoff is real and consequential.

Third is the role of information in wealth creation. The Rothschilds understood before most that information itself was valuable, that knowing something before others knew it could be worth more than physical assets. This presages the information economy of the late 20th and early 21st centuries, where data and information have become primary sources of value.

Fourth is the persistence of wealth across generations, even absent continued business dominance. The Rothschild family lost their position atop the financial world, but they remain wealthy centuries after Mayer Amschel started his coin-dealing business. Wealth, once accumulated on a sufficient scale, becomes extremely difficult to dissipate entirely. This has implications for contemporary debates about wealth inequality and inheritance taxation.

Finally, the Rothschild experience illustrates how political and social context shapes wealth accumulation and preservation. As Jews in Christian Europe, the Rothschilds faced constraints and hostility that limited their options despite their wealth. They couldn't hold certain government positions, faced social discrimination, and during the Nazi era, had assets seized and family members murdered. Wealth provided security and options, but it couldn't fully insulate them from historical forces and social prejudice.

As we move forward to examine other wealth dynasties and individual billionaires, the Rothschild template remains relevant. They pioneered international business organization, grappled with succession and family governance issues that continue to challenge wealthy families, faced the disruption of their business model by technological and institutional change, and navigated the complex relationship between private wealth and public power. Their story, freed from conspiracy theory and examined with historical rigor, reveals that the reality of dynastic wealth is more complex, more interesting, and more instructive than any myth.

Chapter 3

John D. Rockefeller - The Original Oil Baron

On September 29, 1916, John D. Rockefeller's personal wealth surpassed one billion dollars. He was seventy-seven years old, had been retired from active business management for a decade, and was by then more famous as a philanthropist than as an oil magnate. Yet this milestone, becoming the world's first documented billionaire cemented his place in history not just as extraordinarily wealthy, but as the exemplar of a new kind of wealth entirely.

Unlike Mansa Musa, whose fortune was inseparable from territorial control and imperial power, or the Rothschilds, whose wealth came from facilitating transactions between others, Rockefeller built his fortune through industrial dominance of a single commodity, oil. He didn't discover oil or invent new uses for it. What he did, with ruthless efficiency and strategic brilliance, was organize chaos into monopoly, transforming a fragmented, wasteful industry into a vertically integrated machine that would power the modern world while making him incomprehensibly rich.

At his peak, Rockefeller controlled approximately 90% of oil refining in the United States. His company, Standard Oil, was so dominant that the word "trust" entered the American vocabulary as a term for monopolistic business combinations specifically because of the legal structure Rockefeller used to consolidate his empire. His wealth, adjusted for inflation, is estimated at $340 billion to $400 billion in today's currency, making him arguably the wealthiest American who ever lived, and second globally perhaps only to Mansa Musa.

Yet Rockefeller's legacy is profoundly contradictory. He was simultaneously the most hated man in America, depicted in political cartoons as an octopus strangling the nation and its most generous philanthropist, whose giving literally transformed medicine, education, and scientific research. He built monopoly through tactics that ranged from innovative efficiency to outright extortion, yet he lived with almost absurd personal frugality. Understanding Rockefeller requires holding multiple truths simultaneously: visionary and villain, efficiency expert and monopolist, ruthless competitor and thoughtful philanthropist.

From Bookkeeper to Oil Pioneer: The Early Years

John Davison Rockefeller was born in 1839 in Richford, New York, to a family that oscillated between middle-class respectability and precarious poverty. His father, William Avery Rockefeller, was a con man who sold dubious elixirs and patent medicines, frequently absent from the family for months at a time. His mother, Eliza, was a devout Baptist who instilled in young John a sense of discipline, frugality, and religious obligation that would shape his entire life.

The contrast between his parents defined Rockefeller's character. From his father, he inherited boldness, risk tolerance, and a willingness to push ethical boundaries in pursuit of advantage. From his mother, he absorbed discipline, methodical thinking, religious devotion, and a belief that wealth carried moral obligations. This combination, the con man's audacity with the Baptist's accountability created someone uniquely suited to both build and ultimately justify extraordinary wealth.

Rockefeller's formal education ended at sixteen when he completed a three-month business course at Folsom's Commercial College in Cleveland. He learned bookkeeping, penmanship, commercial law, and banking practical skills that would prove more valuable than any liberal arts education. In 1855, at age sixteen, he found work as an assistant bookkeeper at Hewitt & Tuttle, a small firm of commission merchants. His starting salary was fifty cents per day.

This bookkeeping experience profoundly shaped Rockefeller's approach to business. While others saw oil as a glamorous frontier business of wildcatters and speculators, Rockefeller saw it as a bookkeeper would: numbers, costs, efficiencies, and profit margins. He understood from the beginning that wealth came not from drilling oil, a risky, capital-intensive business with highly variable returns but from refining and distributing it, businesses where efficiency and scale created sustainable advantages.

By 1859, at just twenty years old, Rockefeller had saved enough money to enter into a partnership with Maurice Clark, forming Clark & Rockefeller, a commission merchant business. The timing was fortuitous. That same year, Edwin Drake struck oil in Titusville, Pennsylvania, launching the first oil boom in American history. Cleveland, where Rockefeller was based, was ideally positioned, connected by rail and water to both the oil fields and major markets.

Rockefeller saw the opportunity clearly. The problem wasn't finding oil, speculators were drilling everywhere, often producing more oil than the market could absorb. The problem was refining crude oil into useful products like kerosene (then used primarily for lighting), and distributing those products efficiently to customers. In 1863, Rockefeller and Clark, along with Samuel Andrews, a refining expert, built their first oil refinery in Cleveland.

Building the Machine: Horizontal and Vertical Integration

What happened next transformed American business forever and established patterns that tech companies like Amazon and Google would follow a century later. Rockefeller looked at the oil refining industry and saw waste everywhere, dozens of small refineries operating inefficiently, competing viciously, driving prices down until nobody made money. He saw an industry that could be rationalized, consolidated, and optimized. He saw that whoever accomplished this consolidation would control the industry entirely.

His strategy had two components: horizontal integration (buying or destroying competitors) and vertical integration (controlling every step from production to distribution). The horizontal strategy came first. Between 1865 and 1870, Rockefeller systematically bought out competing refineries in Cleveland. His approach was methodical. He would approach a competitor with detailed financial analysis showing how combining operations would reduce costs. He would offer a fair, sometimes generous price for the business. Most importantly, he would make clear that refusing his offer meant facing him as a competitor, and Rockefeller's advantages in efficiency and scale would eventually drive them out of business anyway.

This wasn't entirely bluff. Rockefeller's obsession with efficiency gave him genuine cost advantages. He studied every aspect of the refining process, identifying waste and improving methods. His refineries used every component of crude oil, when competitors discarded byproducts, Rockefeller sold them. He negotiated discounts with suppliers by guaranteeing large, regular orders. He operated at scales that allowed specialization of labor and equipment that smaller refineries couldn't match.

But efficiency alone doesn't explain Standard Oil's dominance. Rockefeller also employed tactics that ranged from aggressive to predatory. The most controversial was his arrangement with railroads. In 1872, Rockefeller negotiated secret rebates with railroads, he would ship large, regular volumes of oil, and in exchange, railroads would charge him significantly less than they charged his competitors. In some cases, railroads even paid Rockefeller rebates on oil his competitors shipped, effectively charging competitors more to subsidize Standard Oil's operations.

When competitors discovered these arrangements and protested, Rockefeller was unapologetic. He argued, with some justification, that his large, regular shipments were more profitable for railroads than sporadic smaller shipments. Loading a train car with Standard Oil barrels required less time and labor than consolidating shipments from multiple small refineries. His shipments reduced railroad costs, so discounts were economically rational, not favoritism.

This argument had merit, but it also revealed the self-reinforcing nature of scale advantages. Because Rockefeller was large, he got discounts. Because he got discounts, he could undersell competitors. Because he undersold competitors, he got larger. Each advantage compounded the others, creating a flywheel that, once spinning, became nearly impossible for competitors to slow.

By 1870, Rockefeller consolidated his various holdings into Standard Oil Company of Ohio. By 1872, Standard Oil controlled about 25% of American oil refining. By 1880, it controlled over 90%. The speed and completeness of this consolidation was unprecedented in American business history.

Vertical integration came next. Rockefeller realized that controlling just refining left him vulnerable to suppliers and distributors who could extract profits from his operations. So Standard Oil began acquiring oil fields, guaranteeing crude supply. It built pipelines to transport crude from fields to refineries, eliminating dependence on railroads for this crucial step. It acquired tank cars, storage facilities, and distribution networks.

Most significantly, Standard Oil developed its own marketing and retail operations. Instead of selling refined oil to distributors who then sold to customers, Standard Oil sold directly through company-owned operations. This required building an entire infrastructure of warehouses, sales staff, and eventually retail stations, massive capital investment but it gave Standard Oil control over the entire value chain from wellhead to customer.

The result was a machine of extraordinary efficiency. Standard Oil could produce kerosene and other petroleum products at costs far below any

competitor. It could guarantee supply even when crude prices fluctuated. It could reach customers in even remote locations. And because it controlled so much of the market, it could set prices at whatever level maximized profit, constrained only by the theoretical threat of new competition, a threat that Rockefeller's scale advantages and reputation for ruthlessness largely neutralized.

The Trust: Legal Innovation and Antitrust Response

Rockefeller's empire faced a significant challenge, corporate law in the 19th century made it difficult for a company incorporated in one state to own property or operate businesses in other states. Standard Oil was an Ohio corporation, but its operations spanned the country. Rockefeller needed a legal structure that would allow centralized control of nationwide operations.

The solution was the trust, a legal mechanism that had existed for estate management but had never been used for corporate organization. In 1882, Rockefeller's lawyers created the Standard Oil Trust. Shareholders of Standard Oil and its affiliated companies exchanged their shares for trust certificates. Trustees including Rockefeller controlled all the companies making unified decisions for the entire organization.

This structure was brilliant and terrifying. Brilliant because it solved the legal problem of interstate corporate control. Terrifying because it created an organizational form that could consolidate entire industries under unified control, potentially creating monopolies across the economy. The word "trust" entered popular vocabulary specifically because of Standard Oil, becoming synonymous with monopolistic combinations that stifled competition.

Public reaction was intense. By the 1880s, Standard Oil was perhaps the most hated corporation in America. Journalists exposed its predatory

practices. Competitors who had been driven out of business testified about Rockefeller's tactics. Small oil producers blamed Standard Oil for low prices that made their operations unprofitable. Consumers, conversely, blamed Standard Oil for high kerosene prices that they believed reflected monopoly pricing rather than fair market value.

Political cartoons depicted Standard Oil as an octopus, its tentacles strangling industry, government, and the common man. Ida Tarbell, whose father had been driven out of business by Standard Oil, wrote a devastating series of articles for McClure's Magazine that exposed the company's practices in exhaustive detail. Her work, later published as "The History of the Standard Oil Company," became the definitive muckraking text of the Progressive Era.

State governments responded first, suing to revoke Standard Oil's charter in Ohio. Rockefeller responded by shifting the trust's base to New Jersey, which had more permissive corporate laws. But pressure continued building. In 1890, Congress passed the Sherman Antitrust Act, intended specifically to address monopolies like Standard Oil.

The legal battle culminated in 1911 when the Supreme Court ruled that Standard Oil violated the Sherman Act and ordered the trust broken into 34 separate companies. These included Standard Oil of New Jersey (later Exxon), Standard Oil of New York (later Mobil), Standard Oil of California (later Chevron), and others. The court found that Standard Oil had engaged in "unreasonable" restraint of trade through predatory practices designed to eliminate competition.

The irony was that this breakup made Rockefeller even richer. He owned significant stakes in all the successor companies, and once freed from unified control, many of them thrived independently. As their stock prices rose, so did Rockefeller's wealth. The government had succeeded in breaking the monopoly but failed to diminish the monopolist's fortune.

The Paradox of Frugality: Living Modestly While Banking Billions

Throughout his life, even as his wealth reached astronomical levels, Rockefeller maintained habits of frugality that bordered on obsessiveness. He kept meticulous personal account books, recording every penny spent. He wore suits until they were threadbare. He lived in comfortable but not ostentatious homes, his New York residence was substantial but modest compared to the Gilded Age mansions of contemporaries like Vanderbilt or Carnegie.

His one indulgence was real estate, but even here his approach was practical. He purchased estates like Kykuit in New York's Westchester County not as showpieces but as investments and family retreats. The properties were well-maintained but reflected Rockefeller's Baptist sensibilities more than Gilded Age excess.

This frugality wasn't affectation or public relations, it was genuine, rooted in the religious principles his mother had instilled. Rockefeller believed wealth was a sacred trust, that God had allowed him to accumulate it for purposes beyond personal consumption. Wasting money on luxuries would be sinful, a violation of his obligation as a steward of resources.

Yet there's something almost grotesque about billionaire frugality. When Rockefeller would haggle over pennies in household accounts while his company was crushing competitors and extracting millions from the oil market, the juxtaposition highlights a moral blind spot. He could be scrupulous about personal spending while seemingly unconcerned about the human costs of his business practices, workers laid off when refineries were shuttered, families ruined when independent oil men were driven out, communities disrupted by Standard Oil's market power.

Rockefeller never seemed to recognize this contradiction, or if he did, he resolved it through his concept of stewardship. In his view, Standard Oil's efficiency was itself a moral good, waste was sin and his company had eliminated enormous waste from the oil industry. That this efficiency was achieved through monopolistic practices that enriched him while limiting opportunities for others was, in his mind, simply the natural order of competitive business.

From Most Hated to Most Generous: The Philanthropic Transformation

If Rockefeller had died in 1900, at age sixty-one, he would be remembered almost exclusively as a robber baron, the personification of monopoly capitalism's excesses. But he lived until 1937, dying just shy of his 98th birthday, and the last four decades of his life were devoted to giving away his fortune in ways that fundamentally transformed American society.

The transition began in the 1890s, when Rockefeller increasingly delegated Standard Oil's management to subordinates and focused on philanthropy. His early giving was haphazard, donations to Baptist churches, education institutions, and various causes. But he quickly realized that giving away money effectively was as challenging as earning it. He needed systematic approaches, professional management, and clear strategic goals.

Enter Frederick Taylor Gates, a Baptist minister who became Rockefeller's principal philanthropic advisor. Gates convinced Rockefeller that charity should be "scientific", targeted at root causes rather than symptoms, based on expert analysis rather than emotion, measured by results rather than intentions. This approach, novel at the time, would become the foundation of modern philanthropy.

The Rockefeller Foundation, established in 1913, embodied these principles. Rather than funding random charitable causes, it identified specific problems that, if solved, would benefit millions. The foundation's early focus on hookworm eradication demonstrates the approach.

Hookworm was endemic in the American South, causing chronic illness, reduced productivity, and perpetuating poverty. The foundation funded research into the parasite's lifecycle, developed treatment protocols, built sanitation infrastructure, and conducted public education campaigns. Within two decades, hookworm was largely eliminated as a public health threat in the United States.

The foundation applied similar approaches to malaria, yellow fever, and other diseases. It funded medical research that led to treatments for diseases that had killed millions. It supported the development of modern medical education, the Flexner Report funded by Rockefeller philanthropy transformed American medical schools from diploma mills into rigorous scientific institutions. Today's medical education system, for better or worse, reflects Rockefeller's influence.

In education, Rockefeller's giving was equally transformative. He founded the University of Chicago in 1890, funding it so generously that it became one of the world's premier research universities within decades. He supported historically Black colleges and universities, including Spelman College (named after his wife's family). He funded public school systems, libraries, and educational research.

By the time of his death in 1937, Rockefeller had given away approximately $540 million, roughly $11 billion in today's currency, but representing an even larger share of total wealth at the time. His son, John D. Rockefeller Jr., continued the philanthropic work, and subsequent generations have maintained the tradition. The Rockefeller Foundation remains one of the world's most influential philanthropic organizations.

This transformation from robber baron to beloved philanthropist raises profound questions. Was Rockefeller's philanthropy genuine atonement for business practices that harmed millions? Was it a calculated effort to rehabilitate his reputation? Was it a sincere expression of religious conviction about stewardship? The answer is probably all of these simultaneously.

There's no doubt that Rockefeller's image benefited enormously from his philanthropy. By the 1920s, the man who had been depicted as an octopus strangling American industry was now celebrated as a generous benefactor whose gifts had saved countless lives. Critics argued that no amount of charity could justify monopolistic practices, that Rockefeller was essentially returning a portion of ill-gotten gains. Defenders countered that his philanthropy accomplished more good than Standard Oil had done harm, and that judging 19th-century business practices by 20th-century standards was anachronistic.

Perhaps the most honest assessment is that Rockefeller contained multitudes. He was capable of ruthless business practices and genuine religious devotion, of crushing competitors and carefully considering how to do maximum good with his wealth, of meticulous penny-pinching and billion-dollar gifts. The same mind that optimized oil refining applied itself to optimizing philanthropy, with results that were genuinely transformative.

The Rockefeller Legacy: Efficiency, Monopoly, and Lasting Influence

More than a century after Standard Oil's breakup, Rockefeller's influence remains pervasive. The oil companies that descended from Standard Oil, ExxonMobil, Chevron, and others remain among the world's largest corporations. The Rockefeller family, through foundations and continued wealth accumulation across generations, remains influential in philanthropy, environmental conservation, and public policy.

But beyond specific institutions, Rockefeller established patterns that define modern corporate capitalism. He demonstrated that systematic efficiency and scale advantages could create dominant market positions. He showed that vertical integration, controlling supply chains from beginning to end could be a sustainable competitive advantage. He proved that professional management and systematic analysis could be applied to both business and philanthropy.

He also illustrated the tensions inherent in concentrated private power. Standard Oil's efficiency genuinely benefited consumers, kerosene prices fell dramatically during Standard Oil's dominance, making lighting affordable for millions. But this efficiency came at the cost of competition, innovation, and economic opportunity for those whom Standard Oil crushed. Was this tradeoff worth it? Economic historians still debate the question.

Rockefeller's life spans the crucial transition from 19th-century entrepreneurial capitalism to 20th-century corporate capitalism. He began his career as a small merchant in a city of small businesses, and by the end, had created a corporate structure that prefigured the large, bureaucratic organizations that would dominate the 20th century. Standard Oil had divisions, management hierarchies, professional staff, and systematic processes; it was a modern corporation decades before most American businesses adopted such structures.

His philanthropic model has proven equally influential. Today's major philanthropists, Gates, Buffett, Bloomberg, and others follow the Rockefeller template. Professional management, strategic focus, measurable outcomes, and willingness to tackle problems at scale. Whether this model is optimal remains debated. Critics argue that it gives unelected billionaires too much influence over public priorities, that "strategic" philanthropy often reflects donor preferences over community needs, and that no amount of charity justifies the economic structures that allow such wealth accumulation in the first place.

Yet even critics acknowledge the real benefits. The diseases eradicated, the universities built, the research funded these represent genuine improvements in human welfare. The question isn't whether Rockefeller's philanthropy did good, but whether the system that allowed him to accumulate such wealth, and then choose how to distribute it, is ultimately just or sustainable.

Lessons from the Oil Baron

John D. Rockefeller's life offers several enduring lessons for understanding extreme wealth. First, efficiency and innovation matter, but market structure matters more. Standard Oil wasn't successful because it refined oil better than anyone else, though it did. It succeeded because Rockefeller understood that controlling market structure through horizontal and vertical integration created advantages that efficiency alone couldn't match.

Second, scale creates self-reinforcing advantages that can lead to monopoly unless actively prevented. Each advantage Rockefeller gained, better railroad rates, more efficient refineries, broader distribution networks made it easier to gain the next advantage. This dynamic appears throughout business history and is particularly visible in modern tech platforms where network effects create winner-take-all markets.

Third, the relationship between business practices and personal ethics is complex. Rockefeller genuinely believed he was doing good, eliminating waste, making oil products affordable and stewarding resources responsibly. That these beliefs coexisted with practices that ruined competitors and concentrated economic power doesn't make them insincere; it reveals how easily ethical frameworks can be constructed to justify self-interest.

Fourth, reputational rehabilitation through philanthropy is possible but complicated. Rockefeller's giving was too sustained, too strategic, and too personally involved to be dismissed as mere public relations. Yet it undeniably served his interests by transforming his public image. Modern billionaires face similar dynamics, their philanthropy is simultaneously genuine and strategic, altruistic and self-interested.

Finally, Rockefeller demonstrates that extreme wealth persists across generations even when actively given away. Despite giving away the equivalent of hundreds of billions in today's currency, the Rockefeller family remains wealthy and influential six generations later. This persistence of dynastic wealth has profound implications for economic opportunity and social mobility.

As we continue examining history's billionaires, Rockefeller stands as perhaps the archetypal American example, the self-made man who built an empire through intelligence and ruthlessness, dominated an industry through systematic strategy, was vilified and then celebrated, and attempted to justify his wealth through transformative giving. His story contains both inspiration and warning, demonstrating both what's possible through capitalist enterprise and what dangers concentrated economic power poses to competition and democracy.

Chapter 4

Andrew Carnegie - From Rags to Riches to Giving It Away

The thirteen-year-old boy stood at his loom in the cotton factory, his fingers bleeding from the rough thread, his lungs choking on lint-filled air. Twelve hours a day, six days a week, for $1.20 weekly wages. This was Andrew Carnegie's introduction to America in 1848, a world away from the stone cottage in Dunfermline, Scotland where his father had once proudly worked as a master weaver before the power looms destroyed that ancient craft.

Young Andrew would occasionally glance out the factory windows at the world beyond, but he couldn't have imagined what lay ahead: that he would become the second-richest man in American history, control more steel production than entire nations, employ hundreds of thousands, and then systematically give nearly all of it away in what would become the template for modern philanthropy. His story is not just one of spectacular wealth creation, but of a man who spent the second half of his life trying to answer a question that still haunts billionaires today: What is wealth actually for?

The Scottish Roots of American Ambition

Carnegie's childhood in Scotland planted seeds that would flower in unexpected ways. His father, William, was a skilled handloom weaver, but industrialization was merciless. Steam-powered looms could do the work of dozens of men, and the Carnegie family watched their modest prosperity evaporate. His mother, Margaret, proved to be the family's backbone, binding shoes to keep the family fed when weaving work disappeared entirely.

But poverty wasn't the only gift Scotland gave young Andrew. His uncle, George Lauder, was a firebrand Chartist who filled the boy's head with ideas about democracy, workers' rights, and the dignity of common people. These weren't abstract concepts in the Scotland of the 1840s, they were fighting words that could get a man imprisoned. The Carnegies lived through the aftermath of the Radical War, when weavers and workers had taken up arms against conditions that ground them into dust.

When Margaret Carnegie borrowed money for passage to America in 1848, she was making a desperate gamble. The family arrived in Allegheny, Pennsylvania, near Pittsburgh, with almost nothing. William Carnegie tried to return to handloom weaving in the new world, but the same industrial forces that had crushed him in Scotland were already at work in America. Within months, thirteen-year-old Andrew was the family's main breadwinner, working in the cotton factory.

The factory was brutal, but Carnegie possessed something beyond physical endurance, a ferocious hunger to learn and advance. He understood instinctively that his hands might be working the loom, but his mind was his real tool. When he moved to a new job as a telegraph messenger boy at $2.50 a week, it felt like liberation. He was out of the factory, moving through the city, seeing how business actually worked.

The Telegraph, The Railroad, and The Education of an Empire Builder

Carnegie's telegraph messenger position was his real university. Pittsburgh in the 1850s was a city transforming itself, and the telegraph office was where information flowed. Carnegie taught himself to recognize the sound of incoming messages, eventually learning to transcribe Morse code by ear, a rare skill that made him invaluable. He read every book he could borrow from Colonel James Anderson, a local benefactor who opened his personal library to working boys each Saturday. This act of generosity would echo through Carnegie's life; decades later, his library philanthropy would make Colonel Anderson's gesture available to millions.

But Carnegie's real education came from watching powerful men operate. Thomas A. Scott, superintendent of the Pennsylvania Railroad's western division, noticed the sharp young telegraph operator and hired him as his personal assistant and telegrapher. This was Carnegie's true lucky break, though he made his own luck by being indispensable. He learned everything about railroad operations, mastered the art of delegating authority, and absorbed Scott's lessons about leverage and capital.

The railroad was the internet of the nineteenth century, the infrastructure on which all other business depended. Carnegie saw how tiny efficiencies multiplied across thousands of miles could generate enormous profits. He learned about bottlenecks and chokepoints, about the power of controlling key assets in a system, about the difference between owning the thing and owning the system.

Scott gave Carnegie something even more valuable than knowledge: access to investment opportunities. In 1856, Scott offered Carnegie a chance to buy ten shares in Adams Express Company for $500. Carnegie didn't have $500, that was more than a year's wages but his mother mortgaged their home. It was another desperate gamble, but this time it paid off. When Carnegie received his first dividend check for $10, he later wrote that it was "the first penny of revenue from capital, something that I had not worked for with the sweat of my brow. 'Eureka!' I cried. 'Here's the goose that lays the golden eggs.'"

This was Carnegie's great revelation, money could make money. The laborer traded hours for dollars, but the capitalist put dollars to work earning more dollars while he slept. It was a profoundly undemocratic insight for a boy raised on Chartist ideals, and it would create a tension in Carnegie's psyche that he'd spend his entire life trying to resolve.

The Civil War Profiteer Becomes an Industrialist

The Civil War made Carnegie rich, though he never fired a shot. He was twenty-six when the war began, working for the Pennsylvania Railroad and investing aggressively in every opportunity that came his way. He bought stock in railroads, oil companies, iron foundries, and bridge building companies. He understood something that most people missed: war was hell for soldiers but heaven for suppliers.

Carnegie's investments in iron and steel were particularly shrewd. The war consumed iron at an astonishing rate, for railroads, bridges, weapons, ships, and armor plating. After the war, the country would need even more to rebuild and expand westward. Carnegie began positioning himself at the intersection of these massive forces.

In 1865, Carnegie left the railroad to focus on his own ventures. He was already earning more from his investments than from his salary. He formed the Keystone Bridge Company, using iron and steel to replace wooden railroad bridges. The company was perfectly positioned, railroads were expanding rapidly, and wooden bridges were constantly burning down or collapsing. Carnegie's bridges were expensive but saved money in the long run.

But Carnegie was thinking bigger than bridges. He traveled to England and saw the Bessemer process, a revolutionary method for mass-producing steel by blowing air through molten iron to remove impurities. Steel was stronger and more versatile than iron, but had been expensive to produce. The Bessemer process changed everything, and Carnegie immediately grasped its implications.

In 1873, Carnegie decided to focus entirely on steel. He later told a friend, "Put all your eggs in one basket, and then watch that basket." At age thirty-seven, he bet everything on steel, building a massive plant near Pittsburgh that would become the Edgar Thomson Steel Works, named strategically after the president of the Pennsylvania Railroad, Carnegie's largest potential customer.

Vertical Integration: Controlling Everything from Mine to Market

Carnegie didn't invent vertical integration, but he perfected it with an almost artistic thoroughness. Other steel makers bought iron ore, coal, and limestone from suppliers. Carnegie decided to own the suppliers. He bought iron mines in Minnesota and Michigan. He bought coal fields in Pennsylvania. He bought limestone quarries. He bought the railroads and ships that transported raw materials to his plants.

When his steel mills needed more efficient transportation, he bought a fleet of Great Lakes steamships. When railroad rates were too high, he built his own railroad lines. At one point, Carnegie's operations included the raw materials, the transportation systems, the manufacturing plants, and even the sales networks. He controlled the entire process from the ore in the ground to the steel beams in a skyscraper.

The advantages were overwhelming. While competitors paid market prices for inputs and shipping, Carnegie's costs were a fraction as much. When steel prices were high, he made enormous profits. When prices crashed, his competitors went bankrupt while Carnegie survived and then bought their plants for pennies on the dollar during the panic.

But vertical integration wasn't just about cost savings. It was about information and control. Carnegie knew exactly how much iron ore was left in his mines. He knew precisely what his transportation costs would be years in advance. He could make long-term contracts with customers at prices competitors couldn't match because he understood his true costs to a degree they never could.

Carnegie also pioneered the use of chemistry and engineering in steel production. He hired university-trained chemists, almost unheard of in industrial plants to analyze the chemical composition of iron ore and optimize the Bessemer process. He installed cost accounting systems that tracked expenses for every single operation. He measured everything, optimized everything, controlled everything. A superintendent who couldn't explain a cost increase would be gone by morning.

His management style was hard-driving and ruthless. He practiced what he called "the Carnegie method", pitting managers against each other, comparing the costs of different plants, publicly praising those who reduced expenses and humiliating those who didn't. He paid well but demanded total dedication. The men who worked for Carnegie either became wealthy or had nervous breakdowns; sometimes both.

The Homestead Strike: When the Champion of Workers Became the Villain

Carnegie presented himself as a friend to working people. After all, hadn't he been a factory boy himself? He wrote articles arguing that labor had rights, that workers deserved dignity, that unions could be a positive force. His book "Triumphant Democracy" praised American workers as the backbone of national prosperity.

But Carnegie's enlightened rhetoric collided brutally with reality in 1892 at his Homestead steel plant outside Pittsburgh. The workers, members of the Amalgamated Association of Iron and Steel Workers, one of the strongest unions in America, were negotiating a new contract. Carnegie's partner and chairman, Henry Clay Frick, a man even more ruthless than Carnegie, decided to break the union completely.

Carnegie was conveniently in Scotland during the crisis, at his castle, Skibo. He left Frick in charge with instructions that most historians believe were deliberately vague, giving Frick permission to take a hard line while allowing Carnegie deniability. When negotiations failed, Frick locked workers out and brought in 300 Pinkerton guards by barge up the river.

What happened next shocked the nation. Workers were waiting on the shore, armed. A gunfight erupted that lasted all day, killing seven workers and three Pinkertons. The governor sent 8,500 state militia troops to occupy Homestead. The union was crushed. Frick survived an assassination attempt by an anarchist who had no connection to the union but was radicalized by the violence.

Carnegie's reputation never fully recovered. His eloquent writings about workers' dignity rang hollow after Homestead. He had always claimed he was different from the other robber barons, that he remembered being a poor boy but at Homestead he showed he would destroy workers as ruthlessly as any Vanderbilt or Gould when they threatened his profits. The champion of labor revealed himself to be, first and foremost, a champion of capital.

Some historians argue Carnegie genuinely believed he could have negotiated a better outcome and that Frick exceeded his instructions. Others see Carnegie's absence as calculated cowardice, letting Frick be the villain while Carnegie preserved his public image. The truth probably lies somewhere in between: Carnegie wanted to win but didn't want blood on his hands. He got both.

The Sale to Morgan: $480 Million and Walking Away

By 1900, Carnegie Steel Company dominated American steel production. Carnegie was sixty-five years old and thinking about mortality. He had no children who could inherit his business empire. His young wife, Louise, whom he'd married in 1887, was decades younger and had no interest in running steel mills. And Carnegie had been writing for years about the moral obligation of wealthy men to give their money away.

J.P. Morgan, the most powerful banker in America, was assembling U.S. Steel, a super-corporation that would control two-thirds of American steel production. He needed Carnegie Steel to make it work. But Carnegie was a notoriously tough negotiator, and Morgan knew a bidding war would be expensive.

The legend goes that Morgan's representative, Charles Schwab, met Carnegie on the golf course. Carnegie scribbled a number on a piece of paper: $480 million. Morgan looked at the figure and said, "I accept this price." There was no negotiation, no haggling. Morgan knew the number was fair, probably even a bargain. When they met later, Morgan said, "Mr. Carnegie, I want to congratulate you on being the richest man in the world."

Carnegie's reply revealed everything about his state of mind, "Mr. Morgan, I think I made a mistake. I should have asked you for $100 million more and you would have paid it."

The sale made Carnegie the richest man in America, though the title would soon pass to Rockefeller as Standard Oil's value soared. But more importantly, it freed Carnegie to pursue what he increasingly saw as his real life's work: giving the money away systematically and strategically.

The Gospel of Wealth: A Philosophy of Giving

Three years before selling his steel company, Carnegie published an essay that would define his legacy more than any amount of steel he ever produced. "The Gospel of Wealth," published in 1889, argued that rich men had a moral obligation to distribute their wealth for the public good during their lifetimes.

Carnegie's argument was complex and, to modern ears, paternalistic. He accepted wealth inequality as natural and even beneficial, the talented and hardworking would always accumulate more than others. He opposed both leaving large inheritances to children (which would make them lazy) and waiting until death to give money away (which was too late to ensure it was well spent). Instead, wealthy men should act as trustees of their fortunes, administering them for the benefit of society.

But not through indiscriminate charity. Carnegie scorned giving money directly to poor people, which he believed encouraged dependence. Instead, wealthy philanthropists should create opportunities for those willing to help themselves. His famous line captured this perfectly: "The man who dies rich dies disgraced."

This philosophy was shaped by Carnegie's own experience. He had risen through access to knowledge (Colonel Anderson's library) and opportunity (his telegraph job). He believed society needed institutions that gave ambitious poor boys the same chances he'd had. He wasn't interested in making poverty comfortable; he wanted to make escape from poverty possible.

Carnegie's philosophy also conveniently justified his own wealth accumulation. If he needed enormous fortune to give away enormous sums, then his ruthless business practices became almost virtuous, a necessary evil on the path to greater good. His critics, including labor leaders who remembered Homestead, found this self-serving. But Carnegie seemed to genuinely believe it.

The Library Builder: 2,509 Monuments to Learning

Carnegie's most visible legacy is the 2,509 libraries he funded across the English-speaking world. The first was in his boyhood home of Dunfermline in 1883. By the time he died in 1919, Carnegie libraries dotted cities and small towns from Pennsylvania to California, from Scotland to Australia.

The Carnegie library formula was specific and strategic. He would donate the building if the town would provide the land and commit to funding ongoing operations through taxes. This ensured local buy-in and sustainability. The buildings were often the most impressive structures in small towns, stone or brick palaces of learning that announced civic pride and possibility.

Carnegie believed libraries were nearly perfect philanthropy. They cost money to build but required users to invest their own time and effort to benefit. They were accessible to everyone but only useful to those willing to read and learn. They didn't create dependency but enabled independence. A poor boy with ambition could educate himself just as Carnegie had done.

The libraries weren't without controversy. Some towns refused Carnegie's offers, seeing them as blood money from Homestead. Labor unions sometimes opposed accepting funds from the man who had crushed their brothers. But most communities eagerly accepted. For many small towns, the Carnegie library was the first public building dedicated purely to intellectual improvement.

Walking into a Carnegie library today as thousands still operate you see Carnegie's philosophy in stone and wood. The architecture is dignified but not pretentious, classical but functional. The message is clear, knowledge is valuable, self-improvement is noble, and democracy requires an educated citizenry. These buildings weren't temples to Carnegie's ego; they were infrastructure for democratic capitalism.

Beyond Libraries: The Diversification of Giving

Libraries were Carnegie's most famous gift, but they were just the beginning. He gave $125 million to the Carnegie Corporation of New York, a foundation designed to continue his philanthropic work after his death. He established the Carnegie Endowment for International Peace, hoping to prevent wars through arbitration and education. He created the

Carnegie Hero Fund to recognize civilians who risked their lives saving others, honoring the kind of everyday courage he valued.

Carnegie also gave heavily to education. He founded Carnegie Mellon University in Pittsburgh, built Carnegie Hall in New York, and donated organs to thousands of churches across America (he loved organ music despite being an avowed skeptic about religion). He funded scientific research, built swimming pools, and supported pension funds for college professors and injured workers.

His giving was strategic but also reflected his personal enthusiasms and quirks. He loved music, so concert halls and organs. He romanticized the Scottish Highlands, so grants to Scottish universities. He believed in peace but also admired heroes, so both peace foundations and hero awards. His philanthropy was systematic but never impersonal.

By his death in 1919, Carnegie had given away roughly $350 million, about 90% of his fortune, equivalent to about $75 billion today. Only the Carnegie Corporation of New York remained with significant endowment to continue his work. His wife Louise inherited the remaining estate, which was modest by his former standards.

The Paradox of Carnegie: Ruthless Builder, Generous Giver

How do we reconcile the two Andrew Carnegies? The man who ground workers into exhaustion and crushed unions with violence, yet believed deeply in workers' dignity and opportunity? The man who monopolized an industry through ruthless competition, yet wrote eloquently about business's social responsibilities? The man who accumulated one of history's great fortunes, yet argued that dying rich was disgraceful?

Some see Carnegie as a hypocrite whose philanthropy was merely reputation laundering, buying back the respect that Homestead destroyed. Others view him as a man of his time, operating within the brutal rules of nineteenth-century capitalism while trying to ameliorate its worst effects. Still others see him as genuinely conflicted, believing simultaneously in ruthless competition and moral obligation, never fully resolving the contradiction.

Perhaps the most generous interpretation is that Carnegie was a man who changed. The poor Scottish immigrant who fought his way up saw competition as survival. The middle-aged industrialist building his steel empire saw business as war. But the elderly billionaire looking back saw waste and moral failure in a system that created such extremes of wealth and poverty. His philanthropy wasn't just reputation management; it was an attempt to build the infrastructure, libraries, universities, research institutions that might make the next generation's climb less brutal than his own.

Carnegie himself seemed aware of the paradox. In his autobiography, written near the end of his life, he described his working years with pride but his giving years with joy. He didn't apologize for his business practices, he believed he'd earned his fortune fairly within the system as it existed. But he also believed that keeping it all would be a moral failure.

The Carnegie Template: Blueprint for Modern Philanthropy

Carnegie's influence on modern philanthropy is impossible to overstate. He established principles that billionaires still follow more than a century later:

Strategic giving: Don't just donate randomly; identify high-impact causes and fund them systematically.

Institutional building: Create libraries, universities, and foundations that outlive the donor.

Matching requirements: Carnegie's library formula, making communities invest their own resources ensured local buy-in and sustainability.

Living giving: Don't wait until death; give while you can oversee distribution and adjust strategy.

Public advocacy: Carnegie didn't just give privately; he publicly argued that wealth carried obligations.

When Bill Gates and Warren Buffett created the Giving Pledge, asking billionaires to commit to giving away at least half their fortunes, they were following Carnegie's template. When Mark Zuckerberg pledged to give away his Facebook shares, he echoed Carnegie's arguments. When contemporary philanthropists debate effective altruism and how to maximize impact per dollar, they're continuing conversations Carnegie started.

But Carnegie's template also raised questions we still struggle with, Who should decide how billions are spent, democratic governments or individual billionaires? Does philanthropy excuse business practices that created extreme wealth in the first place? Can systematic giving address the structural inequalities that produce billionaires? Is it enough to build libraries and universities if the economic system keeps recreating poverty?

The Final Years: A Man Haunted by Homestead

Carnegie spent his final years at Skibo Castle in Scotland, his purchased Highland retreat. He continued to manage his philanthropic foundations but gradually withdrew from public life. The First World War devastated him, his peace foundation had failed to prevent the exact catastrophe it was created to stop. He saw his optimistic faith in inevitable human progress shattered by industrial-scale slaughter.

Friends noted that Carnegie remained haunted by Homestead. He would bring it up unprompted, still defending his actions, still insisting he would have negotiated if only he'd been there, still unable to escape the shadow of that July day in 1892 when workers and Pinkertons shot each other on the banks of the Monongahela River.

When Carnegie died in 1919 at age eighty-three, obituaries struggled with how to sum up his life. Industrialist and philanthropist. Robber baron and benefactor. Ruthless monopolist and generous donor. All were true, and none captured the full complexity.

His grave is simple, befitting a man who preached that dying rich was disgraceful. He succeeded in giving away most of his fortune, though the Carnegie Corporation of New York continues his work with an endowment of several billion dollars, the gift that keeps giving more than a century later.

Legacy: The Library Builder and the Questions He Left Behind

Walk into almost any American town of a certain age and you'll likely find a Carnegie library, even if it's been converted to a community center or museum. These buildings are Carnegie's most visible monuments, solid, dignified structures that embody his belief in self-improvement through education.

But Carnegie's deeper legacy is the question he forced into American consciousness: What is vast wealth actually for? He couldn't accept that accumulation was its own purpose. He needed his fortune to mean something beyond the steel it came from. His answer, systematic philanthropy guided by the donor's vision became the model for American billionaire giving.

Yet Homestead's shadow never quite lifts from Carnegie's legacy. He wanted to be remembered as the poor Scottish boy who made good and gave back, the champion of workers who built institutions for their advancement. But he's also remembered as the man whose fortune was built on twelve-hour days, seven-day weeks, and ultimately on violence against the very workers he claimed to champion.

Perhaps that's the most honest legacy, Carnegie as a man who embodied all the contradictions of American capitalism, its tremendous productive power and its brutal human costs, its capacity for incredible generosity and its foundation in ruthless competition, its promise of opportunity and its reality of exploitation. He made a fortune through means he later seemed uncomfortable with, then tried to redeem both himself and the system through philanthropic works that continue benefiting millions.

The question Carnegie left us is whether this bargain, ruthless wealth creation followed by systematic giving is enough. Can philanthropy balance the scales that business tips? Should we celebrate the libraries while remembering the workers who paid for them? Or should we see Carnegie whole, neither saint nor devil but a man whose life contained both remarkable achievement and moral compromise, whose legacy includes both opportunity created and dignity destroyed?

There's no simple answer, which is perhaps fitting for a man who spent his life wrestling with contradictions he never fully resolved. Andrew Carnegie died having given away his fortune, but the questions his life raised about wealth, power, and responsibility remain as urgent today as they were in the Gilded Age he helped create.

Chapter 5

Cornelius Vanderbilt - The Commodore's Empire

Cornelius Vanderbilt stood six feet tall in an era when most men barely reached five-foot-six. He had ice-blue eyes that could make grown men flinch, fists that had won countless street fights, and a vocabulary that made sailors blush. At sixteen years old, in 1810, he borrowed $100 from his mother to buy a small sailing vessel to ferry passengers and cargo between Staten Island and Manhattan. He named it *Swiftsure*, and it was the first piece of what would become the largest transportation empire in America.

Sixty years later, Vanderbilt would be worth over $100 million, approximately $200 billion in today's money making him the richest American of his time. He would control more miles of railroad track than some countries had roads. His name would become synonymous with wealth, power, and the kind of ruthless business practices that defined the Gilded Age. Yet within two generations of his death, his descendants would squander nearly every penny, turning one of history's great fortunes into a cautionary tale about the difference between building wealth and preserving it.

Vanderbilt's story is about timing, toughness, and an almost supernatural ability to know when to abandon a dying industry for a thriving one. But it's also about what happens when the empire builder's work ethic doesn't transfer to his heirs, when mansions replace businesses, and when the hunger that built the fortune is satisfied by the inheritance that destroys it.

The Staten Island Ferry Boy Who Learned to Fight

Cornelius Vanderbilt was born in 1794 on Staten Island, then a rural backwater, to a poor farming family of Dutch descent. His father operated a small ferry service, and young Cornelius grew up on the water, learning to sail before he could properly read. School held no interest for him, he dropped out at eleven and never returned. Throughout his life, he would spell phonetically and write in a crude hand, but his mathematical mind could calculate profit margins and compound interest faster than most educated men with pencil and paper.

The $100 loan from his mother came with conditions, earn it back by plowing and planting an eight-acre field, then deliver the harvest. Vanderbilt, already over six feet tall and strong as an ox, completed the task in weeks. His mother gave him the money, and he bought the small sailing vessel. He was in business.

But this wasn't gentle business. The New York harbor was controlled by established operators who didn't welcome competition. They tried to undercut his prices, bribe his customers, and even sabotage his boat. Vanderbilt responded with a combination of lower prices, better service, and physical intimidation. More than once, disputes were settled with fists on the docks. He earned a reputation as someone who would fight, literally and figuratively to protect his interests.

During the War of 1812, Vanderbilt secured a military contract to supply forts around New York Harbor. He expanded his fleet to six boats, working eighteen-hour days, captaining vessels himself while learning every aspect of the business. He saved obsessively, living frugally despite growing income. By age nineteen, he had paid back his mother and accumulated $9,000 in savings, a small fortune for someone who'd started with borrowed money just three years earlier.

But Vanderbilt's real education came from watching Thomas Gibbons, a wealthy New Jersey lawyer and businessman who hired the twenty-three-year-old Vanderbilt to captain his steamboat. Steamboats were the cutting-edge technology of the 1810s, and Gibbons was locked in a legal and business war with Robert Fulton and Robert Livingston, who claimed a monopoly on steamboat traffic in New York waters granted by the state legislature.

Vanderbilt captained Gibbons's steamboat in deliberate violation of the monopoly, daring the authorities to stop him. He was arrested multiple times and developed a taste for legal warfare that would serve him throughout his career. More importantly, he saw how monopolies worked and how much money they made. The experience taught him that controlling infrastructure was more valuable than simply using it, and that legal barriers to competition were worth fighting to obtain.

Breaking Monopolies to Build His Own

By 1829, Vanderbilt had saved $30,000 working for Gibbons. He was thirty-five years old, and he saw his opportunity. The steamboat business was expanding rapidly on the Hudson River and Long Island Sound. Established operators charged high prices and provided mediocre service, protected by various informal monopolies and price-fixing agreements.

Vanderbilt launched his own steamboat line with a simple strategy, drastically undercut competitors on price while providing better, faster service. He would operate at a loss initially if necessary, driving competitors to financial exhaustion. Once he'd forced them out or absorbed them, he'd raise prices to profitable levels. It was a strategy he'd use repeatedly throughout his career, and it worked devastatingly well.

His competitors tried everything to stop him. They cut their own prices, sometimes offering free passage. Vanderbilt cut his prices further and improved service. They tried to buy him out. Vanderbilt demanded astronomical sums, then used the money to expand his fleet and attack new routes. They appealed to legislatures for protective laws. Vanderbilt hired better lawyers and bribed more effectively.

One famous story captures his approach: a competitor offered Vanderbilt $100,000 plus $5,000 monthly for ten years to simply stay off a particular route. Vanderbilt took the money, then used it to fund cutthroat competition on other routes, destroying the same competitor's business elsewhere. When accused of accepting money not to compete while competing anyway, Vanderbilt pointed out the agreement only covered one specific route. He had kept the letter of the deal while gutting its spirit.

By the 1840s, Vanderbilt controlled most steamboat traffic in the New York region. He operated faster ships with better amenities at lower prices than competitors. He made enemies of nearly every established businessman in New York, but customers loved him because he made travel cheaper and more accessible. The public nicknamed him "Commodore" in tribute to his maritime empire, and the name stuck for life.

But Vanderbilt was already looking ahead. Steamboats were profitable, but the railroad was the future. He began studying the emerging railroad industry with the same intensity he'd once studied steamboat operations, waiting for his moment to make the leap.

The Gold Rush Gamble: Nicaragua and Near-Disaster

In 1849, gold was discovered in California, and Americans went mad with gold fever. Getting to California meant either a dangerous overland journey across the continent or an equally dangerous sea voyage around Cape Horn, the southern tip of South America. Vanderbilt saw opportunity in the gap.

He proposed a revolutionary route: steamship from New York to Nicaragua, a quick overland transit across Nicaragua at its narrowest point, then another steamship up the Pacific coast to San Francisco. It would cut weeks off the journey and avoid both the western wilderness and the treacherous Cape Horn passage.

Vanderbilt personally traveled to Nicaragua to negotiate transit rights and survey the route. At age fifty-five, he hacked through jungles and navigated rivers, displaying the same hands-on approach that had characterized his ferry days. He formed the Accessory Transit Company and began running the route in 1851, charging less than competitors while making enormous profits on volume.

For a few years, it was spectacularly successful. Vanderbilt's Nicaragua route carried thousands of gold seekers and made millions of dollars. Then it collapsed in a combination of business betrayal and international politics that nearly destroyed him.

Two of Vanderbilt's business associates, Charles Morgan and Cornelius Garrison, conspired to take control of the Accessory Transit Company while Vanderbilt was taking a rare vacation, a European tour on his private yacht. They bribed Nicaraguan officials, manipulated company stock, and positioned themselves to steal the company Vanderbilt had built.

When Vanderbilt discovered the betrayal, he sent Morgan a letter containing one of the most famous lines in business history: "Gentlemen: You have undertaken to cheat me. I won't sue you, for the law is too slow. I'll ruin you. Yours truly, Cornelius Vanderbilt."

It wasn't an idle threat. Vanderbilt systematically destroyed their business. He funded a rival route through Panama, undercutting their prices so severely they couldn't compete. He manipulated shipping schedules and bribed officials. He even backed a rival faction in Nicaragua's civil war, the faction that revoked Morgan and Garrison's transit rights. Within a few years, both men were financially ruined, their company destroyed, their reputations in tatters.

But the victory came at a cost. The Nicaragua route was caught up in Central American political instability and eventually became untenable. Vanderbilt extracted himself profitably but recognized that maritime transportation, while lucrative, was vulnerable to political upheaval and competition. The future lay in railroads, ribbons of steel that once laid were hard to replicate, that couldn't be stolen by political coups, and that were becoming the circulatory system of American commerce.

The Pivot to Railroads: An Old Man's New Empire

In 1862, Vanderbilt was sixty-eight years old, ancient by nineteenth-century standards. Most men his age were retired or dead. Vanderbilt was just getting started on his greatest project: consolidating American railroads into an integrated system.

He began by buying the New York and Harlem Railroad, a struggling line that ran from Manhattan to upstate New York. It was poorly managed, deep in debt, and losing money. Vanderbilt saw potential: it was one of only two rail connections between Manhattan and the mainland. He bought control, installed new management, invested in track improvements, and turned it profitable within a year.

Then he executed one of the most audacious stock manipulations in financial history. Vanderbilt learned that corrupt New York City councilmen were planning to revoke his streetcar franchise in Manhattan; they wanted bribes he'd refused to pay. He also knew they planned to short the stock, betting its price would fall then profit from the revocation announcement.

Vanderbilt quietly bought every share he could find. When the councilmen announced the franchise revocation, the stock initially fell as expected. The corrupt politicians tried to buy shares to cover their short positions but Vanderbilt owned nearly all available shares. He could name his price. The councilmen faced infinite losses unless Vanderbilt agreed to sell. He squeezed them mercilessly, forcing them to buy at ruinous prices, bankrupting several in the process. The public reveled in seeing corrupt politicians crushed by someone even more ruthless.

With the New York and Harlem Railroad secured, Vanderbilt began acquiring other railroads: the Hudson River Railroad, then the New York Central Railroad. His strategy was similar to his steamboat days: identify weak, poorly managed railroads that controlled strategic routes, buy control, improve operations, eliminate redundancy, and connect them into an integrated system.

By 1867, Vanderbilt controlled an unbroken railroad line from New York City to Buffalo, connecting the nation's largest city to the Great Lakes and westward expansion. He merged the individual railroads into the New York Central, creating one of the most powerful companies in America. He was seventy-three years old and worth approximately $40 million, but he wasn't finished.

The Erie War: Vanderbilt Meets His Match

Vanderbilt's next target was the Erie Railroad, which ran parallel to his New York Central line from New York to Buffalo. Controlling both would give him a near-monopoly on rail transport in upstate New York. But the Erie was controlled by three men who would prove to be Vanderbilt's most formidable opponents: Jay Gould, James Fisk, and Daniel Drew, a trio of speculators and manipulators whose corruption and creativity exceeded even Vanderbilt's.

What followed was the most spectacular financial battle of the nineteenth century. Vanderbilt began buying Erie stock, intending to acquire majority control. Gould, Fisk, and Drew responded by simply printing more stock, literally running printing presses in the Erie offices to create new shares as fast as Vanderbilt could buy existing ones. It was blatantly illegal, but they had bribed judges and legislators who looked the other way.

Vanderbilt bought millions of dollars worth of Erie stock, but his ownership percentage never increased, the denominator kept growing as

Gould's printing presses churned out new certificates. Finally, Vanderbilt got a friendly judge to issue arrest warrants for the trio. They fled to New Jersey with millions in cash, setting up headquarters in a Jersey City hotel fortified with guards and cannons.

The "Erie War" dominated newspapers for months. Vanderbilt controlled New York courts and police. Gould controlled New Jersey and had enough cash to bribe the New York legislature. Both sides bought politicians wholesale, with Albany legislators openly auctioning their votes. Estimates suggest over $1 million in bribes changed hands, an astronomical sum at the time.

Eventually, Vanderbilt accepted reality: he couldn't win. Gould's printing presses could create stock faster than Vanderbilt could buy it, and Gould had sufficient political protection to make the fraud legal retroactively. Vanderbilt negotiated a truce: Gould would buy back Vanderbilt's Erie stock at a small loss, and Vanderbilt would abandon his takeover attempt.

It was one of the few times in his life Vanderbilt lost a business fight. He was reportedly philosophical about it: "Never kick a skunk" became his assessment of tangling with Gould. But the loss stung, and Vanderbilt focused the rest of his energy on expanding and improving the New York Central rather than acquiring competitors.

The Last Years: King of the Railroads

Vanderbilt's final decade was spent consolidating his railroad empire. He extended the New York Central westward to Chicago, connecting the Atlantic coast to the heartland. He upgraded tracks, built new terminals, improved scheduling, and reduced rates. The New York Central became the standard against which other railroads were measured, efficient, profitable, and powerful.

He also built Grand Central Depot (predecessor to today's Grand Central Terminal) in Manhattan, creating a grand entrance to his railroad empire. The building was both functional, consolidating three separate rail stations and symbolic, announcing Vanderbilt's dominance in marble and iron.

Personally, Vanderbilt remained the same rough, profane, pragmatic man he'd always been. He never learned to spell properly, never read literature for pleasure, never developed refined tastes or sophisticated manners. He played whist for high stakes, bet heavily on horse racing, and made crude jokes. High society found him embarrassing but couldn't ignore his wealth.

His family life was troubled. His first wife, Sophia, died in 1868 after a long illness. Against his family's wishes, the seventy-five-year-old Vanderbilt married a thirty-year-old cousin, Frank Crawford. His children were scandalized, particularly when Vanderbilt seemed more energetic and engaged with his young wife than he'd been in years.

His relationship with his children was complicated. He had thirteen children with Sophia, but only four survived to adulthood. He showed open contempt for most of them, particularly his eldest son Cornelius Jeremiah, who suffered from epilepsy and gambling addiction. Vanderbilt cut him off financially multiple times and publicly stated his disappointment. Only his second son, William Henry Vanderbilt, earned his respect by demonstrating business acumen managing the Staten Island Railroad.

As death approached, Vanderbilt faced the question that haunts every empire builder, succession. He could divide his fortune equally among his children, but that would fragment his railroad empire and give control to people he considered incompetent. Or he could concentrate it with one heir, preserving the business but creating resentment.

The Will That Preserved an Empire (Temporarily)

When Vanderbilt died in January 1877 at age eighty-two, his will shocked New York society. He left approximately $95 million to his second son, William Henry Vanderbilt, the largest personal fortune ever transferred at that point in American history. His widow Frank received the Manhattan house and $500,000. Each of his eight surviving daughters received a trust fund worth between $250,000 and $500,000.

His eldest son, Cornelius Jeremiah, received only the interest on $200,000, with the principal held in trust. Within two years, Cornelius Jeremiah would commit suicide, shooting himself in a New York hotel room. His suicide note blamed his father's rejection.

The will was immediately challenged by Vanderbilt's other children, leading to a sensational trial that captivated the nation. Lawyers argued that the will was unfair, that Vanderbilt had been mentally incompetent, that William had exercised undue influence. Spiritualists testified (bizarrely) that Vanderbilt had been communicating with the dead. Former employees testified about his crude behavior and temper.

The trial revealed embarrassing details about the Commodore's life, his profanity, his contempt for most of his children, his relationship with spiritualists, and his coarse manners. But it also revealed his sharp mind and clear business judgment right until the end. The will was upheld. William inherited the empire intact.

Vanderbilt's decision to concentrate his fortune was strategically sound in the short term. William proved to be a capable manager who doubled the fortune during his nine years controlling it, leaving $200 million when he died in 1885. But concentrating the fortune also set the stage for its eventual squandering by heirs more interested in spending than building.

The Gilded Descendants: How the Fortune Vanished

William Henry Vanderbilt inherited his father's business acumen but not his frugality. He lived more lavishly, built grander houses, and began the family's transformation from builders to spenders. But William still worked, still managed the railroads actively, still thought like a businessman. His sons would not.

When William died in 1885, he split the fortune more evenly among his children, but still concentrated the majority with his two eldest sons, Cornelius II and William K. Vanderbilt. Now the floodgates truly opened. The third generation of Vanderbilts built some of the most extravagant mansions in American history.

Cornelius II built The Breakers in Newport, Rhode Island, a 70-room Italian Renaissance palace that cost $7 million and took 2,500 workers to build. William K. built Marble House, also in Newport, literally importing 500,000 cubic feet of marble from Italy. Alva Vanderbilt, William K.'s wife threw a costume ball that cost $250,000, approximately $6 million today for a single party.

The mansions multiplied, Biltmore Estate in North Carolina (largest private home in America, 178,926 square feet), multiple Fifth Avenue palaces in Manhattan, summer "cottages" in Newport, European castles, yachts that rivaled ocean liners. The Vanderbilts became American royalty, defining the Gilded Age aesthetic of ostentatious consumption.

But none of these Vanderbilts worked in any meaningful sense. They managed investments, sat on corporate boards, and attended social events. They spent their time decorating mansions, organizing balls, racing yachts, and competing for social status. They married European aristocrats, buying noble titles with American money. They lived like royalty because they could, never questioning whether they should.

The fortune hemorrhaged. Maintaining multiple massive estates required armies of servants and constant repairs. Throwing elaborate parties required enormous expenditure. Competing socially with other wealthy families demanded ever-greater displays. The railroads that generated the fortune were sold or their value diluted through stock issues and dividends extracted to fund lifestyles.

By the 1920s and 1930s, the Vanderbilt fortune was evaporating. The Great Depression accelerated the decline. The massive mansions became impossible to maintain, property taxes and upkeep consumed whatever income remained. One by one, the palaces were sold, often for pennies compared to their construction costs, or simply demolished because no one wanted to buy them.

The Last Vanderbilt Fortune: A Warning Unheeded

In 1973, roughly 120 descendants of Cornelius Vanderbilt gathered for a family reunion at Vanderbilt University, which Cornelius had endowed (ironically, it's one of his few lasting legacies). Not a single attendee was a millionaire. The largest fortune in American history had completely evaporated within four generations.

The decline wasn't due to bad luck or economic catastrophe. It was the predictable result of systematic overconsumption, lack of business engagement, and the false assumption that immense wealth was permanent. Each generation inherited less, spent more, and contributed nothing to wealth regeneration. The third generation built mansions. The fourth generation sold them. The fifth generation worked regular jobs.

The Vanderbilts violated every principle of dynasty building that contemporary wealthy families now follow. They didn't diversify investments meaningfully. They didn't instill work ethic in heirs. They didn't create trust structures that prevented total dissipation. They didn't require heirs to be productive. They confused spending with status and consumption with legacy.

Several Vanderbilt descendants have written about this cautionary tale. Anderson Cooper, the CNN journalist and Vanderbilt descendant through his mother Gloria Vanderbilt, has spoken publicly about the family fortune's disappearance and his mother's explicit decision not to leave him an inheritance, believing he needed to work for his own success. Gloria herself, once called "the poor little rich girl," saw multiple family fortunes squandered and chose to break the pattern.

The Commodore's Lessons: What Vanderbilt Got Right and Wrong

Cornelius Vanderbilt's business career offers several enduring lessons about wealth creation:

Know when to pivot: Vanderbilt's greatest skill was recognizing when an industry was maturing and moving capital to emerging opportunities. Sailing to steamboats to railroads, each time he abandoned a profitable business for a more promising one, even when competitors thought him foolish.

Control infrastructure, not just operations: Vanderbilt understood that owning the tracks was more valuable than running trains, just as owning steamboat companies was better than captaining individual boats. He always sought to control the bottlenecks and the infrastructure.

Be ruthless when necessary: Vanderbilt's competitors learned that he would fight without mercy, using price wars, legal manipulation, political bribery, and any other tool available. His reputation for ruthlessness sometimes won battles before they started.

Focus creates power: Unlike many wealthy contemporaries who diversified into many businesses, Vanderbilt concentrated on transportation. This focus allowed him to understand his industry deeply and to accumulate market-dominating positions.

Tough times reveal character: Vanderbilt worked into his eighties, personally surveying rail lines and managing operations. The work ethic that lifted him from poverty never left him.

But Vanderbilt also demonstrated fatal weaknesses in planning for succession:

Wealth without purpose dies: Vanderbilt built an empire but never articulated a larger purpose beyond accumulation. His heirs inherited money but no mission, fortune but no philosophy.

Work ethic isn't genetic: Vanderbilt assumed his descendants would naturally value work as he did. They didn't. Growing up wealthy, they never experienced the hunger that drove him.

Concentration creates vulnerability: By leaving nearly everything to one son, Vanderbilt preserved his empire temporarily but created enormous inequality among heirs. The resentment and entitled spending by subsequent generations accelerated the decline.

No institutional structures: Unlike Carnegie or Rockefeller, who created foundations and institutions, Vanderbilt left only businesses. When the businesses were sold or declined, nothing remained.

The Empty Palaces: What Remains of Vanderbilt's Empire

Today, Vanderbilt's most visible legacy consists of empty palaces converted to museums. The Breakers in Newport welcomes tourists who pay admission to gawk at the excess. Biltmore Estate operates as a winery and tourist attraction. Marble House hosts weddings and events. These monuments to spending have outlasted the fortune that built them, teaching visitors more through their emptiness than they ever taught their residents through their grandeur.

Vanderbilt University remains, though the family long ago lost control of it. Grand Central Terminal in New York, rebuilt on the site of Vanderbilt's original depot, still bears his name. A few streets and parks carry the Vanderbilt name. Otherwise, the largest fortune in nineteenth-century America has vanished almost without trace.

The contrast with Carnegie is instructive. Carnegie was worth less than Vanderbilt but built institutions, libraries, universities, foundations that continue operating 100+ years after his death, touching millions of lives annually. Vanderbilt was worth more but built only businesses that were eventually sold, and mansions that became museums of excess.

Perhaps the cruelest irony is that Vanderbilt's name is now most commonly associated not with transportation innovation or business genius, but with the rapid squandering of dynastic wealth. Business schools teach the "Vanderbilt effect", how fortunes disappear across generations without proper planning. Financial advisors cite the Vanderbilts when warning clients about the dangers of failing to prepare heirs.

The Ghost of Staten Island: A Poor Boy's Ambition

There's a story, possibly apocryphal, that in his final months, the dying Vanderbilt would sometimes speak as if he were back on Staten Island, calling out navigation instructions as if captaining a ferry across New York Harbor. His mind returned to the beginning, to the sixteen-year-old boy with borrowed money and unlimited ambition.

That boy would have been astounded to see what he built: railroads spanning states, a fortune exceeding most national treasuries, a name synonymous with American wealth. But would he have been proud of what became of it? Would he have recognized the mansion-building, party-throwing, yacht-racing descendants as his legacy? Or would he have been disgusted by their softness, their idleness, their transformation of his life's work into decorating budgets?

Vanderbilt himself provided no answer because he never seriously addressed the question. He assumed strength, competitiveness, and work ethic were natural human traits rather than products of circumstance. He assumed his descendants would want to build as he had built, to work as he had worked, to fight as he had fought. His greatest miscalculation wasn't in business, it was in human nature.

The Commodore died the richest man in America, but his true legacy isn't the fortune he built, it's the fortune his descendants lost. And in that loss lies perhaps his most valuable lesson: that creating wealth and preserving wealth require different skills, that work ethic doesn't transfer through inheritance, and that without purpose beyond accumulation, even the greatest fortunes return to dust as surely as the empire builders themselves.

The boy who started with one boat and $100 borrowed from his mother ended up proving something he never intended: that it's not enough to build an empire. You have to build something that survives you. And that requires either institutions that outlast individuals, or descendants who share your values. Vanderbilt achieved neither, and so the greatest transportation empire of the nineteenth century vanished like morning mist over New York Harbor, leaving behind only empty palaces as monuments to ambition without legacy, fortune without purpose, and wealth that taught its heirs everything about spending and nothing about building.

PART II: THE INDUSTRIAL AGE MOGULS (1900-1970s)

Chapter 6

Henry Ford - The Assembly Line Revolutionary

In the spring of 1903, a forty-year-old engineer with two failed companies behind him convinced a handful of investors to give him one more chance. Henry Ford had already burned through the patience of Detroit's business elite. His first venture, the Detroit Automobile Company, had collapsed after producing vehicles so unreliable that customers demanded refunds. His second attempt, the Henry Ford Company, ended with him being forced out by his own investors. Most men would have accepted defeat and returned to steady employment. Henry Ford was not most men.

What happened next would transform not just the automobile industry, but the entire architecture of modern manufacturing, reshape the American economy, redefine the relationship between workers and wages, and make Ford one of the richest men who ever lived. It would also reveal a personality of stunning contradictions, a man who revolutionized worker compensation while harboring deep prejudices, who democratized mobility while resisting change, whose innovations made him a billionaire but whose stubbornness nearly destroyed everything he built.

The Failed Ventures Before the Model T

Henry Ford's path to greatness was paved with spectacular failures that would have crushed a less obstinate man. Born in 1863 on a Michigan farm, Ford showed an early aptitude for machinery and a deep distaste for agricultural labor. While his father hoped he would inherit the family farm, young Henry spent his time disassembling and reassembling watches, dreaming of mechanisms far more complex than plows and threshers.

His first attempt at building a commercial automobile company, the Detroit Automobile Company, launched in 1899 with $150,000 in capital from prominent Detroit businessmen. It was a disaster from the start. Ford, ever the perfectionist, couldn't stop tinkering. Each vehicle rolled out differently from the last. Quality was inconsistent. Prices were too high. Production was agonizingly slow. Within eighteen months, the company had produced just twenty vehicles and was hemorrhaging money. The investors shuttered the operation in January 1901.

Most entrepreneurs would have slunk away in shame. Ford, however, had identified the fundamental problem: automobiles were being built like custom furniture, one piece at a time, by craftsmen who assembled each vehicle from start to finish. This artisanal approach meant cars were expensive, inconsistent, and accessible only to the wealthy. Ford's vision was radically different, he wanted to build cars the way his heroes, Samuel Colt and Cyrus McCormick, had built guns and reapers: through standardization and mass production.

But vision without execution means nothing, and Ford needed to prove he could actually build something people wanted. He pivoted to racing, the motorsport of the era that captivated public attention and attracted wealthy enthusiasts. In October 1901, Ford personally drove a race car he'd built to victory against Alexander Winton, the country's most famous driver. The win generated publicity and attracted new investors, including coal merchant Alexander Malcomson.

The Henry Ford Company was born from this success in November 1901, but it lasted barely four months. Ford and his new investors clashed immediately over direction. They wanted to produce luxury cars for the wealthy. Ford wanted to build simple, affordable vehicles for the masses. The investors brought in engineer Henry M. Leland to assess Ford's designs. Leland, a perfectionist who would later found Cadillac and Lincoln, found Ford's work substandard. The board sided with Leland. Ford walked away or was pushed taking $900 and the rights to his name.

Two failures before age forty. Most of Detroit's business community now considered Henry Ford unreliable, stubborn, and possibly delusional in his obsession with cheap cars. Who, after all, wanted cheap cars? The automobile was a luxury item, a toy for the rich. The conventional wisdom held that quality manufacturers should focus on wealthy buyers who could afford their products.

Henry Ford thought the conventional wisdom was backward.

The Third Time's the Charm: Ford Motor Company

In June 1903, Ford and Malcomson, who still believed in him, scraped together twelve investors and $28,000 to launch the Ford Motor Company. The amount would be worth roughly $900,000 today, not exactly a shoestring budget, but far from the deep pockets backing his earlier failures. One investor, the Dodge brothers, contributed $10,000 worth of parts in exchange for stock. Another, lawyer John Anderson, invested $5,000 and later remarked it was "the most profitable decision I ever made in my life." That stake would eventually be worth hundreds of millions.

The early Ford Motor Company operated out of a converted wagon factory on Mack Avenue in Detroit. The operation was modest: Ford didn't actually manufacture most components. Instead, following common practice of the era, he assembled cars from parts made by suppliers. The Dodge brothers supplied engines and transmissions. Other vendors provided wheels, bodies, and hardware. Ford's innovation wasn't in what he made, but in how he organized production.

The company's first product, the Model A (not to be confused with the later, more famous Model A of 1927), sold for $850, expensive for the time, but cheaper than most competitors. It was a simple, sturdy vehicle with an eight-horsepower engine. More importantly, it worked. Ford had finally learned the lesson of his first failure: don't ship the prototype. The Model A was tested, refined, and reliable.

Sales exceeded all projections. The company sold 1,708 Model As in the first fifteen months and turned a profit almost immediately. Ford and his team followed with Models B, C, F, K, N, R, and S over the next few years, an alphabetical progression that seems quaint now but represented Ford's methodical approach to learning what customers wanted and what his operation could efficiently produce.

The more expensive models sold poorly. The cheaper, simpler models flew out of showrooms. Ford was learning what he had long suspected: there was an enormous untapped market of people who wanted automobiles but couldn't afford the luxury vehicles that dominated the industry. Most manufacturers were pursuing 10,000 wealthy customers willing to pay $3,000. Ford wanted to pursue 1,000,000 middle-class customers willing to pay $500.

By 1908, Ford was ready to bet everything on his vision.

The Model T: The Car That Changed Everything

On October 1, 1908, the Ford Motor Company introduced the Model T. It was ugly, a boxy, utilitarian vehicle with none of the elegance of luxury automobiles. It came in one color: black (contrary to popular belief, Ford actually said "Any customer can have a car painted any color that he wants so long as it is black" much later, in 1922, after years of offering multiple colors). Early Model Ts came in gray, green, blue, and red. Black eventually became standard because black paint dried fastest, speeding production.

The Model T wasn't the cheapest car in America, that honor belonged to various short-lived competitors. It wasn't the fastest or most powerful. What made it revolutionary was the combination of price, durability, and simplicity. At $825, it cost roughly half what most cars sold for, yet it was rugged enough to handle America's terrible roads. It was light enough that a farmer could pull it out of mud. Its 22-horsepower engine could reach 40-45 miles per hour. Most crucially, it was designed to be repaired by owners with basic tools.

The Model T was an instant sensation. Ford sold 10,000 in the first year. By 1912, sales reached 170,000 annually. The company couldn't build them fast enough. And this is where Ford made the leap that would transform him from successful businessman to historical titan.

Mass Production Innovation: The Assembly Line

The conventional approach to manufacturing in 1913 involved skilled craftsmen building products from start to finish. A team of workers would gather around a chassis and spend twelve hours assembling a complete automobile, walking back and forth to retrieve parts, adjusting components, solving problems. It was inefficient, required highly skilled labor, and was expensive.

Ford had toured slaughterhouses (or more accurately, "disassembly" plants) and watched butchers break down cattle carcasses in a line, each worker performing one specific cut as the carcass moved past. He'd also studied the work of Frederick Winslow Taylor, whose "scientific management" principles applied engineering precision to human labor. Ford wondered: if disassembly could be optimized with a moving line, why not assembly?

In 1913, at Ford's new Highland Park plant, the company experimented with moving assembly lines. Instead of workers moving to the car, the car moved to the workers. Each worker performed one specific task, attaching a wheel, bolting in seats, installing the engine as the chassis moved steadily along a conveyor belt. The worker didn't need comprehensive automotive knowledge, just expertise in their particular task.

The results were staggering. Assembly time for a Model T dropped from twelve hours to ninety-three minutes. Then, as Ford refined the process, to just over ninety minutes. Productivity exploded. Costs plummeted. Ford passed the savings to customers, cutting the Model T's price from $825 in 1908 to $360 by 1916 (remember, this was during a period of inflation—the price dropped by more than half even as general prices rose). Lower prices meant more sales, which meant greater economies of scale, which meant even lower prices. It was a virtuous cycle that competitors couldn't match.

By 1914, Ford Motor Company was producing more cars than all other manufacturers combined. The Highland Park plant churned out a Model T every twenty-four seconds. Ford had achieved what no one thought possible: he'd made the automobile affordable for ordinary working people. In 1908, there were roughly 200,000 cars in America. By 1920, there were 8 million, and half of them were Model Ts.

The assembly line didn't just transform Ford Motor Company, it became the template for modern manufacturing. Every factory producing complex products, from radios to refrigerators to airplanes, would adopt Ford's innovation. The assembly line stands alongside the steam engine and electricity as one of the fundamental innovations that enabled modern industrial society.

Henry Ford's personal wealth exploded. He owned 58.5% of Ford Motor Company stock. As the company's value soared into the hundreds of millions, Ford became one of the richest men in the world. By the early 1920s, his personal fortune exceeded $1 billion, equivalent to roughly $15-20 billion today. And he was just getting started.

The $5 Workday: Revolution or Calculation?

On January 5, 1914, Ford Motor Company made an announcement that shocked the business world and made front-page news across America: the company would pay workers $5 per day, more than double the prevailing industrial wage of $2.34. Additionally, the workday would be reduced from nine hours to eight hours, and the company would move to three shifts instead of two, creating additional jobs.

The reaction was immediate and explosive. The New York Times covered it extensively. Business leaders called Ford a socialist, a madman, and a traitor to his class. The Wall Street Journal warned Ford was injecting "spiritual principles into a field where they do not belong" and undermining the entire industrial system. Crowds of job-seekers mobbed Highland Park, with 10,000 men showing up in frigid winter weather hoping to be hired.

Workers across America suddenly had a benchmark for fair wages. Labor organizers pointed to Ford as proof that industrial companies could afford to pay more. Other manufacturers fumed that Ford was driving up labor costs across the economy.

Was Ford's $5 day a revolutionary act of enlightened capitalism and social engineering, or brilliant business strategy dressed up as benevolence? The truth is both.

Ford faced a serious problem by early 1914. The assembly line had made production incredibly efficient, but it had also made work mind-numbingly repetitive. Worker turnover was catastrophic, Ford had to hire 52,000 people per year to maintain a workforce of 14,000. The cost of constantly training new workers was eating into profits. Absenteeism was rampant. Many workers simply walked off the job, unable to tolerate the mechanical repetition.

The $5 day solved these problems immediately. Turnover plummeted. Absenteeism dropped. Workers fought to keep their jobs. Productivity soared as experienced workers stayed longer and worked harder. Ford got a more stable, efficient workforce and generated enormous positive publicity that cemented his reputation as a friend to working people.

But the $5 day came with strings attached that revealed Ford's paternalistic streak and desire to control workers' lives beyond the factory floor. To qualify for the full $5, workers had to pass inspection by Ford's

"Sociological Department," a creepy quasi-investigative unit that sent staff to workers' homes to ensure they met Ford's standards of middle-class respectability.

The investigators checked whether workers drank alcohol, gambled, or engaged in other behavior Ford deemed immoral. They verified that homes were clean and that families were intact. Immigrant workers had to attend English classes. Single men under twenty-two were disqualified unless they were supporting family members. Women were generally excluded unless they were single and supporting dependents.

Workers who failed inspection received only the base wage until they reformed their behavior to Ford's satisfaction. It was enlightened capitalism with a heavy dose of social control. Ford would pay you well but in return he expected to mold you into his vision of a proper citizen.

The Dark Side: Anti-Semitism and Controversial Views

As Ford's wealth and influence grew, so did the platform for his increasingly troubling views. During the 1920s, Ford used his fortune to promote conspiracy theories and anti-Semitic propaganda that would forever stain his legacy and raise uncomfortable questions about separating innovation from ideology.

In 1919, Ford purchased a small newspaper called The Dearborn Independent. Over the next seven years, the paper published a series of articles blaming Jewish people for virtually every social problem facing America. The articles claimed Jews controlled banking, media, and government. They pushed conspiracy theories about Jewish plots to undermine Christian civilization. The paper serialized "The International Jew," a four-volume collection of anti-Semitic propaganda that was translated into multiple languages.

Adolf Hitler praised Ford in Mein Kampf, and Ford was the only American mentioned by name. In 1938, Ford accepted the Grand Cross of the German Eagle, the highest honor Nazi Germany could bestow on a foreigner. While Ford's defenders note he later expressed some regret about The Dearborn Independent and closed it in 1927 after lawsuits, the damage was done. His ideas influenced the darkest chapter of the 20th century.

How could the same man who revolutionized manufacturing and improved workers' lives harbor such vile prejudices? It's a question that highlights the uncomfortable reality that genius in one domain doesn't translate to wisdom in others, and that transformative innovations can come from deeply flawed people. Ford's anti-Semitism wasn't incidental to his worldview, it reflected his broader tendency toward rigid thinking, suspicion of outsiders, and belief that he understood society better than the experts.

Stubbornness Nearly Destroys the Empire

The same obstinacy that drove Ford to succeed against repeated failures eventually became his greatest liability. By the 1920s, Ford had achieved everything he'd set out to accomplish. The Model T had put America on wheels. Ford Motor Company dominated the industry. Henry Ford was one of the richest, most famous men in the world.

And he was completely convinced that the Model T should never change.

While competitors like General Motors introduced new models with improved features, colors, and style, Ford remained committed to the basic black Model T design. His son Edsel, who served as company president, begged his father to develop new models. Engineers presented designs for updated vehicles. Everyone could see that consumer preferences were changing, people wanted more than bare-bones transportation. They wanted style, comfort, and variety.

Henry Ford refused to listen. "We've got a pretty good car," he insisted. The Model T had made him a billionaire; why fix what wasn't broken?

By 1926, the Ford Motor Company's market share had collapsed from 55% to less than 30%. General Motors, under the leadership of Alfred Sloan, had introduced the concept of yearly model changes and cars for different price points, from Chevrolet to Cadillac. Chrysler was gaining ground. The Model T, once revolutionary, was now obsolete.

Finally, in May 1927, Ford admitted defeat. The last Model T rolled off the assembly line on May 26, 1927. Ford shut down production for six months, an eternity in the automotive industry to retool factories for the Model A. During this period, Ford lost even more market share and laid off thousands of workers. The shutdown cost the company roughly $250 million (over $4 billion today).

The Model A was a success and saved the company, but Ford never fully recovered its dominance. The man who had revolutionized the industry had nearly destroyed his own company through sheer stubbornness.

Family Feuds and the Battle for the Company

The Ford family drama reads like Shakespearean tragedy. Henry Ford's relationship with his son Edsel was complex and often cruel. Edsel was everything his father was not: refined, diplomatic, interested in aesthetics and design, and open to new ideas. Henry valued toughness and repeatedly undermined his son's authority, overruling his decisions and belittling him in front of employees.

Edsel pushed for the innovations that kept Ford Motor Company competitive, the Model A, the V-8 engine, the Mercury brand, and sleeker designs. Henry resisted and sabotaged many of these initiatives. The psychological toll on Edsel was immense. In 1943, at age forty-nine, Edsel died from stomach cancer, though many believed the stress of dealing with his father contributed to his death.

After Edsel's death, the eighty-year-old Henry Ford briefly reassumed the company presidency, a decision that nearly proved catastrophic. By this point, Ford was suffering from cognitive decline and was making increasingly erratic decisions. The company hemorrhaged money, losing $10 million per month by 1945.

Edsel's widow, Eleanor Clay Ford, allied with Henry Ford's wife Clara to force Henry into retirement. The women essentially staged a coup, threatening to sell their stock if Henry didn't step aside in favor of Edsel's son, Henry Ford II. In September 1945, Henry Ford finally relinquished control. He died two years later, on April 7, 1947, at age eighty-three.

Henry Ford II, "Hank the Deuce" saved the company his grandfather nearly destroyed. He brought in professional management, including the famous "Whiz Kids" team that included Robert McNamara, implemented modern accounting and management practices, and rebuilt Ford into the global powerhouse it remains today.

Legacy: The Man Who Changed How We Make Everything

Henry Ford died with a fortune estimated at $200 billion in today's dollars, making him one of the wealthiest people who ever lived. But his legacy extends far beyond his personal fortune.

Ford's assembly line innovation fundamentally changed manufacturing and made modern consumer society possible. The ability to mass-produce complex products cheaply and consistently enabled the spread of automobiles, appliances, electronics, and countless other goods that we now consider basic necessities. Ford didn't invent the automobile, but he made it accessible, transforming it from a luxury toy for the rich into a tool that reshaped how and where people lived, worked, and traveled.

The $5 day, despite its paternalistic aspects, demonstrated that paying workers well could be profitable, not just charitable. Ford proved that well-compensated workers could be both producers and consumers, buying the very products they made. This insight helped fuel the growth of the American middle class and influenced labor policies for generations.

Yet Ford's legacy is inextricably tied to his bigotry. His anti-Semitic propaganda did real harm and provided intellectual ammunition for hatred that culminated in genocide. His stubborn resistance to change nearly destroyed the company he built. His cruel treatment of his son revealed how ruthless business brilliance can coexist with personal failings.

Perhaps the deepest irony of Henry Ford's life is that the man who revolutionized production through constant optimization became fatally unable to adapt. The innovator became the dinosaur. The revolutionary became reactionary. He demonstrated both the power of obsessive vision and the danger of rigid thinking.

Ford's story teaches us that genius is domain-specific, that transformative success can breed dangerous arrogance, and that the traits that build an empire, obsession, stubbornness and confidence in one's own judgment can just as easily destroy it. He was neither a hero nor a villain, but something more complex and more human: a revolutionary who couldn't quite let go of his revolution, a man who changed the world but couldn't change himself.

In the end, Henry Ford's greatest invention wasn't the Model T or the assembly line. It was the demonstration that the same principles of engineering and optimization could be applied to human systems, a lesson that shaped the 20th century for better and, sometimes, for worse.

Chapter 7

J. Paul Getty - The Paradox of Penny-Pinching Billions

In 1957, Fortune magazine declared J. Paul Getty the richest living American, with a fortune estimated at between $700 million and $1 billion. Getty was irritated by the publicity. Not because it was inaccurate, he was indeed spectacularly wealthy but because the attention brought him nothing but trouble. Strangers begged for money. Kidnappers plotted schemes. Tax authorities scrutinized his affairs. Getty concluded that being known as the world's richest man was "a distinct handicap" that brought him "nothing but headaches."

This was quintessential J. Paul Getty, a man who accumulated more wealth than he could ever spend, yet resented the attention it brought and lived in constant fear of losing it. He installed pay phones in his English mansion so guests couldn't make calls on his dime. He rewrote his will countless times to punish relatives who displeased him. He refused to pay ransom when his grandson was kidnapped, relenting only after receiving the boy's severed ear in the mail. He married five times but died alone, bitter, and estranged from most of his family.

Getty's life poses uncomfortable questions about the psychology of wealth accumulation: What drives a man to keep amassing money long after achieving more security than a hundred lifetimes could require? Why do some billionaires clutch every penny while others give fortunes away? And what happens to the soul when the pursuit of wealth becomes detached from any larger purpose?

The answer lies in Getty's formative years, his relationship with his domineering father, and a personality shaped by the trauma of the Great Depression, a man who accumulated billions but never escaped the fear of poverty that haunted his psyche.

Oil in the Blood

Jean Paul Getty was born in Minneapolis in 1892 to George Franklin Getty and Sarah Catherine McPherson Risher Getty. His father was a lawyer who had struggled financially before moving the family to the Oklahoma Territory in 1903, lured by rumors of oil discoveries. George Getty started as an independent operator buying mineral rights and leases, wildcatting in fields where major companies feared to tread.

The elder Getty had a gift for reading geological surveys and making calculated gambles. He drilled wells that came up dry, but he also hit enough producers to build a modest fortune. More importantly, he taught his son the fundamentals of the oil business: how to read drilling reports, assess risk, negotiate leases, and understand the relationship between supply, demand, and price.

Young Paul was bright, privileged, and aimless. He attended the University of Southern California and then Oxford University, studying politics, economics, and literature while living the life of a wealthy young gentleman. He developed expensive tastes in art, antiques, women, and luxury that would last his entire life, tastes that clashed spectacularly with the miserliness that defined his later years.

At Oxford, Getty affected the persona of an aristocratic aesthete. He threw parties, traveled Europe, collected art, and showed little interest in the grimy business of drilling for oil. His father, who had by now become wealthy through shrewd investments in Oklahoma oil fields, despaired that his son would amount to anything. George Getty was a hard-driving businessman who believed in work, discipline, and the Protestant ethic. His son seemed to believe in pleasure.

The tension between them defined Paul's psychology. He desperately wanted his father's approval but resented his domineering nature. George Getty had made his fortune; Paul wanted to prove he could do the same on his own terms. This toxic mixture of ambition, insecurity, and need for validation would drive Paul Getty to accumulate wealth far beyond reason or necessity.

Wildcatting in Oklahoma: The Compulsion Begins

In 1914, at age twenty-one, Paul Getty reluctantly entered the family oil business. His father offered him a challenge: make his own fortune wildcatting in Oklahoma, and if he succeeded, he could return to his life of leisure. George Getty would provide some capital and guidance but insisted Paul work independently.

Getty threw himself into the Oklahoma oil fields with unexpected intensity. He studied geological reports, bought mineral leases, and personally supervised drilling operations. The work was brutal, oil fields in the 1910s were rough frontier environments populated by speculators, drunks, prostitutes, and desperate men gambling their last dollars on holes in the ground.

Getty discovered he had a talent for calculated risk-taking. He bought leases on land where major companies saw little promise, conducted his own geological analysis, and drilled in locations others dismissed. Some wells came up dry, but enough struck oil to generate substantial profits. Within two years, Getty had made his first million dollars.

He was twenty-three years old, wealthy in his own right, and free to pursue the life of leisure he'd promised himself. Getty traveled to Los Angeles, bought expensive clothes, dated beautiful women, and lived in fine hotels. He convinced himself he was retired, that he'd achieved his goal and could now enjoy the fruits of success.

It lasted less than a year. Getty discovered that he couldn't stop thinking about oil. He read drilling reports compulsively. He analyzed price movements. He calculated the fortune he wasn't making while he wasted time enjoying himself. The pursuit of wealth had become something deeper than desire for money, it had become an addiction, a compulsion he couldn't shake even when he tried.

In 1916, Getty returned to the oil fields. He would never truly leave again.

Building an Empire Through Depression

The 1920s were boom years for American oil. Automobile ownership exploded, and with it demand for gasoline. Getty expanded aggressively, acquiring leases, buying up small operators, and investing in producing wells across California and Oklahoma. He also began acquiring shares in Pacific Western Oil Company, seeing an opportunity to build something larger than a collection of wells.

But Getty's approach to business was shaped profoundly by the Depression. When the stock market crashed in 1929 and the economy collapsed, Getty saw opportunity where others saw catastrophe. While competitors sold assets to raise cash and major oil companies retrenched, Getty bought aggressively. Oil stocks traded for pennies. Companies with real assets were valued as if they might disappear tomorrow.

Getty, who'd been accumulating cash, went on a buying spree. He purchased shares in Pacific Western Oil Company and the Tide Water Associated Oil Company at Depression-era discounts. These were real companies with producing wells, refineries, and distribution networks selling for fractions of their intrinsic value because everyone else was terrified.

This experience burned into Getty's psyche a permanent lesson: fear creates opportunity, and cash is power. He would never forget the advantage he'd gained by having liquid resources when everyone else was desperate. It helps explain why, even after becoming a billionaire, Getty hoarded cash and lived frugally. Some part of him never stopped preparing for the next

Depression, the next collapse, the next opportunity that would require capital while everyone else was broke.

Throughout the 1930s, Getty consolidated control over Pacific Western and accumulated a significant stake in Tide Water. But progress was slow and contentious. He fought bitter proxy battles with entrenched management and other shareholders. The struggle for control of Tide Water would consume two decades and create enemies who accused Getty of ruthless tactics and manipulation.

Getty didn't care. He'd identified undervalued assets and was determined to extract their value, regardless of who he offended. This single-minded focus on financial value over personal relationships became a defining characteristic in business and in his personal life.

The Middle East Gamble: The Deal That Changed Everything

By the late 1940s, Getty controlled significant oil assets in America, but the really transformative opportunity lay overseas. The major oil companies, the "Seven Sisters" that dominated global petroleum, had locked up the most promising territories in the Middle East through exclusive concessions with monarchs and governments. Saudi Arabia, Iran, Iraq, and Kuwait were either controlled by the majors or closed to Western companies.

But there was one exception: the Neutral Zone, a 2,200-square-mile diamond-shaped territory on the border between Saudi Arabia and Kuwait. Both countries claimed it, but neither had full sovereignty. It was considered marginal territory, desert wasteland where geologists doubted significant oil deposits existed. The majors had passed on it.

In 1948, Getty negotiated a sixty-year concession for the Saudi Arabian portion of the Neutral Zone. The terms were expensive by contemporary standards: $9.5 million signing bonus plus $1 million annually, even if no oil was found, plus generous royalties to Saudi Arabia if production began. Other oil companies thought Getty had lost his mind. He was in his mid-fifties, betting a substantial portion of his fortune on marginal desert acreage that might contain nothing.

Getty didn't see it that way. He'd studied the geology obsessively. He believed the same formations that produced oil in nearby Kuwait extended into the Neutral Zone. More importantly, he was willing to offer terms more favorable to the Saudis than the major companies would consider. While the majors treated Middle Eastern monarchs as supplicants, Getty treated them as business partners, not out of progressive politics, but because he wanted access to oil the majors couldn't get.

For four years, Getty's crews drilled in the Neutral Zone and found nothing. The annual payments and drilling costs mounted into the millions. Industry observers began referring to the venture as "Getty's Folly." He was hemorrhaging money with nothing to show for it. Some of his own staff urged him to cut losses and walk away from the concession.

Getty refused. He'd committed to the gamble and wouldn't fold until he'd exhausted all possibilities. In 1953, Getty's crews finally struck oil, enormous quantities of it. The reserves in the Neutral Zone proved vast, among the largest and most productive fields ever discovered. The wells that came online produced thousands of barrels per day. Getty had hit the jackpot.

The Neutral Zone oil transformed Getty from a wealthy oilman into one of the richest men in the world. By the mid-1950s, his various companies were generating profits of $100 million annually. His personal fortune exceeded half a billion dollars and was growing exponentially. The gamble that everyone had mocked had paid off spectacularly.

Fortune's 1957 declaration that Getty was the richest living American was based primarily on the Neutral Zone success. Getty's net worth would continue to grow throughout the 1960s and early 1970s, eventually exceeding $2 billion, equivalent to roughly $15 billion today. He'd achieved wealth beyond imagination.

And he was miserable.

The Paradox of Penny-Pinching: Pay Phones and Dog Food

Here's where Getty's story becomes truly strange. As his fortune grew into the billions, Getty's personal habits became increasingly parsimonious to the point of absurdity. The stories of his stinginess became legendary, some apocryphal, others well-documented and even more bizarre than the myths.

The most famous example: Getty installed a pay phone in the entrance hall of Sutton Place, his Tudor manor in Surrey, England. The phone was for guests, Getty didn't want them making calls on his line. When questioned about this, Getty explained that guests had abused his hospitality by making expensive international calls. The pay phone ensured they paid their own costs.

The public and press mocked him mercilessly. Here was a man worth over a billion dollars, installing a coin-operated phone in his mansion to save a few pounds on phone bills. Getty was genuinely bewildered by the criticism. To him, it was a simple matter of principle: why should he subsidize other people's phone calls? The fact that the cost was trivial relative to his wealth was irrelevant. It was the principle that mattered.

Other examples of Getty's parsimony bordered on pathological. He wrote letters to newspaper editors complaining about the cost of newspapers. He reused envelopes and wrote on both sides of paper to save money. He stayed in modest hotels when traveling, avoiding luxury establishments.

When the Duke and Duchess of Windsor visited Sutton Place, Getty served them dog food, an error, he later insisted, though guests noted he seemed unconcerned about the mistake.

He rewrote his will compulsively, adding and removing beneficiaries based on perceived slights. Family members who asked for money found themselves disinherited. Those who maintained independence and didn't request funds were rewarded until they did something that displeased him, at which point they too were written out.

Getty seemed to derive genuine satisfaction from these penny-pinching exercises, as if each small economy represented a victory over waste and disorder. Money saved was money protected from the chaos of the world. He'd seen fortunes lost in the Depression and knew that wealth could vanish. His frugality was a form of control, a way to maintain order in an uncertain universe.

But there was something deeper and darker at work. Getty's miserliness wasn't just about saving money, it was about power and control. Money was the medium through which he related to people. He gave it grudgingly, strings attached, always with the implicit threat of withdrawal. Love, approval, and affection were commodities to be rationed like oil from a well.

Five Marriages and Emotional Bankruptcy

Getty married five times and divorced five times. Each marriage followed a similar pattern: passionate beginning, Getty's emotional distance and obsession with work, growing resentment, and bitter ending. He fathered five sons with four of his wives, but maintained minimal relationships with most of them.

His first marriage, to Jeanette Dumont in 1923, lasted three years. His second, to Allene Ashby in 1926, produced his first son George Franklin

Getty II, and ended in divorce after five years. His third marriage, to Adolphine Helmle in 1928, lasted two years. His fourth, to Ann Rork in 1932, produced two sons (J. Paul Getty Jr. and Gordon Getty) and ended in divorce after three years. His fifth and final marriage, to Louise Dudley Lynch in 1939, produced his son Timothy and ended in divorce in 1958.

The pattern reveals a man incapable of sustaining intimate relationships. Getty was most comfortable alone, working, accumulating wealth, and maintaining emotional distance. His letters to his sons were often cold and formal, more like business correspondence than familial communication. He criticized them constantly, comparing them unfavorably to himself, and expressing disappointment in their achievements, a pattern he'd learned from his own father.

Getty rarely saw his children when they were young. He was either traveling for business, living abroad, or simply too absorbed in work to make time for family. His sons grew up largely without him, raised by their mothers, seeking approval from a distant father who offered it sparingly if at all.

The emotional damage was profound. George Franklin Getty II struggled with substance abuse and personal demons throughout his life. J. Paul Getty Jr. battled heroin addiction and descended into a life of excess and tragedy. Timothy Getty died of a brain tumor at age twelve, Getty didn't attend the funeral, claiming business obligations prevented him from leaving Europe. Gordon Getty, the youngest, survived relatively intact but maintained a cautious distance from his father.

Getty seemed genuinely confused by his children's problems and his family's dysfunction. He'd provided financial security, hadn't he? What more could they want? The idea that love, attention, and emotional presence might matter as much or more than money seemed to elude him entirely. Or perhaps he understood it perfectly well but was simply incapable of providing what he'd never received from his own father.

The Kidnapping: When Penny-Pinching Became Monstrous

On July 10, 1973, sixteen-year-old John Paul Getty III, grandson of J. Paul Getty and son of J. Paul Getty Jr. was kidnapped in Rome by members of the 'ndrangheta, the Calabrian mafia. The kidnappers demanded $17 million in ransom.

Getty Sr.'s response was chilling: he refused to pay. His reasoning, which he explained to the press, was that he had fourteen grandchildren, and if he paid ransom for one, the others would become targets. Better to refuse and discourage future kidnapping attempts. It was a coldly logical calculation that ignored the terror his teenage grandson was experiencing.

The Italian police and Getty family members begged the billionaire to reconsider. J. Paul Getty Jr., the boy's father, had already been effectively disinherited and lacked the resources to pay himself. Getty Sr. was unmoved. He offered to loan his son money for the ransom at four percent interest.

The standoff lasted five months. The kidnappers grew increasingly desperate and violent. They sent letters threatening to harm the boy if payment wasn't received. Getty Sr. insisted it was a hoax, that the boy had staged his own kidnapping to extract money. He offered no proof for this theory, but used it to justify his refusal.

On November 10, 1973, an envelope arrived at a Rome newspaper. Inside was a human ear, along with a lock of hair and a note: "This is Paul's ear. If we don't get some money within 10 days, then the other ear will arrive. In other words, he will arrive in little bits."

The ear was genuine. Getty III had been mutilated by his captors.

Even then, Getty Sr. hesitated. Eventually, under enormous pressure from family and facing a public relations catastrophe, he agreed to pay $2.2 million, the maximum tax-deductible amount under Italian law. He loaned his son the remaining ransom at interest. On December 15, 1973, after five months of captivity and torture, Getty III was released.

The psychological damage was permanent. Getty III never fully recovered from the ordeal. He struggled with substance abuse, and in 1981 suffered a stroke that left him paralyzed and nearly blind for the rest of his life. He died in 2011 at age fifty-four.

Getty Sr.'s behavior during the kidnapping revealed something monstrous at the core of his personality. Here was a man worth $2 billion who wouldn't immediately pay $17 million to save his grandson from torture. The explanation he offered, that paying would encourage more kidnappings rings hollow given that he eventually paid anyway. The real reason seems to have been a pathological inability to part with money under any circumstances, combined with a fundamental lack of empathy.

The kidnapping destroyed what little remained of Getty's public reputation. He'd been seen as eccentric and miserly but not necessarily malicious. After the kidnapping, he was seen as something worse: a man whose love of money exceeded his love of family, who would let his own blood suffer rather than part with a fraction of his vast fortune.

The Final Years: Alone in the Palace

Getty spent his final years at Sutton Place, surrounded by priceless art, rare antiquities, and an enormous fortune. He was seventy-three when his grandson was released, and he would live another three years. They were not happy years.

Getty had always been something of a loner, but by the 1970s he was almost completely isolated. He'd alienated most of his family through his cold behavior and the kidnapping crisis. His few remaining friends were employees or people dependent on him financially. He communicated primarily by phone and letter, managing his business empire from his estate, rarely leaving the grounds.

He spent his time cataloging his art collection, writing his memoirs, and revising his will. He was still worth over $2 billion, still worried about money, still making deals and tracking oil prices and calculating returns. The compulsion to accumulate never left him.

Getty had collected art throughout his life, one area where he spent lavishly. He owned works by Rembrandt, Gainsborough, and Titian. He'd built a replica of a Roman villa in Malibu to house his collection and open it as a museum, a gesture toward legacy, an attempt to be remembered for something beyond wealth and stinginess.

But even his philanthropy was grudging. He donated art but never cash. He built the museum but ran it on a tight budget. He seemed to want the prestige of being a cultural patron without the actual generosity patronage requires.

On June 6, 1976, J. Paul Getty died at Sutton Place at age eighty-three. The cause was heart failure, but one could argue he'd died years earlier in any meaningful sense. He left behind the bulk of his fortune to the J. Paul Getty Museum Trust, $1.2 billion at the time, which would grow to over $7 billion today. His family received relatively modest bequests by billionaire standards, some with strings attached.

His funeral was sparsely attended. Many family members stayed away, their grief complicated by years of emotional neglect and the trauma of the kidnapping. Getty was buried next to his mother at the Getty family plot in Pacific Palisades, California. The boy who'd desperately sought his father's approval, the man who'd amassed one of history's great fortunes, the grandfather who'd let his namesake suffer was finally at rest.

The Psychology of Never Enough

J. Paul Getty's life raises profound questions about the psychology of wealth accumulation. What drives someone to continue amassing money long after achieving more security than they could ever need? Why do some billionaires give generously while others clutch every penny?

Part of the answer lies in Getty's relationship with his father and his formation during the Depression. George Franklin Getty was a hard-driving, critical man who never seemed satisfied with his son's achievements. Paul Getty spent his life seeking approval he would never receive, his father died in 1930, before Paul's greatest successes. The compulsion to accumulate wealth became a way to prove his worth to a father who couldn't witness it.

The Depression reinforced Getty's sense that catastrophe lurked around every corner. He'd seen fortunes evaporate overnight, watched desperate men lose everything. His frugality and hoarding of cash were defenses against a repeat of that chaos. He never felt secure, no matter how many billions he accumulated, because he'd witnessed how quickly wealth could vanish.

But there's something deeper and more disturbing at work in Getty's psychology. His treatment of his family suggests a fundamental inability to connect emotionally with other people. Money was the only language he spoke fluently. He related to people through financial transactions, loans, gifts, bequests and disinheritances. Love and approval were commodities he rationed carefully, always ready to withdraw them as punishment.

Psychologists would recognize in Getty's behavior elements of what we now call attachment disorder and narcissistic personality traits. His inability to form secure emotional bonds, his view of relationships as transactional, his need for control, and his lack of empathy are all consistent with deep psychological damage likely rooted in his own childhood.

The ultimate tragedy of J. Paul Getty is not that he was rich and unhappy, plenty of people are unhappy regardless of wealth. The tragedy is that his pursuit of wealth actively destroyed his capacity for the things that might have made him happy suah as love, family, connection, and purpose beyond accumulation.

Legacy: A Cautionary Tale

Getty left behind one of the world's greatest art collections, now housed in the Getty Center and Getty Villa in Los Angeles. The Getty Trust funds scholarships, conservation projects, and art education globally. It's a substantial philanthropic legacy, though one Getty established more for immortality than from any deep commitment to improving the world.

His business legacy is more ambiguous. Getty Oil, the company he built, was eventually sold to Texaco in 1984 for $10 billion in a deal that triggered decades of litigation. The Getty family has produced some notable figures, Gordon Getty became a successful classical composer, and various descendants have engaged in philanthropy and activism but none have matched the old man's wealth accumulation.

Getty's real legacy is as a cautionary tale about the psychology of wealth and the danger of letting accumulation become detached from purpose. He demonstrated that it's possible to win the game of capitalism utterly, to accumulate more wealth than you could spend in a thousand lifetimes and still lose at life. His billions bought him art, property, and a place in history, but they couldn't buy him love, peace of mind, or happiness.

The pay phone in the mansion stands as the perfect symbol of his life: a man with unlimited resources who remained forever in a state of scarcity, unable to enjoy what he had, unable to stop accumulating what he didn't need, unable to connect with the people who might have loved him if he'd let them.

Getty proved that you can indeed be the richest man in the world and simultaneously the poorest, if poverty is measured not in dollars but in joy, connection, and meaning. His life poses a question every person accumulating wealth should ask themselves: At what point does having more become meaningless? And what are you willing to sacrifice to find out?

Chapter 8

Howard Hughes - Genius, Madness, and Mystery

On April 5, 1976, a frail, skeletal figure died aboard a plane en route from Acapulco to Houston. The body weighed ninety-three pounds, with long, unkempt hair and fingernails that curled like talons. The man had needle marks covering his arms, rotting teeth, and tumors on his head. The FBI had to use fingerprints to confirm his identity because he was so physically unrecognizable.

This was Howard Hughes, billionaire industrialist, film producer, aviation pioneer, once the most famous playboy in America, and arguably the most accomplished person of the 20th century. He had broken aviation speed records, built an aircraft empire, produced Hollywood blockbusters, dated the most beautiful actresses in the world, and amassed a fortune worth billions. He had also descended into a paranoid, drug-addicted isolation so complete that he spent his final years locked in darkened hotel rooms, communicating with the outside world through a handful of Mormon attendants who followed increasingly bizarre instructions.

How does someone go from being a brilliant, charismatic achiever who seemed capable of anything to a drug-addled recluse who stored his urine in jars and refused to cut his hair or nails? Hughes's story is a tragedy in the classical sense, a tale of extraordinary gifts undermined by fatal flaws, of genius consumed by madness, of a man who conquered the business world but couldn't conquer his own mind.

The Golden Child: Inheriting Fortune and Ambition

Howard Robard Hughes Jr. was born on December 24, 1905, in Houston, Texas, into a family already wealthy and climbing higher. His father, Howard Hughes Sr., had invented a revolutionary rotary drill bit that could penetrate rock formations previously impervious to drilling. The Hughes Tool Company held patents on this essential technology, and every oil company in America paid licensing fees to use it.

Young Howard grew up in privilege but also in the shadow of an ambitious, driven father and an overprotective, anxiety-ridden mother. Allene Hughes was obsessed with germs and disease, constantly warning young Howard about contamination and illness. She monitored his diet obsessively, restricted his contact with other children, and created an environment of heightened vigilance against invisible threats. These childhood lessons about unseen dangers would later metastasize into full-blown paranoia.

Hughes Sr. had different concerns. He wanted his son to be tough, accomplished, and worthy of the family fortune. He pushed Howard academically and physically, setting high standards and expressing disappointment when the boy fell short. Young Howard was bright but struggled with what was likely undiagnosed dyslexia and possibly other learning differences. He excelled in mathematics and mechanics but struggled with reading and writing. His father's criticism cut deep.

Two events in Hughes's youth would shape his entire life. First, at age fourteen, he took his first airplane ride with a barnstormer in Houston. The experience was transformative, Hughes felt he'd found his calling. Flying represented freedom, control, and mastery in a way nothing else did. From that moment, aviation would be his obsession.

Second, his parents died within three years of each other, his mother in 1922 when he was sixteen, his father in 1924 when he was eighteen. Suddenly, Howard Hughes Jr. was alone, grieving, and in control of 75% of the Hughes Tool Company, one of the most profitable enterprises in America.

Most eighteen-year-olds inheriting such wealth would have been placed under guardianship until they came of age. But Hughes, displaying the determination that would define his life, convinced family members to grant him control. He bought out other shareholders, gaining complete ownership of Hughes Tool Company. The patents and licensing fees generated roughly $2 million annually, over $35 million in today's money without requiring his active involvement. It was the perfect foundation for whatever ambitions he might pursue.

Hughes decided to pursue them all.

Hollywood: Making Movies and Making Headlines

In 1926, at age twenty, Hughes moved to Los Angeles with his young wife, Ella Rice (a marriage that would dissolve within a few years). He announced his intention to produce motion pictures. Hollywood insiders dismissed him as another rich playboy dabbling in show business. They were about to learn otherwise.

Hughes's first films were expensive failures. He lost hundreds of thousands learning the business, but he was a quick study. In 1927, he produced "Two Arabian Knights," a comedy that won the first Academy Award for Best Director of a Comedy Picture. The following year, he produced "The Racket," which received a Best Picture nomination. Hughes was proving he wasn't just a dilettante with money, he had genuine talent and vision.

But his masterpiece was still to come. In 1928, Hughes began production on "Hell's Angels," an aviation epic about World War I fighter pilots. Hughes poured money into the project with abandon, insisting on authenticity and spectacular aerial combat sequences. He purchased dozens of vintage aircraft, hired stunt pilots, and personally flew some of the most dangerous sequences himself.

When "talkies" revolutionized the industry mid-production, Hughes scrapped much of what he'd shot and started over, reshooting with sound. The budget ballooned to $3.8 million, equivalent to roughly $70 million today and the most expensive film ever made at that time. Studios and industry observers predicted disaster.

"Hell's Angels" premiered in May 1930 to massive commercial and critical success. The aerial combat sequences were unlike anything audiences had seen, thrilling, realistic, and spectacular. The film made a star of Jean Harlow (replacing the original lead actress Greta Nissen, whose Norwegian accent didn't work for talkies) and confirmed Hughes as a serious filmmaker. It also established a pattern: Hughes would spare no expense pursuing his vision, would personally involve himself in dangerous activities, and would bet enormous sums on his own judgment.

Throughout the 1930s and early 1940s, Hughes produced more films including "Scarface" (1932), a controversial gangster film that battled censors and became a landmark of the genre, and "The Outlaw" (1943), which created a sensation and censorship battles by marketing Jane Russell's cleavage. Hughes understood both cinematic art and publicity stunts, a combination that made him wealthy and famous.

He also dated nearly every beautiful actress in Hollywood: Katharine Hepburn, Ava Gardner, Ginger Rogers, Rita Hayworth, and many others. He was tall, handsome, wealthy, charming when he wanted to be, and utterly focused on whatever or whoever interested him at any given moment. He pursued women with the same intensity he pursued aviation records and business deals.

But even then, there were warning signs. Hughes could be obsessive, controlling, and prone to abrupt mood changes. He would become fixated on minor details to the exclusion of everything else. He had strange rituals and increasing anxiety about germs and contamination. Those close to him chalked it up to eccentricity, the quirks of a brilliant mind. They didn't recognize the early symptoms of something darker.

Aviation Pioneer: Breaking Records and Building Planes

While conquering Hollywood, Hughes was simultaneously building a reputation as one of the world's great aviators. Flying was more than a hobby, it was an obsession that combined his love of engineering, his competitive drive, and his need for control and solitude.

In 1935, flying a plane he'd designed himself the Hughes H-1 Racer Hughes set a new world land speed record of 352 miles per hour. The plane was a marvel of engineering: streamlined, powerful, and incorporating innovations that would influence aircraft design for decades. Hughes had essentially taught himself advanced aeronautical engineering through obsessive study and hands-on experimentation.

In 1937, he broke the transcontinental airspeed record, flying from Los Angeles to New York in 7 hours, 28 minutes, and 25 seconds. In 1938, he flew around the world in 91 hours, shattering the previous record. He was feted with ticker-tape parades, met with presidents, and became an American hero. Charles Lindbergh had conquered the Atlantic; Howard Hughes had conquered the globe.

But Hughes wasn't just a daredevil pilot, he was a serious aircraft designer and manufacturer. In 1932, he founded the Hughes Aircraft Company, initially as a division of Hughes Tool Company. Through the 1930s and 1940s, he employed some of the best aeronautical engineers in the world and gave them resources to pursue cutting-edge designs.

Hughes Aircraft developed military planes during World War II, though the relationship between Hughes and the military was often contentious. Hughes refused to be rushed, insisted on perfection, and frequently missed deadlines. He also insisted on personally test-flying prototype aircraft, which nearly killed him on multiple occasions.

The most serious crash occurred in July 1946, when Hughes was test-flying the XF-11, a prototype reconnaissance aircraft. The plane malfunctioned and crashed in Beverly Hills. Hughes was pulled from the burning wreckage with a crushed chest, collapsed lung, broken ribs, third-degree burns, and other severe injuries. Doctors didn't expect him to survive.

He did survive, but recovery required massive doses of morphine for pain management. Hughes became addicted. He would struggle with opiate addiction for the rest of his life, and many observers believe this was the turning point, the moment when Hughes's existing psychological issues combined with drug dependency to create the paranoid recluse of his later years.

The Spruce Goose: Ambition Meets Criticism

The most controversial and emblematic project of Hughes's career was the Hughes H-4 Hercules, forever known by the nickname Hughes hated: the "Spruce Goose." It was conceived as a solution to a genuine World War II problem, how to transport troops and materials across the Atlantic when German U-boats were sinking cargo ships.

Hughes proposed a massive flying boat, larger than anything ever built, capable of carrying 750 troops or two M4 Sherman tanks. The military gave him a contract for three prototypes, with Henry J. Kaiser as a partner. The specifications were audacious: it would have a wingspan of 320 feet (longer than a football field) and be powered by eight engines. Due to wartime aluminum shortages, it would be built primarily from laminated birch not spruce, despite the nickname.

Construction began in 1942, but the project immediately encountered problems. Hughes was a perfectionist who insisted on approving every design decision personally. He frequently redesigned components, stopped work to reconsider approaches, and clashed with Kaiser, who eventually withdrew from the partnership. The military grew increasingly frustrated with delays and cost overruns.

By the time the war ended in 1945, the Hercules was nowhere near completion. The military canceled the remaining two prototypes, and suddenly the project looked like a boondoggle, $23 million in taxpayer money (over $350 million today) for a plane that might never fly. Congressional investigations ensued, and Hughes found himself testifying before the Senate War Investigating Committee in 1947.

Hughes, naturally, took the criticism personally. He'd worked obsessively on the Hercules and considered it his masterpiece of aviation engineering. To prove his critics wrong, he decided to personally fly the completed aircraft not just taxi it, but actually take it into the air despite having no authorization and substantial safety concerns.

On November 2, 1947, with reporters and skeptics watching, Hughes piloted the Hercules on a test run in Long Beach harbor. He was only supposed to taxi the massive plane across the water. Instead, at full throttle, Hughes lifted the 400,000-pound aircraft seventy feet into the air and flew it for a mile at 135 miles per hour before landing.

It was a vindication, proof that the Hercules could fly, that Hughes's design was sound, that his critics were wrong. It was also the only time the plane ever flew. Hughes had made his point and apparently lost interest. The Hercules was placed in climate-controlled storage, where it remained until Hughes's death. Today it's displayed at the Evergreen Aviation Museum in Oregon, a monument to Hughes's brilliance, his stubbornness, and his inability to complete what he started.

Building an Empire: TWA and Las Vegas

While pursuing his aviation dreams, Hughes was also building a business empire. In 1939, he began acquiring stock in Transcontinental & Western Air, which later became Trans World Airlines (TWA). By the late 1940s, he controlled the airline.

Under Hughes's ownership, TWA expanded dramatically, pioneering transatlantic service and introducing the Lockheed Constellation, a plane Hughes had helped design. TWA became one of the world's premier airlines, and Hughes's stake made him even wealthier. However, his management style, making decisions in isolation, refusing to attend meetings and disappearing for weeks at a time created enormous operational challenges.

But Hughes's most lasting business legacy came in Las Vegas. In November 1966, Hughes arrived in Las Vegas by train (he'd stopped flying years earlier, his aviator days behind him). He checked into the top two floors of the Desert Inn hotel and never checked out.

By this point, Hughes was already deep into his paranoid, reclusive phase. He lived in darkened rooms, saw no one except a small group of Mormon male attendants, and communicated with the outside world through handwritten memos. When the Desert Inn's owner tried to evict him (Hughes's permanent residence was costing the casino money from high-roller suites), Hughes simply bought the hotel for $13.2 million.

Over the next few years, from his blacked-out hotel suite, Hughes went on a buying spree. He purchased the Sands, the Frontier, the Castaways, and the Silver Slipper casinos. He bought the Landmark hotel and casino. He acquired substantial real estate throughout Las Vegas and a local television station (reportedly because he didn't like the programming and wanted to control what aired).

Hughes poured over $300 million into Las Vegas, transforming it from a mob-controlled gambling town into a legitimate corporate enterprise. His involvement encouraged other large corporations to invest in Vegas, laying the groundwork for the modern casino industry. It was Howard Hughes, a recluse who barely left his room who helped transform Las Vegas into the entertainment capital it is today.

The irony was profound: Hughes was conducting major business deals while barely conscious, often high on codeine, speaking to no one in person, and displaying increasing signs of mental illness. His empire was being run by proxies and executives who received cryptic instructions via handwritten notes. That it worked at all was remarkable. That it worked as well as it did was testimony to the quality of people Hughes had hired in his more lucid days.

Descent into Paranoia: The Dark Side of Genius

The warning signs had been there for years, but by the 1950s, Hughes's psychological deterioration accelerated dramatically. The exact diagnosis is debated, most experts believe he suffered from obsessive-compulsive disorder (OCD), possibly bipolar disorder, and drug addiction, all worsening over time.

His fear of germs became pathological. He wrote detailed memos to his staff about how to handle objects to avoid contamination. Items had to be wrapped in tissue paper and handled with gloves. Foods had to be prepared according to elaborate protocols. Hughes himself rarely bathed, reasoning that bathing exposed him to waterborne germs, a logic that makes sense only to someone in the grip of severe OCD.

He became obsessed with minute details while ignoring major issues. He might spend hours ensuring that a can of peaches was opened according to precise specifications while ignoring urgent business decisions. His attention became increasingly fractured and his priorities increasingly irrational.

Hughes's drug use, primarily codeine and Valium, later supplemented with other medications exacerbated his psychological problems. He was taking doses that would have killed most people, administered via injection by his aides. The drugs dulled his pain but clouded his thinking and reinforced his paranoid delusions.

He stopped cutting his hair and nails. He sat naked on paper towels to avoid contaminating himself with furniture. He watched the same movies repeatedly, particularly movies featuring his old girlfriends like Jean Harlow and Katharine Hepburn while consuming nothing but chicken, chocolate bars, and milk. He conducted business from bed, often in the middle of the night, issuing instructions that became increasingly bizarre.

His staff, primarily Mormon men chosen because Hughes believed they were trustworthy and wouldn't drink or steal from him, followed his instructions without question. They enabled his worst behaviors, administered his drugs, maintained his isolation, and controlled all access to him. Whether they were helping him or enabling a sick man's delusions became an increasingly troubling question.

The Final Years: A Ghost in the Machine

In 1970, Hughes left Las Vegas in the middle of the night, spirited away by his aides to the Bahamas. For the next six years, he moved between hotels in the Bahamas, Nicaragua, Vancouver, London, and Acapulco, always occupying sealed-off floors, always isolated, always deteriorating.

The business empire continued operating largely on momentum. Hughes's companies, Hughes Tool Company, Hughes Aircraft, TWA (from which he'd eventually been forced out), and his Las Vegas properties were mostly run by professional managers who rarely if ever spoke to Hughes directly. Decisions that required Hughes's approval often took weeks or months as aides tried to get him lucid enough to consider them.

There were occasional signs of the old Hughes. He would sometimes emerge from his drug haze with sudden clarity, making brilliant business decisions or offering insights that reminded people why he'd been so successful. But these moments became rarer and shorter.

His physical health collapsed along with his mental state. He refused medical treatment, didn't eat properly, and received no dental care. He developed anemia, kidney problems, and malnutrition. The man who had once been a tall, handsome leading man now looked like a concentration camp survivor.

On April 5, 1976, Hughes finally agreed to be transported from Acapulco to Houston for medical treatment. He died en route, most likely from kidney failure, though the exact cause of death remained somewhat unclear given his terrible overall health. He was seventy years old but looked ancient, a skeleton with long hair and talons, barely recognizable as human.

The Will Mystery and Legal Battles

Hughes's death triggered one of the most complex legal battles in American history. He had no children, no clear will, and an estate worth an estimated $2.5 billion (over $13 billion today). Dozens of people claimed to be heirs or beneficiaries. Over forty purported wills surfaced, most obvious forgeries.

The most famous was the "Mormon Will," allegedly found in the Church of Jesus Christ of Latter-day Saints headquarters in Salt Lake City. It left substantial portions of the estate to various charities and, bizarrely, to Melvin Dummar, a Utah gas station owner who claimed to have once picked up a disheveled hitchhiker who turned out to be Howard Hughes. The will was almost certainly a forgery, Dummar probably created it himself and was rejected by the courts.

After years of litigation, judges ruled that Hughes had died intestate, without a valid will. His estate was divided among his cousins and other relatives he'd barely known or spoken to in decades. The Hughes Tool

Company was eventually sold to other corporations. Hughes Aircraft became a major defense contractor before being acquired by General Motors and later Boeing. The Las Vegas properties were sold off. The empire Hughes built was dismantled and distributed.

Legacy: What Genius Costs

Howard Hughes left behind technological innovations in aviation and film, a transformed Las Vegas, and one of the great fortunes in American history. He also left behind a cautionary tale about the relationship between genius and madness, success and self-destruction.

Hughes's story raises uncomfortable questions: Was his genius inseparable from his madness? Did the same obsessive focus that allowed him to break aviation records and build an empire ultimately destroy him? Could he have been helped with modern psychiatric treatment and drug rehabilitation, or was his personality structure too fragmented to save?

The tragedy of Howard Hughes is that he accomplished extraordinary things but couldn't enjoy them. He built an aviation empire but stopped flying. He dated the most beautiful women in the world but died alone. He amassed billions but spent his final years in darkened hotel rooms, paranoid and drug-addled. He had everything money could buy and nothing that money couldn't.

There's evidence that Hughes knew what was happening to him, that in lucid moments, he recognized his deterioration but felt powerless to stop it. A man who could design revolutionary aircraft and run multiple businesses couldn't fix his own mind. The ultimate control freak lost control of the only thing that really mattered.

Hughes's legacy lives on in aviation technology he pioneered, in the Hughes Medical Institute (created as a tax shelter but now one of the world's largest philanthropic organizations funding biomedical research), and in the modern Las Vegas he helped create. But his most lasting legacy might be as a warning: genius is not enough, success is not enough, wealth is not enough. Without mental health, without connection to others, without some anchor to reality and meaning beyond achievement, even the most extraordinary talents and accomplishments can crumble into tragedy.

The image that haunts his story is the final one: a ninety-three-pound skeleton with long nails and hair, barely recognizable as the handsome aviator who'd once broken world records and dated movie stars. Howard Hughes proved you could conquer the world and still lose yourself. He demonstrated that there are forms of poverty that have nothing to do with money, the poverty of connection, of sanity, of simple human dignity.

He died as he'd lived his final years: alone, isolated, and unreachable, a ghost haunting the empire he'd built, a genius consumed by the darkness in his own mind. The question that remains is whether his tragedy was inevitable, the price of his particular form of brilliance or whether it was preventable, a waste of extraordinary gifts that better treatment or intervention might have saved.

We'll never know. What we do know is that Howard Hughes stands as both an inspiration and a warning: a reminder that the human mind can accomplish incredible things, but also that it is fragile, that talent and wealth provide no protection against mental illness, and that success without wellness is its own form of failure.

Chapter 9

Sam Walton - Walmart and the Discount Revolution

In 1985, Forbes magazine declared Sam Walton the richest man in America, with a fortune estimated at $2.8 billion. Walton's response was characteristically down-to-earth: he kept driving his 1979 Ford pickup truck with the dog cages in the back. When reporters asked him about his wealth, he seemed genuinely uncomfortable with the attention. "It's just paper," he'd say, referring to his Walmart stock. "It's not like I can spend it."

This wasn't false modesty or a billionaire's affectation, it was genuine. Sam Walton lived in the same modest house in Bentonville, Arkansas, that he'd bought decades earlier. He ate breakfast at the local Ramada Inn coffee shop. He got his hair cut at the local barbershop for $5. He flew coach when he had to fly commercial. His one indulgence was a private plane, but even that was justified as a business necessity for visiting his stores across rural America.

Walton's story is different from the other billionaires in this book. He didn't inherit wealth like J. Paul Getty or Howard Hughes. He didn't build a technological monopoly like Rockefeller or Gates. He didn't create revolutionary products or break speed records. What Sam Walton did was perfect the art of selling everyday items to ordinary people at slightly lower prices and he did it with such relentless efficiency that he built the largest retail empire in human history.

Walmart's story is also America's story over the last half-century: the transformation from local merchant economies to big-box retail dominance, the shift of manufacturing to Asia, the rise of supply chain management as a competitive advantage, and the complex relationship between low prices for consumers and low wages for workers. Sam Walton didn't just create a successful business he fundamentally altered the landscape of American commerce and small-town life.

The Education of a Merchant

Samuel Moore Walton was born on March 29, 1918, in Kingfisher, Oklahoma, to Thomas and Nancy Walton. His father was a farm mortgager who struggled financially during the Depression, moving the family frequently as he looked for work. Sam grew up watching his family scrape by, watching his father struggle with financial insecurity, and developing the frugality that would define his life and business philosophy.

But young Sam also learned something else: the value of hard work and persistence. He delivered newspapers, sold magazine subscriptions, raised and sold rabbits and pigeons, and did whatever odd jobs he could find. He was naturally competitive, he became an Eagle Scout, was president of his high school class, and quarterbacked his football team. He attended the University of Missouri on a partial scholarship, waiting tables and delivering papers to cover expenses, graduating in 1940 with a degree in economics.

After a brief stint with J.C. Penney (where he learned valuable lessons about customer service and retail operations), Walton served in the Army during World War II, supervising security at aircraft plants and POW camps. He never saw combat, but the military taught him organizational skills and the value of systems and procedures, lessons he'd later apply to retail.

In 1945, with the war over and $5,000 in savings plus a $20,000 loan from his father-in-law, Sam and his wife Helen bought a Ben Franklin variety store franchise in Newport, Arkansas. Walton was twenty-seven years old, full of energy, and convinced he could out-work and out-think any competitor.

The Newport store became Walton's laboratory. He worked long hours, experimented with different displays and pricing strategies, sought out lower-cost suppliers, and personally greeted customers. He studied what sold and what didn't, which displays attracted attention and which were ignored. Most importantly, he discovered something crucial: if you sold items for slightly less than competitors, you could make it up in volume.

The concept sounds simple, but executing it requires discipline. Most retailers mark up goods by a standard percentage, 50% or 100% and maintain those margins religiously. Walton realized that if he could reduce his markup to 30% but sell three times as many items, he'd make more money. Lower prices meant higher volume, which meant he could negotiate better deals with suppliers, which allowed even lower prices. It was a virtuous cycle, but only if you had the discipline to resist the temptation of higher margins.

Within five years, Walton's Ben Franklin store in Newport was the most successful in the six-state region. He was making good money and learning the retail business from the ground up. Everything seemed perfect.

Then disaster struck. Walton had neglected to secure a renewal clause in his lease. When the lease expired in 1950, the landlord refused to renew, he wanted to give the successful store to his own son. Walton had built a thriving business only to have it taken away due to a legal oversight. It was a devastating lesson he would never forget.

Building the Foundation: Walton's Five and Dime

Forced to start over, Walton moved his family to Bentonville, Arkansas, a town of 3,000 people in the Ozark mountains and bought a "Five and Dime" store on the town square. The store was run-down and losing money, but the lease was secure this time. Walton called it "Walton's Five and Dime" and got to work.

Throughout the 1950s, Walton opened more stores across Arkansas, Missouri, and Kansas, operating them as franchises under the Ben Franklin banner. But he was constantly frustrated by the limitations of the franchise model. The parent company dictated which suppliers to use, and those suppliers charged premium prices. Walton knew he could get goods cheaper by buying directly from manufacturers, but the franchise agreement prevented it.

He also noticed something interesting about location. While conventional retail wisdom said stores needed to be in cities of at least 50,000 people to be profitable, Walton was succeeding in towns of 5,000 to 10,000. He realized that if he could offer variety and low prices, small-town customers who currently drove to cities for shopping would stay local. This insight would become the foundation of Walmart's strategy.

By 1960, Sam and his brother Bud (who'd joined the business) operated fifteen Ben Franklin stores. They were successful by any reasonable measure, but Walton wasn't satisfied. He saw the future coming: discount department stores like Kmart and Woolco that operated on thin margins and high volume. He believed this model could work in small towns if executed properly.

Walton approached the Ben Franklin executives with his idea for discount stores in rural markets. They rejected it. They didn't believe the economics would work in small towns. Walton disagreed, and in 1962, at age forty-four, he made the gutsy decision to leave the franchise system and launch his own discount chain.

On July 2, 1962, the first Walmart opened in Rogers, Arkansas, with the slogan "We Sell for Less." The store was nothing fancy, 16,000 square feet of concrete floors, exposed ceiling pipes, and bargain-priced merchandise stacked on tables. But prices were genuinely low, up to 20% below competitors and customers responded enthusiastically.

The Walmart Formula: Efficiency as Strategy

What made Walmart different wasn't revolutionary technology or a breakthrough product, it was operational excellence executed with religious discipline. Walton had developed a formula, and he applied it systematically to every store:

Location Strategy: Open stores in small towns (10,000-25,000 people) that big chains ignored. Saturate a region before moving to the next, allowing for efficient distribution and management oversight. Never pay premium prices for real estate.

Everyday Low Prices (EDLP): Instead of the typical retail strategy of regular prices with frequent sales, maintain consistently low prices. This builds customer trust and reduces operational complexity. The tradeoff: thinner profit margins that must be made up through volume and efficiency.

Inventory Management: Keep inventory lean. Track what sells and what doesn't, reorder popular items quickly, discontinue slow movers. This was revolutionary in the 1960s, when most retailers guessed at inventory needs and warehouses were full of unsold merchandise.

Cost Control: Minimize every expense. Keep stores simple and utilitarian. Use inexpensive fixtures. Negotiate ruthlessly with suppliers. Share hotel rooms when traveling. Turn off lights when not needed. The saved pennies add up to millions when multiplied across hundreds of stores.

Employee Culture: Treat workers as "associates" and give them small ownership stakes through profit-sharing. Hold store-level meetings to get input from frontline workers. Create competitions between stores. Make people feel invested in the company's success, even as you keep wages low.

Walton didn't invent any of these strategies individually, but his genius was combining them into an integrated system and executing with fanatical discipline. Where other retailers might cut corners in one area but splurge in another, Walton demanded efficiency everywhere.

Growth in the 1960s was steady but not explosive. By 1970, Walmart had 32 stores and $31 million in revenue. The company went public in 1970, raising capital for expansion but maintaining Walton family control. The timing was perfect, Walmart was positioned to capitalize on demographic and technological shifts that would transform retail.

The Distribution Revolution

The real breakthrough came in the 1970s when Walton invested heavily in distribution centers and logistics technology. This is where Walmart separated itself from competitors and built an almost insurmountable advantage.

Traditional retail logistics were inefficient. Stores ordered from multiple suppliers who delivered on different schedules. Inventory sat in back rooms. Stores frequently ran out of popular items while overstocking slow sellers. The entire system was reactive rather than proactive.

Walton envisioned something different: massive distribution centers strategically located to serve clusters of stores. Walmart would buy in huge quantities directly from manufacturers, deliver to these warehouses, and then use its own fleet of trucks to resupply stores on precise schedules. The system required massive upfront investment in warehouses, trucks, and eventually computer systems to track everything but the payoff was enormous.

By the early 1980s, Walmart had perfected this approach. A store manager could check what was selling and what wasn't, place an order that went directly to a distribution center, and receive delivery within 48 hours. This was light-years ahead of competitors. Walmart could respond to customer demand almost in real-time, keeping shelves stocked with what people wanted while minimizing capital tied up in excess inventory.

The distribution centers also gave Walmart negotiating leverage with suppliers. When you're ordering 100,000 units at a time for delivery to a single warehouse rather than asking suppliers to deliver 100 units each to 1,000 stores, you can demand dramatically lower prices. Suppliers who didn't agree to Walmart's terms found themselves replaced by those who would.

Walton also invested early in computer systems to track sales and inventory. In the mid-1980s, Walmart installed a satellite communication system, at the time the largest private satellite network in the United States allowing real-time data sharing between stores, warehouses, and headquarters. This was years before the internet made such connectivity common. The investment was enormous, but it gave Walmart an information advantage competitors couldn't match.

By 1990, Walmart had become the nation's largest retailer, surpassing Sears a position it has never relinquished. The secret wasn't lower prices alone, plenty of retailers tried discount strategies. The secret was the integrated system that made those low prices sustainable and profitable.

The Man Behind the Empire: Humble or Shrewd?

As Walmart exploded in size and Sam Walton became one of the richest people in the world, he maintained his remarkably modest lifestyle. This wasn't an act, everyone who knew Walton confirmed that he genuinely preferred simplicity to luxury.

He still drove that old pickup truck, still ate at local diners, and still lived in the same house. When traveling to visit stores (which he did constantly), he stayed at budget motels and often shared rooms with executives to save money. He shopped at Walmart, naturally, and bought generic brands. He got his hair cut for $5 at the local barbershop. His favorite recreation was quail hunting with his bird dogs.

This frugality extended to Walmart's corporate culture. The company headquarters in Bentonville was (and remains) deliberately modest, utilitarian office space with inexpensive furniture. Executives flew coach. The company cafeteria served basic, cheap food. There were no lavish corporate perks or executive dining rooms. The message was clear: every dollar spent on overhead was a dollar that couldn't be passed on to customers in lower prices.

But was Walton's modesty genuine humility or brilliant branding? The answer is probably both. Walton genuinely seemed uncomfortable with wealth and luxury; he'd grown up poor and never developed expensive tastes. But he also understood that his personal frugality was excellent marketing. The billionaire in the pickup truck was a powerful image that differentiated Walmart from "greedy" corporate competitors.

Walton cultivated relationships with Walmart associates, visiting stores constantly, learning employees' names, asking their opinions, and occasionally leading the company cheer ("Give me a W! Give me an A! Give me an L!"). He created profit-sharing programs that gave workers stock ownership. He held open meetings where any associate could ask questions.

Critics pointed out that these gestures cost relatively little compared to simply paying higher wages. Walmart's average wage was low, often at or near minimum wage and the company fought fiercely against unionization efforts. The profit-sharing and stock ownership were meaningful only for long-term employees, while turnover was high. Was Walton genuinely creating a family culture, or was he manufacturing loyalty while keeping labor costs minimal?

The truth is complicated. Walton genuinely seemed to care about his employees and believed he was creating opportunities for people in small towns who had few other options. But he also ran a ruthlessly efficient business that kept labor costs as low as legally possible. He was both the friendly small-town merchant who knew your name and the corporate titan who built systems that commodified and minimized human labor.

The Walmart Effect: Transformation and Destruction

As Walmart expanded across America in the 1980s and 1990s, it fundamentally altered the economic landscape of small-town America, for better and worse.

The benefits were real and significant. Walmart brought lower prices to rural communities, making everything from groceries to electronics more affordable. A family could save thousands of dollars per year shopping at Walmart instead of local stores. For poor and working-class families, this was transformative. Walmart also brought jobs, often becoming the largest employer in small towns.

But the costs were also significant. When Walmart entered a new market, local businesses struggled to compete. The hardware store, the clothing shop, the pharmacy all faced an opponent with deeper pockets, better supply chains, and lower prices. Many went out of business. Main Street retail districts that had been thriving for generations became ghost towns, with empty storefronts and decaying buildings.

The jobs Walmart created often paid less than the jobs at the local businesses it displaced. Small business owners who'd been middle-class found themselves working as Walmart associates at near-minimum wage. The tax base in many towns shifted from multiple small businesses to a single large employer with sophisticated tax minimization strategies.

Walmart also accelerated the shift of American manufacturing overseas. The company's relentless focus on low costs put enormous pressure on American manufacturers. Suppliers who couldn't meet Walmart's price demands found themselves replaced by Chinese factories. Walmart became the largest importer of Chinese goods in the world, facilitating the hollowing out of American manufacturing that transformed the economy.

Economists debate the net effect. Studies show that Walmart's lower prices effectively gave American consumers a raise, especially benefiting poor and working-class families. But those same families often faced wage stagnation or job loss as local businesses closed and manufacturing moved overseas. Walmart saved shoppers money while simultaneously reducing the incomes of many of those same shoppers.

Sam Walton believed he was helping ordinary Americans by giving them access to affordable goods. Critics argued he was destroying local economies and accelerating inequality. Both perspectives contain truth.

Family Succession: Passing the Empire

Unlike many billionaires who clung to control until death or saw their empires collapse in succession battles, Walton managed the transition remarkably well. He'd always intended Walmart to be a family business, and he structured ownership to keep control with his wife and four children: Rob, John, Jim, and Alice.

Walton stepped down as CEO in 1988, though he remained chairman and stayed deeply involved until his death. His chosen successor, David Glass, was a professional manager rather than a family member, a recognition that running a company as large as Walmart required specialized skills. This willingness to cede operational control while maintaining family ownership proved crucial to Walmart's continued success.

When Walton died of bone cancer on April 5, 1992, at age seventy-four, he was worth an estimated $25 billion making him the richest man in America at the time of his death. His fortune was divided among his widow and four children, creating one of the great American family fortunes.

The Walton family has maintained significant Walmart ownership through subsequent generations. As of 2024, the family owns roughly 50% of Walmart stock, worth over $200 billion, making them collectively among the wealthiest families in the world. The individual Walton heirs regularly appear on Forbes' richest people lists.

The children have taken different approaches to their inherited wealth. Rob Walton served as Walmart chairman for many years before retiring. Jim Walton stays involved in Walmart governance and banking interests. Alice Walton founded the Crystal Bridges Museum of American Art in Bentonville, creating a world-class art museum in rural Arkansas, perhaps the most visible Walton philanthropy. The family maintains a relatively low profile compared to other billionaire dynasties, though their political influence through campaign contributions and lobbying is substantial.

Walmart itself has continued to evolve and grow. It became a global giant, operating thousands of stores across multiple countries. It adapted to e-commerce competition from Amazon, though not without struggle. It remains the world's largest retailer by revenue, employing over 2 million people worldwide. Sam Walton's creation outlasted and outgrew him.

Legacy: The Merchant Who Changed Everything

Sam Walton's legacy is inseparable from Walmart's impact on American life, and that impact is profound and contested. He demonstrated that efficiency and scale could revolutionize retail, that supply chain management could be a source of competitive advantage, and that vast fortunes could be built not through innovation but through execution.

Walton proved that you didn't need to be flashy or glamorous to build an empire, discipline, persistence, and relentless focus on fundamentals could achieve extraordinary results. His personal modesty and down-home image made him more relatable than most billionaires, even as he built systems that concentrated unprecedented wealth and power.

But Walmart's success poses uncomfortable questions about the costs of efficiency. The benefits of lower prices are diffuse and invisible, shoppers save a few dollars here and there, adding up to significant savings over time. The costs are concentrated and visible, shuttered stores on Main Street, displaced workers, manufacturing towns that became ghost towns as factories moved to China.

Walton believed in a kind of populist capitalism, that by driving costs down and passing savings to consumers, he was helping ordinary Americans live better lives. His critics argued that he was simply transferring wealth from workers and local business owners to consumers and shareholders, while concentrating unprecedented power in corporate hands.

The truth is that both perspectives are valid. Walmart made life materially better for millions of Americans, particularly poor families for whom every dollar saved matters. It also disrupted millions of lives, destroyed thousands of local businesses, and accelerated economic trends that increased inequality and reduced economic security.

Sam Walton died believing he'd built something good, something that helped people. He almost certainly had no idea that his name would become controversial, that "Walmart" would be a political term, that people would debate whether his life's work was beneficial or harmful. He thought he was just a merchant selling goods at fair prices.

Perhaps that's the most important lesson of Sam Walton's story: the same forces that create efficiency and affordability can also create disruption and hardship. Progress helps some while hurting others. And the man driving that change might be a genuinely modest person in a pickup truck who never intended to hurt anyone but built systems whose consequences extended far beyond his imagination or control.

Walton's pickup truck, his $5 haircuts, and his small-town sincerity were all genuine. So was the massive transformation of American commerce, the destruction of local retail, and the concentration of wealth that his company caused. He was both the friendly neighbor and the force of creative destruction. He proved you could be personally humble while building something that changed everything for better, or for worse.

PART III: THE TECH REVOLUTION (1980s-2000s)

Chapter 10

Bill Gates - The Software Monopolist

In the late 1990s, Bill Gates was the most hated man in technology. Rivals called him ruthless. The Department of Justice accused Microsoft of illegal monopolistic practices. Tech luminaries testified that Gates had threatened them, copied their ideas, and crushed their companies. In depositions, Gates was evasive, combative, and dismissive. He seemed to embody everything people feared about concentrated corporate power.

Two decades later, Bill Gates was one of the most beloved figures in the world. He'd given away over $50 billion to fight disease and poverty. He'd convinced other billionaires to pledge their fortunes to charity. He'd helped eradicate polio in multiple countries and saved millions of lives through vaccines and health initiatives. Public opinion polls ranked him among the most admired people on Earth.

How did the same person go from monopolistic villain to humanitarian hero? The transformation of Bill Gates is one of the most remarkable redemption arcs in modern history, a story about the seductive power of winning at all costs, the limitations of business success as a measure of worth, and the possibility of reinvention even after achieving everything the business world has to offer.

But Gates's story starts long before his transformation, with a brilliant, competitive, socially awkward kid who discovered computers and became utterly obsessed with them.

The Prodigy Finds His Calling

William Henry Gates III was born on October 28, 1955, in Seattle, Washington, to a well-off family. His father, William Gates Sr., was a prominent attorney. His mother, Mary Maxwell Gates, served on corporate boards and was active in civic affairs. Bill grew up in an environment of high expectations, intellectual stimulation, and competitive achievement.

Young Bill was clearly gifted but also difficult. He was intensely competitive, argumentative, and prone to rocking back and forth when thinking, a habit he maintains to this day. He read voraciously, had an exceptional memory, and excelled academically. He was also socially awkward and didn't fit in naturally with other children.

In 1968, when Gates was thirteen, his parents enrolled him at Lakeside School, an exclusive private school in Seattle. That decision changed the trajectory of computing history. Lakeside had something almost no schools possessed in 1968: computer access. The Mothers' Club had used proceeds from a rummage sale to buy a teletype terminal connected to a General Electric computer that students could access via time-sharing.

Gates was transfixed. He spent every available moment programming, often staying at the computer lab until he was kicked out late at night, then sneaking back in whenever possible. He and a group of other students, most notably Paul Allen, who would become his business partner became obsessed with these machines and the possibilities they represented.

The teletype time was expensive, charged by the minute. Gates and his friends quickly exhausted the school's computer budget. They found creative solutions: exploiting bugs to get free time, getting hired by local companies to test software in exchange for computer access, even breaking into a computer company's system to steal time. They got caught, Gates was briefly banned from computer use but his hunger for access was insatiable.

What attracted Gates to programming wasn't just the intellectual challenge, though he loved that. It was the sense of control and the immediate feedback. In the social world, Gates struggled. He didn't understand the unwritten rules, couldn't read subtle cues, and often alienated people with his bluntness and competitiveness. But in programming, everything was logical. You wrote code, it either worked or it didn't, and you could see the results immediately. For someone like Gates, programming was not just interesting, it was a way to interact with the world that actually made sense.

By his mid-teens, Gates and Allen were getting paid programming jobs. They wrote scheduling software for Lakeside, a payroll program for a local company, and traffic-counting software for the city of Seattle. Gates was good at programming, but what set him apart was his understanding that software had commercial value. Many programmers saw it as an intellectual pursuit or a hobby. Gates saw it as a business.

Harvard Dropout: The Microsoft Beginning

In 1973, Gates enrolled at Harvard University, ostensibly to study law like his father. But he spent more time playing poker, taking math and computer science classes, and hanging out with other brilliant oddballs than attending his required courses. He was clearly brilliant, he famously got one of the highest scores in his class on the notoriously difficult Math 55 but he was also rudderless, unsure what to do with his talents.

The answer arrived in December 1974, when Paul Allen showed Gates a magazine with the Altair 8800 on the cover, the first commercially available personal computer kit. It was primitive by modern standards, essentially a box with switches and lights, but Gates and Allen saw its potential immediately. If people were going to have computers at home, they'd need software.

Without access to an Altair (they couldn't afford one), Gates and Allen wrote a version of the BASIC programming language for the machine using just the published specifications and a simulation they wrote. It was an audacious gambit, spending weeks writing software for hardware they'd never touched, hoping it would work when they finally got to test it.

In March 1975, Allen flew to Albuquerque, New Mexico, to demonstrate their BASIC interpreter to MITS, the company making the Altair. He'd never actually run the program on a real Altair, it might crash immediately, might not work at all. Allen loaded the paper tape into the machine, held his breath, and watched the program execute flawlessly. MITS agreed to distribute their software.

Gates dropped out of Harvard (though he never officially withdrew, leaving open the possibility of return) and moved to Albuquerque. He was nineteen years old. He and Allen founded a company they called "Micro-Soft" (later dropping the hyphen). The name perfectly captured their vision: software for microcomputers.

The early years of Microsoft were chaotic. Gates and Allen hired a small team of programmers who worked insane hours writing software for the emerging personal computer market. Gates proved to be a demanding, sometimes brutal manager. He'd review code line by line, often declaring it "garbage" and demanding rewrites. He'd challenge everything, argue ferociously, and push his team relentlessly.

But Gates also had a vision that extended beyond the immediate market. He famously wrote an "Open Letter to Hobbyists" in 1976, complaining that people were copying their BASIC interpreter instead of paying for it. This outraged the hobbyist community, where sharing software was the norm. Gates didn't care. He understood something crucial: if software was going to be a real business, it had to be treated as valuable intellectual property, not something to be freely shared.

This philosophical battle, software as product versus software as commons would define the next several decades of computing. Gates stood firmly on the side of proprietary software, and he would build a fortune defending that position.

The DOS Deal: Buying an Operating System for $50,000

The deal that made Bill Gates a billionaire happened almost by accident. In 1980, IBM approached Microsoft about providing an operating system for their upcoming personal computer. IBM was the dominant force in business computing, and their entry into the personal computer market would legitimize the entire industry.

Microsoft didn't have an operating system. Gates and Allen had focused on programming languages and applications. But Gates understood this was an extraordinary opportunity and told IBM that Microsoft could provide what they needed.

He then scrambled to find an operating system to deliver on that promise. He discovered that Seattle Computer Products had created 86-DOS (also called QDOS, Quick and Dirty Operating System), a basic operating system for Intel 8086 processors. In what would prove to be one of the most lopsided business deals in history, Microsoft bought the rights to 86-DOS for $50,000.

Microsoft modified 86-DOS, rebranded it as MS-DOS, and licensed it to IBM. But here's the crucial detail that would make Gates's fortune: Microsoft retained the right to license MS-DOS to other companies. IBM got non-exclusive rights to the operating system for their PC.

Why did IBM agree to this? They didn't think the operating system was particularly important or valuable. The real value, in their view, was the hardware. They assumed customers would buy IBM PCs because they were IBM products, not because of the software. It was a catastrophic miscalculation.

As the IBM PC became successful, dozens of companies built "IBM-compatible" computers, cheaper machines that could run the same software as IBM PCs because they used MS-DOS. Every one of those companies had to license MS-DOS from Microsoft. IBM made money only on computers they manufactured. Microsoft made money on every IBM-compatible computer sold, regardless of manufacturer.

Gates understood something that IBM missed: in the computer industry, whoever controls the platform controls the market. Hardware would become commoditized, different manufacturers competing on price. But the operating system created "lock-in." Once businesses invested in MS-DOS software and trained employees to use it, they couldn't easily switch to a different operating system. And since most software developers wrote programs for MS-DOS (because that's where the largest market was), the advantage became self-reinforcing.

The DOS deal didn't make Microsoft an instant monopoly, but it established the foundation. Through the 1980s, MS-DOS became the dominant operating system for business computers. Microsoft's revenue grew from $16 million in 1981 to $140 million by 1985. Gates, who owned a substantial stake in the company, was becoming very wealthy. But the real fortune was still to come.

Windows: From Imitation to Domination

In 1984, Apple launched the Macintosh with a graphical user interface, instead of typing commands, users could point and click with a mouse. It was revolutionary, making computers accessible to people who'd never learned command-line interfaces. The Mac was expensive and had limited software, but the interface was clearly superior to DOS's command-line prompt.

Gates recognized immediately that graphical interfaces were the future. Microsoft had already been working on "Interface Manager" (later renamed Windows), their own graphical interface that would run on top of DOS. Apple's Steve Jobs was furious, he believed Gates was stealing

Apple's ideas. (Ironically, Apple had taken inspiration from Xerox PARC's research, so the question of who "invented" the graphical interface was complicated.)

The first version of Windows, released in 1985, was mediocre, slow, buggy, and unpopular. Windows 2.0 in 1987 was better but still not a serious threat to Apple. Gates kept pushing. Windows 3.0, released in 1990, was finally good enough to gain significant market adoption. Windows 3.1 in 1992 became hugely successful.

But the real breakthrough was Windows 95, launched with enormous fanfare in August 1995. Microsoft spent $300 million on marketing, including buying the rights to the Rolling Stones' "Start Me Up" and hosting a massive launch event. Windows 95 was genuinely good, more stable, more user-friendly, and compatible with the massive installed base of MS-DOS software.

More importantly, Windows 95 benefited from network effects and Microsoft's platform control. Software developers wrote programs for Windows because that's where the customers were. Customers bought Windows computers because that's where the software was. Computer manufacturers pre-installed Windows because that's what customers expected. Each element reinforced the others, creating a monopolistic cycle that competitors couldn't break.

By the late 1990s, Windows was installed on over 90% of personal computers worldwide. Microsoft's revenue exceeded $14 billion annually. Bill Gates's personal fortune surpassed $50 billion, making him the richest person in the world. He was forty-one years old, and Microsoft dominated personal computing the way Standard Oil once dominated petroleum.

Ruthless Competition: Building and Defending the Empire

Microsoft's rise to dominance wasn't just about superior products, it was about ruthless, aggressive competition that often crossed ethical and legal lines. Gates and Microsoft developed a reputation for identifying promising technologies, copying them, bundling them with Windows, and destroying the original innovators.

Netscape Navigator was the dominant web browser in the mid-1990s. Microsoft introduced Internet Explorer, bundled it free with Windows, and leveraged their operating system monopoly to crush Netscape. The browser itself wasn't necessarily better, Microsoft simply used their control of Windows to make Internet Explorer the default, pre-installed browser.

The same pattern repeated with numerous products. WordPerfect dominated word processing until Microsoft Office (bundled together and integrated with Windows) drove them out. Lotus 1-2-3 ruled spreadsheets until Excel took over. Innovative small companies would create promising products, Microsoft would develop competing versions, and the smaller companies would wither and die.

Competitors accused Microsoft of "vaporware", announcing products that didn't exist to discourage customers from buying competitors' products. They accused Microsoft of modifying Windows to make competitors' software run poorly. They accused Microsoft of using their inside knowledge of Windows to give their own applications unfair advantages.

Much of this was true. Microsoft played hardball in ways that went beyond normal competition. Gates and other Microsoft executives made threats, used their market power as leverage, and aggressively defended their territory. In depositions and meetings, Gates could be dismissive, combative, and evasive. He seemed to view business as warfare where the goal was total victory, not coexistence.

The irony is that this ruthlessness wasn't particularly unusual in business history. Rockefeller, Carnegie, and other robber barons had employed similar tactics. What was different was that by the 1990s, antitrust law was more robust, and Microsoft's dominance was happening in full public view in a highly visible industry.

The Antitrust Battle: The Government vs. Microsoft

In May 1998, the U.S. Department of Justice and twenty state attorneys general filed antitrust charges against Microsoft. The case focused on Microsoft's bundling of Internet Explorer with Windows and their agreements with computer manufacturers that prevented them from pre-installing competing browsers.

The trial was a public relations disaster for Microsoft and particularly for Gates. Video deposition footage showed Gates being evasive, claiming not to remember key events, and parsing questions with lawyer-like precision that came across as dishonest. At one point, prosecutors spent an entire day getting Gates to admit what "market share" meant; he kept claiming he didn't understand the term, which was absurd for a CEO.

Gates's behavior during the trial revealed both his brilliance and his blindness. He was technically correct in many of his answers, parsing language with extreme precision but completely failed to understand how he appeared to the public. He seemed arrogant, evasive, and contemptuous of the legal process.

In November 1999, Judge Thomas Penfield Jackson issued his findings of fact, concluding that Microsoft held monopoly power in the operating system market and had used that power to harm competitors and consumers. In June 2000, he ordered that Microsoft be broken into two companies, one for operating systems, one for applications.

Microsoft appealed. The breakup order was overturned, but the company was still found to have violated antitrust law. Eventually, a settlement was reached: Microsoft would face oversight and restrictions on certain business practices but would remain intact. It was a partial victory for Microsoft but a humiliating process for Gates personally.

The trial changed Gates. He stepped down as CEO in 2000 (remaining as chairman and chief software architect) and gradually reduced his involvement with Microsoft over the following years. The public drubbing, the portrayal as a ruthless monopolist, and the stress of the trial seemed to prompt serious reflection about his life and legacy.

The Transformation: From CEO to Philanthropist

In 2000, Bill and Melinda Gates (whom he'd married in 1994) consolidated their charitable efforts into the Bill & Melinda Gates Foundation. Initially, it was a side project while Gates remained focused on Microsoft. But over the next several years, it became his primary focus.

The transformation wasn't sudden, it was gradual and, at first, tentative. Gates approached philanthropy the same way he approached software: analytically, systematically, focused on measurable outcomes. He read extensively about global health, education, and poverty. He met with experts, challenged assumptions, and asked difficult questions. He applied the same intensity to understanding malaria eradication that he'd once applied to understanding operating systems.

What Gates discovered was that his wealth could save lives on an extraordinary scale. Diseases that killed millions in developing countries, malaria, tuberculosis, HIV/AIDS, polio could be prevented or treated with vaccines and medicines that were cheap but unavailable to poor populations. The problem wasn't scientific, it was distribution, funding, and political will. Gates realized that his billions could address those gaps in ways governments and NGOs couldn't or wouldn't.

The Gates Foundation began funding vaccine distribution, supporting research into neglected tropical diseases, and partnering with governments to strengthen health systems in developing countries. The scale was unprecedented, eventually committing over $50 billion to these efforts.

In 2006, Warren Buffett announced he would donate the bulk of his fortune, over $30 billion to the Gates Foundation, effectively doubling its resources. Buffett's donation was a remarkable vote of confidence: the Oracle of Omaha, known for his careful evaluation of investments, was betting that Gates could deploy charitable capital more effectively than anyone else.

Gates stepped away from day-to-day Microsoft management in 2008 to focus full-time on philanthropy. The man who'd once been obsessed with crushing Netscape was now obsessed with eradicating polio. The competitive drive remained, Gates tracked metrics, set ambitious targets, and pushed for results with the same intensity he'd shown in business. But the target had shifted from market share to lives saved.

The Giving Pledge and Legacy Building

In 2010, Gates and Buffett launched the Giving Pledge, a commitment by billionaires to give away at least half their wealth during their lifetimes or in their wills. It wasn't legally binding, just a public promise, but it had moral weight. Over 200 billionaires have signed the pledge, committing over $600 billion to charitable causes.

The Giving Pledge revealed Gates's evolution. The man who'd once fought to defend every percentage point of market share was now encouraging other billionaires to give away their fortunes. He'd concluded that accumulating wealth beyond a certain point was meaningless, that the real measure of success was what you did with that wealth to improve the world.

Gates's philanthropic work has had genuine, measurable impact. The Gates Foundation played a crucial role in nearly eradicating polio, cases dropped from 350,000 per year in 1988 to just a handful annually by the 2020s. The foundation's funding for malaria research and prevention has saved millions of lives. Its investments in agricultural development have improved food security in Africa. Its education initiatives have had mixed results, but the willingness to experiment, measure outcomes, and adjust approaches represents a more sophisticated approach to philanthropy than simply writing checks.

Critics note that billionaire philanthropy, even well-intentioned, is fundamentally undemocratic, one person deciding how to spend resources that arguably should be spent by elected governments. They question whether Gates's foundation inadvertently reinforces the power structures and inequalities that created those problems. They point out that Gates made his fortune through monopolistic practices that harmed innovation and consumers, and that no amount of charity erases that harm.

These criticisms aren't entirely wrong. But they also can't erase the reality that Gates's wealth has funded vaccines, medicines, and research that have saved millions of lives. Children who are alive because of Gates Foundation funding don't care whether the foundation model is perfectly democratic.

The Complete Picture: Monopolist and Humanitarian

Bill Gates's story forces us to grapple with uncomfortable complexity. The same traits that made him a ruthless monopolist, competitive intensity, unwillingness to accept defeat, obsessive focus on winning are part of what makes him an effective philanthropist. The same analytical approach that helped him crush competitors helps him identify the most effective charitable interventions.

Gates in his twenties and thirties was brilliant, driven, and ruthless. He wanted to win, and he was willing to bend or break rules to do it. He created immense value through software that made computers useful to billions of people, but he also stifled innovation, crushed competitors, and extracted monopolistic profits.

Gates in his sixties is still brilliant and driven, but channeled toward different ends. He's genuinely committed to using his wealth to improve lives, particularly for the world's poorest people. His foundation operates with unusual transparency and accountability for a private charity. He's thought seriously about the responsibility that comes with extreme wealth.

The public loves the redemption narrative, villain becomes hero, monopolist becomes philanthropist. But the reality is more nuanced. Gates didn't become a different person. He's still competitive, still analytical, still convinced that his approach is the right one. What changed was his target: from market share to malaria, from crushing Netscape to crushing polio.

Perhaps the real lesson of Bill Gates isn't about redemption at all. It's about the separate evaluation of different domains. Gates was wrong to abuse Microsoft's monopoly power, and the antitrust case was justified. He's right to fund vaccines and health research, and deserves credit for that work. These facts coexist. The good doesn't erase the bad, and the bad doesn't invalidate the good.

Legacy: The Two Gates

Gates will be remembered for two distinct legacies, and history will debate which matters more.

The business legacy: Gates and Microsoft helped make personal computers ubiquitous, created software that billions use daily, and demonstrated how platform control and network effects could create enduring monopolies. Whether that contribution is net positive, weighing the value of Windows and Office against the harm from stifled innovation and monopolistic practices remains contested.

The philanthropic legacy: Gates has given away over $50 billion and counting, saved millions of lives through health initiatives, and convinced other billionaires to give away their fortunes. Whether billionaire philanthropy is the right model for addressing global problems, versus higher taxes and government action remains debated, but the lives saved are real.

The transformation from the first legacy to the second is remarkable. Gates went from being booed at technology conferences to being applauded at health conferences. He went from the face of corporate monopoly to the face of effective philanthropy. He proved that it's possible to be terrible at one phase of your life and admirable at another, that change is possible even for someone who seemed locked into a particular path.

For those seeking simple narratives, Gates is frustrating. Was he good or bad? Did he help or harm? The answer is: both. He built a monopoly that harmed innovation while creating software that helped billions. He accumulated obscene wealth through questionable practices and then gave most of it away to save lives.

Perhaps that complexity, the refusal to fit into a simple hero or villain narrative is the most important lesson Gates offers. People are capable of both great achievement and significant wrongdoing. Success in one domain doesn't guarantee wisdom in others. And the story isn't over until it's over, there's always the possibility of reinvention, of choosing a different path, of using power for better purposes than the ones that acquired it.

Bill Gates started as a brilliant, socially awkward kid who found meaning in computer code. He became a ruthless monopolist who dominated an industry. He transformed into a philanthropist committed to improving lives. All three versions are the real Bill Gates. The question isn't which one is authentic, they all are. The question is what we learn from watching someone evolve across such different roles, and whether that evolution represents genuine growth or merely the deployment of the same competitive instincts toward more socially acceptable targets.

The jury is still out. Gates is still alive, still active, still deploying his fortune toward the causes he's identified as most important. The final assessment of his legacy won't be possible until the story is complete. But the transformation itself, from most hated to most admired, from monopolist to humanitarian remains one of the most remarkable journeys in the history of wealth and power.

Chapter 11

Steve Jobs - The Creative Genius Who Died Too Soon

On October 5, 2011, the world learned that Steve Jobs had died at age fifty-six after a long battle with pancreatic cancer. The outpouring of grief was extraordinary and unprecedented for a business figure. People left flowers and handwritten notes at Apple Stores worldwide. Heads of state issued statements. Strangers wept openly. It was the kind of mourning typically reserved for beloved artists, humanitarian leaders, or cultural icons not corporate executives.

But Steve Jobs was never just a corporate executive. He was a visionary who convinced the world that technology could be beautiful, intuitive, and even spiritual. He didn't invent the personal computer, the smartphone, or the tablet, but he reimagined each of them so completely that his versions became definitive. He built Apple into one of the most valuable companies in human history. And he did it all with a personality that was by turns inspiring and appalling, a creative genius who could be cruel, manipulative, and impossible, yet who pushed everyone around him to achieve things they didn't think possible.

Jobs's death at fifty-six adds a tragic dimension to his story that makes it fundamentally different from other billionaire narratives. He never got to enjoy a long retirement, never spent decades managing his fortune, never had the chance to transform into an elder statesman or philanthropist. His legacy was frozen at the peak of his creative powers, making him simultaneously more heroic and more human than billionaires who lived into old age. He proved that mortality shapes legacy in ways that money cannot, that dying at the height of achievement can be its own kind of immortality.

The Adopted Son: Searching for Identity

Steven Paul Jobs was born on February 24, 1955, in San Francisco to Joanne Schieble and Abdulfattah "John" Jandali, unmarried graduate students who gave him up for adoption. He was adopted by Paul and Clara

Jobs, a working-class couple in Mountain View, California. Paul was a machinist and carpenter who loved working with his hands. Clara was an accountant who never finished college.

The adoption shaped Jobs profoundly, though he spent much of his life insisting it didn't. Being adopted gave him a sense of being special, chosen, not merely born but also a sense of abandonment that he never fully resolved. In later life, he tracked down his biological parents but maintained complicated, distant relationships with them. He discovered he had a biological sister, novelist Mona Simpson, with whom he formed a genuine bond.

Jobs grew up in what would become Silicon Valley, though it wasn't called that yet. It was the 1960s, and the area south of San Francisco was transitioning from agricultural to technological. Engineers from companies like Hewlett-Packard lived in modest suburban homes and tinkered in their garages. Young Steve would wander the neighborhood, watching these men work on electronics projects, asking questions, and absorbing the culture of engineering and innovation.

Paul Jobs encouraged his son's curiosity, teaching him basic electronics and showing him how to build things. Jobs later credited his father with teaching him the importance of craftsmanship, that the back of a cabinet should be as beautiful as the front, even if no one sees it. This philosophy would later manifest in Apple products with meticulously designed interiors that users never saw.

But young Steve was also difficult. He was bored in school, acted out, played pranks, and challenged authority. Teachers found him brilliant but exasperating. In fourth grade, a teacher bribed him to study by giving him money and candy. It worked, Jobs later said she was one of the most important people in his life because she helped him realize that learning could be rewarding.

In seventh grade, Jobs met Bill Fernandez, who introduced him to Steve Wozniak, an electronics whiz five years older than Jobs. Wozniak was a brilliant engineer who loved building things for the pure joy of creation. Jobs immediately recognized that Wozniak's technical genius could be channeled into something commercial. This partnership, the creative engineer and the visionary marketer would change technology history.

The Blue Box and the Birth of Apple

Jobs and Wozniak's first collaboration was illegal. They built and sold "blue boxes", devices that hacked the phone system to make free long-distance calls. Wozniak designed the boxes; Jobs sold them. It was technically phone fraud, but it taught them crucial lessons: hardware could be built cheaply, sold for profit, and there was a market for clever technology.

Jobs dropped out of Reed College after one semester, he couldn't see the value in required courses and convinced himself he could get more education by auditing classes that interested him. He hung around campus for another eighteen months, sleeping on friends' floors, returning Coke bottles for food money, and getting free meals at the local Hare Krishna temple. He took a calligraphy course that taught him about typography and beautiful letterforms, knowledge that would later influence the Mac's revolutionary fonts and design.

Jobs's time as a dropout and seeker was formative. He experimented with LSD (later calling it one of the most important experiences of his life), traveled to India seeking spiritual enlightenment, adopted Buddhism, and cultivated an aesthetic that valued simplicity and minimalism. He was searching for meaning, for authenticity, for something deeper than conventional middle-class life.

In 1974, Jobs returned to California and got a job at Atari, the pioneering video game company. He was hired despite being difficult to work with, showing up barefoot, insisting his vegetarian diet meant he didn't need to shower (his coworkers disagreed), and being generally abrasive. But he was smart and effective, so Atari kept him, eventually moving him to night shifts so he wouldn't annoy other employees.

Meanwhile, Wozniak was working at Hewlett-Packard and spending his free time designing what would become the Apple I, a personal computer built around a microprocessor. In 1975, he showed his creation to the Homebrew Computer Club, a gathering of electronics hobbyists. Club members were excited but saw it as a hobby. Jobs saw it as a business.

Jobs convinced Wozniak they should start a company to sell his computer. They'd build the machines in Jobs's parents' garage and sell them to hobbyists. Wozniak was hesitant, he had a good job at HP and enjoyed engineering as a hobby. Jobs persisted, and Wozniak finally agreed. They called the company Apple Computer. Jobs claimed the name came from his time working at an apple orchard, but it also evoked simplicity, healthfulness, and positioned them alphabetically before Atari.

They needed capital. Jobs sold his Volkswagen van; Wozniak sold his HP calculator. They scraped together $1,300 and started building computers. The Apple I was essentially a circuit board that hobbyists had to put in their own cases and connect to their own keyboards and monitors. Jobs convinced a local computer store to order fifty units for $500 each. Apple was in business.

The Apple II: Building a Company

The Apple I was a start, but Jobs and Wozniak knew they needed something better, a complete computer that ordinary people could use. Wozniak designed the Apple II, a revolutionary machine with color graphics, expansion slots, and a plastic case. It looked like a consumer product, not a hobbyist's project.

Jobs obsessed over the design. He wanted the case to be a specific shade of beige. He wanted the edges smooth and friendly. He rejected dozens of prototypes. Wozniak and other engineers thought Jobs was crazy, what did the color matter? But Jobs understood that for computers to move from hobbyists' basements to living rooms and offices, they had to be approachable and attractive. Technology had to be humanized.

To manufacture and market the Apple II, they needed serious capital. Jobs convinced Mike Markkula, a retired Intel executive, to invest $250,000 and provide business guidance. Markkula became Apple's third partner and brought adult supervision to the operation. In April 1977, the Apple II launched at the West Coast Computer Faire.

The Apple II was a massive success. It had a killer app: VisiCalc, the first spreadsheet program, which made the Apple II essential for businesses. By 1980, the company had sold over 100,000 Apple IIs and generated over $100 million in revenue. When Apple went public in December 1980, Jobs's stake was worth over $200 million. He was twenty-five years old and on the cover of magazines as the face of the personal computer revolution.

But success brought challenges. Apple was no longer a garage operation, it was a real company with hundreds of employees, complex operations, and investors expecting continued growth. Jobs was brilliant at vision and marketing but terrible at management. He inspired people with his enthusiasm but also berated them cruelly, calling their work "shit" when it didn't meet his standards. He played favorites, creating rivalries between teams. He denied paternity of his daughter Lisa (from a relationship with Chrisann Brennan) for years, claiming he was sterile, even as Apple's Lisa computer bore her name.

Jobs was immature, arrogant, and convinced of his own genius. He believed the rules that applied to other people didn't apply to him, he parked in handicapped spaces, drove without license plates, and treated people as disposable. His reality distortion field, his ability to convince people that impossible things were possible was powerful but also destructive. He'd promise products that couldn't be built, deadlines that couldn't be met, and then blame engineers when they failed to achieve the impossible.

The Macintosh: Triumph and Downfall

In the early 1980s, Jobs became obsessed with a new project: a computer that would be revolutionary in its simplicity and design. The Macintosh would have a graphical user interface inspired by technology Jobs had seen at Xerox PARC. Instead of typing commands, users would point and click with a mouse. It would be "insanely great," Jobs promised.

Jobs took over the Macintosh project from other Apple engineers and made it his personal mission. He recruited the best engineers, promised they were changing the world, and worked them to exhaustion. The Mac team wore pirate flags and saw themselves as rebels within Apple, superior to other divisions. Jobs encouraged this elitism while simultaneously making their lives miserable with his demands and criticism.

The original Macintosh, released in January 1984 with a famous Super Bowl commercial directed by Ridley Scott, was revolutionary. The graphical interface was intuitive and beautiful. But it was also underpowered, with too little memory and too few software applications. It was expensive at $2,495. Initial sales were strong, driven by curiosity and brilliant marketing, but then stalled as limitations became apparent.

Meanwhile, Jobs's relationship with Apple's board and CEO John Sculley (whom Jobs had recruited from Pepsi with the famous line "Do you want to sell sugar water for the rest of your life, or do you want to come with me and change the world?") deteriorated. Jobs was increasingly erratic, clashing with other executives, undermining colleagues, and destabilizing the company.

In 1985, the board faced a choice: Jobs or stability. Sculley maneuvered to strip Jobs of operational responsibilities. Jobs tried to organize a counter-coup. He failed. In September 1985, at age thirty, Steve Jobs resigned from Apple, the company he'd founded.

It was a stunning fall. Jobs had gone from cover-boy billionaire to ousted founder in less than five years. Most observers assumed his career was over, he'd been exposed as too difficult, too unstable, too immature to run a company. They were wrong.

The Wilderness Years: NeXT and Pixar

Jobs spent the next twelve years in what he later called "the wilderness", banished from Apple, working on projects that seemed promising but delivered limited success. These years were crucial to his development. He matured, learned from failures, and discovered capabilities beyond computer hardware.

First, he founded NeXT Computer with $7 million of his own money and $20 million from Ross Perot. NeXT would build high-end workstations for universities and businesses. Jobs applied his perfectionist aesthetic to every detail, the cube-shaped computer, the black magnesium case, the innovative operating system. The NeXT Computer was beautiful and technically advanced. It was also expensive, late to market, and commercially unsuccessful. NeXT sold perhaps 50,000 computers total, a tiny fraction of the market.

But NeXT's software, particularly the NeXTSTEP operating system, was genuinely innovative. It featured object-oriented programming, a sophisticated development environment, and elegant design. Tim Berners-Lee would use a NeXT computer to create the World Wide Web.

The technology would eventually prove more valuable than anyone initially realized.

Jobs's second venture was even more unexpected. In 1986, he bought the computer graphics division of Lucasfilm for $10 million. The division, which he renamed Pixar, made high-end graphics hardware and software. It was hemorrhaging money, but Jobs kept funding it, believing in its potential.

Pixar's hardware business failed, but the animation team led by John Lasseter and Ed Catmull began creating short films using computer graphics. The shorts won awards and attracted attention. In 1991, Pixar signed a deal with Disney to produce a computer-animated feature film.

That film was Toy Story, released in 1995. It was a revolutionary achievement, the first fully computer-animated feature film, and a critical and commercial success. Pixar went public a week after Toy Story's release. Jobs's stake, purchased for $10 million, was suddenly worth over $1 billion. He'd become a billionaire again, but through animation rather than computers.

The wilderness years humbled Jobs and taught him crucial lessons. At NeXT, he learned the costs of perfectionism unconstrained by market reality. At Pixar, he learned to trust creative people and not micromanage every detail, he gave Lasseter and the animation team space to work, something he'd never done at Apple. He also matured personally, marrying Laurene Powell in 1991 and starting a family. The arrogant twenty-something had become a more thoughtful, if still difficult, forty-something.

The Return: Saving Apple

By 1996, Apple was dying. The company had lost its way after Jobs's departure, releasing mediocre products while Microsoft's Windows dominated the market. Apple's market share had collapsed to about 3%. The company was losing money and considering selling itself.

In a twist of fate, Apple needed a new operating system and decided to buy NeXT for $429 million. The deal brought Jobs back to Apple as an advisor. Within months, he'd engineered the ouster of CEO Gil Amelio and took over as "interim CEO" (a title he'd hold for three years before dropping "interim").

Jobs immediately made brutal decisions. He killed dozens of products, reducing Apple's offerings from hundreds of variants to four: professional and consumer, desktop and laptop. He cut deals with former enemies, including a $150 million investment from Microsoft that provided crucial capital and ended debilitating patent litigation. He refocused the company on design and user experience.

In 1998, Apple introduced the iMac, a colorful, translucent all-in-one computer that looked like nothing else in the market. It was friendly and fun, the antithesis of beige box PCs. The iMac was a hit, selling 800,000 units in its first five months and returning Apple to profitability.

Jobs had saved Apple from bankruptcy, but he was just getting started. Over the next thirteen years, he would lead the most remarkable run of innovation in business history.

iPod, iPhone, iPad: Redefining Multiple Industries

In 2001, Apple introduced the iPod, a portable music player that could hold "1,000 songs in your pocket." It wasn't the first MP3 player, but it was the best: elegant design, intuitive interface, and seamless integration with iTunes software. The iPod became a cultural phenomenon, making Apple cool again and generating billions in revenue.

But Jobs saw the iPod as merely a step toward something bigger. In 2007, Apple launched the iPhone, a device that combined a phone, iPod, and internet communicator. It had a revolutionary multitouch interface, no physical keyboard, and elegant software. Industry experts were skeptical. Microsoft's Steve Ballmer laughed at the $499 price and lack of physical keyboard. They were all wrong.

The iPhone redefined mobile phones and created the smartphone era. Within a few years, iPhones were generating more revenue than all of Microsoft. The App Store, launched in 2008, created an entire ecosystem of third-party software that made the iPhone endlessly expandable. Apple had moved from computers to music to phones, redefining each industry.

In 2010, Jobs introduced the iPad, a tablet computer that created a new category between smartphones and laptops. Critics called it a big iPod Touch. Jobs insisted it was a new type of computing device for consuming content. Again, Jobs was right. The iPad became another multi-billion-dollar product line.

Jobs also transformed Apple's retail strategy. Apple Stores, launched in 2001 despite widespread skepticism, became the highest revenue per square-foot retail locations in America. They weren't just stores, they were temples to Apple products, with glass staircases, Genius Bars, and carefully trained staff.

By 2011, Apple was the most valuable technology company in the world. Jobs's stake was worth billions. But more importantly, he'd achieved something unprecedented: creating revolutionary products in multiple categories (computers, music players, phones, tablets) and building a brand that people loved with religious intensity.

The Dark Side: Cruelty and Consequences

Jobs's success came at a cost, often borne by those around him. His cruelty was legendary. He'd tell people their work was "shit" to their faces. He'd cry when frustrated. He'd scream at subordinates. He created a culture of fear where people worked insane hours because they were terrified of disappointing him.

Jobs denied paternity of his daughter Lisa for years, even swearing in court documents that he was sterile (he wasn't, he went on to have three more children). He finally acknowledged Lisa but remained a distant, difficult father. His relationship with his other children was reportedly warmer but complicated by his intensity and self-absorption.

His personal hygiene remained odd, he believed his vegetarian diet eliminated body odor, allowing him to shower infrequently. It didn't. Colleagues learned to have difficult conversations with him while walking outside for fresh air.

Most tragically, when diagnosed with pancreatic cancer in 2003, Jobs initially refused conventional medical treatment. He had a rare, treatable form of pancreatic cancer that surgery could likely cure. But Jobs, convinced he knew better than doctors, tried alternative therapies, dietary changes, acupuncture, herbal remedies. He wasted nine months before finally agreeing to surgery. By then, the cancer might have spread. Whether his delay was fatal is debated, but it certainly didn't help.

This decision, refusing effective medical treatment in favor of alternatives, was classic Jobs. He believed his intuition and willpower could bend reality, that he could solve problems through force of personality. Sometimes this worked brilliantly (creating revolutionary products). Sometimes it failed catastrophically (cancer doesn't negotiate).

The Final Act: Leading While Dying

After his 2004 surgery, Jobs returned to work, but his health continued to decline. He had a liver transplant in 2009. He took multiple medical leaves of absence. By 2011, he was visibly ill, gaunt, weak and struggling. Yet he continued working, introducing products, making decisions, driving Apple forward.

Jobs's final major public appearance was introducing the iPad 2 in March 2011. He was shockingly thin, his voice weak, but his enthusiasm genuine. Two months later, he appeared even more frail at Apple's Worldwide Developers Conference. In August 2011, he resigned as CEO, handing leadership to Tim Cook while remaining chairman.

Jobs died at home on October 5, 2011, surrounded by family. His sister Mona Simpson later revealed his last words, looking at Laurene and their children: "Oh wow. Oh wow. Oh wow."

Legacy: Frozen at the Peak

Jobs's death at fifty-six fundamentally shapes how we remember him. Unlike Gates or Buffett, who could transition to philanthropy and elder statesman roles, Jobs's legacy is frozen at his creative peak. We never saw old Steve Jobs. We never learned if he would have mellowed further, devoted himself to charity, or found new mountains to climb.

This matters because mortality shapes legacy powerfully. Jobs died having just created the most successful products of his career. There was no decline, no failed comeback, no diminishment. He went out at the top, which makes him simultaneously more tragic (cut down too soon) and more heroic (forever in his prime).

Jobs revolutionized six industries: personal computers (Apple II and Mac), animated films (Pixar), music (iPod and iTunes), mobile phones (iPhone), tablets (iPad), and retail (Apple Stores). No other business figure can claim such broad transformative impact. He proved that technology could be beautiful, intuitive, and even spiritual, that great design was about simplicity and removing complexity, not adding features.

But Jobs also demonstrated the costs of genius driven by cruelty. His "reality distortion field" pushed people to achieve impossible things but also broke spirits and destroyed relationships. His perfectionism created beautiful products but made working with him agonizing. He was a singular visionary who was often a terrible human being.

Perhaps the deepest legacy Jobs left is the proof that design matters, that technology should serve humans rather than requiring humans to adapt to technology, and that thinking differently, really differently, not just as a slogan can change the world. Apple's products work not because they have the most features or the fastest processors, but because someone obsessed over every detail of how humans would interact with them.

Jobs never engaged in significant philanthropy, which sets him apart from other billionaires in this book. He closed Apple's charitable programs when he returned as CEO and never reopened them. He gave relatively little to charity personally (though his widow Laurene Powell Jobs has become a major philanthropist). When asked about this, Jobs suggested that creating products that enriched people's lives was his contribution.

This is a fundamentally different philosophy than Gates's that the contribution is the work itself, not what you do with the money afterward. It's a view that some find selfish and others find honest. Jobs wanted to be remembered for his creations, not his donations.

The Irreplaceable Visionary

After Jobs's death, Apple continued to thrive under Tim Cook's leadership, becoming even more valuable. But it hasn't produced another product as revolutionary as the iPhone. It's refined existing products, expanded services, and executed brilliantly but it hasn't created new categories.

This raises a question: Was Jobs irreplaceable? The answer seems to be yes, at least for certain types of innovation. Apple became excellent at incremental improvement and operational excellence but lost something of the visionary leap that characterized the iPod, iPhone, and iPad era.

Jobs proved that a single individual with sufficient vision and will can bend entire industries. But he also proved that such individuals are rare, difficult, and mortal. His death removed something from the world that hasn't been replaced, a visionary who could see around corners, who had the taste and judgment to know what people would want before they knew themselves, and who had the force of personality to make it real.

The question of whether Jobs was a genius or just in the right place at the right time will continue to be debated. But the evidence suggests genius: he did it multiple times in multiple industries. That's not luck, it's vision, taste, and execution coming together in ways that happen perhaps once in a generation.

Steve Jobs was the adopted son searching for where he belonged, the dropout seeking meaning, the brash young entrepreneur building computers in a garage, the ousted founder wandering in the wilderness, the returning hero saving his dying company, and the visionary who saw the future and made it real. He was also cruel, arrogant, and difficult, someone who hurt people and pushed away those who loved him.

His death at fifty-six means we'll never know what else he might have created or whether he would have evolved into something gentler and wiser. We're left with the work, revolutionary products that changed how billions of people interact with technology and the legend of a complicated man who refused to accept the world as it was and bent reality to his vision.

In the end, Jobs achieved a kind of immortality that money alone can't buy: his creations outlived him, his influence shaped industries, and his story inspired millions. He died too soon, but he died having changed everything. That might be the purest form of legacy possible.

Chapter 12

Larry Ellison - Oracle's Brash Fighter Pilot

In the summer of 1977, a thirty-three-year-old programmer named Larry Ellison sat in a cramped office in Silicon Valley, reading a research paper that would change his life. The paper, published by IBM researcher Edgar F. Codd described something called a "relational database", a revolutionary way to store and retrieve information that made existing database systems look like filing cabinets compared to a library's card catalog system. IBM, in characteristic fashion, had published the research but wasn't aggressively commercializing it. They were too busy protecting their mainframe business.

Ellison saw the gap immediately. This was his moment.

But Larry Ellison's path to that moment and to becoming one of the world's wealthiest and most controversial tech billionaires began in circumstances far removed from the elite corridors of computing power.

The Unwanted Child Who Wanted Everything

Lawrence Joseph Ellison was born in New York City in 1944 to an unwed nineteen-year-old Jewish mother. His father was an Italian-American Air Force pilot who never married his mother and remained absent from his life. When Larry contracted pneumonia at nine months old, his mother, struggling and unable to cope, made a decision that would haunt and drive him for decades: she gave him up to her aunt and uncle in Chicago.

His adoptive father, Louis Ellison, was a Russian immigrant who had failed at multiple businesses and settled into a life of middle-class disappointment. Louis was cold, critical, and seemed to take particular pleasure in telling young Larry that he would never amount to anything. "You'll never be a success," Louis told him repeatedly. It was a prophecy that Larry Ellison spent his entire life proving wrong with a fury that never quite subsided.

"My father thought I was a loser," Ellison would later say in interviews, the bitterness still evident decades later. "He told me I'd never amount to anything. I think about that a lot."

Young Larry was brilliant but unfocused, a student who tested at genius level but couldn't conform to institutional expectations. He attended the University of Illinois at Urbana-Champaign but dropped out during his second year after his adoptive mother died. He enrolled at the University of Chicago the following year but dropped out again after just one semester. He had, however, discovered something during his brief college stint: computers. In the mid-1960s, when computers were still room-sized machines tended by specialists in white coats, Ellison found something that made sense to him. Code had rules. Code was logical. Code didn't care about your background or tell you that you'd never succeed.

In 1966, at age twenty-two, Ellison packed his things and drove to California with his first wife in a car so unreliable it barely made it across the Nevada desert. He had $100 in his pocket and no real plan beyond a vague sense that California was where the future was happening.

The Wilderness Years

For the next decade, Larry Ellison wandered through the emerging tech landscape of Northern California, a brilliant programmer who couldn't quite find his footing. He worked for a company called Ampex, where he learned to program mainframe computers. He worked on database projects for the CIA (codename: Oracle, remember that name). He moved from job to job, company to company, always talented enough to get hired, always restless enough to leave or get fired.

His personal life was equally chaotic. His first marriage ended in divorce. He was married and divorced again before age thirty. He had an intensity that people found either magnetic or exhausting, with little middle ground. He worked obsessively, talked constantly about his ideas, and had an ego that even his friends found oversized.

"Larry doesn't have an off switch," a colleague from those years remembered. "He's either at 100% intensity or he's asleep. There's no middle setting."

But the wandering years weren't wasted. Ellison was learning the database business from the inside. He was understanding what customers needed, what the technology could do, and most importantly what the competition was missing. By 1977, working as a programmer at Ampex, he had the skills, the knowledge, and the burning ambition. What he needed was an opportunity.

IBM's research paper was that opportunity.

The Birth of Oracle

Ellison convinced two of his Ampex colleagues, Bob Miner and Ed Oates, to join him in starting a company. They called it Software Development Laboratories, a deliberately boring name that hid ambitious dreams. The plan was simple, at least in concept: build a commercial relational database management system before anyone else could.

They had one immediate advantage: a contract from the CIA for a database project that would provide cash flow while they developed their commercial product. That CIA project was codenamed Oracle. When they finally released their commercial database product in 1979, they called it Oracle too. The name suggested mystery, power, and the promise of hidden knowledge made accessible, perfect for a database system.

But they had virtually no money. Ellison, Miner, and Oates each contributed $2,000 to start the company, $6,000 total. For context, Bill Gates and Paul Allen had launched Microsoft four years earlier with more funding and better connections. Ellison was starting late and starting broke.

What he had instead of money was audacity and a willingness to bet everything on being first to market.

Oracle's first commercial customer was the CIA. The second was the Air Force. Ellison understood something crucial: enterprise software wasn't sold, it was *sold*, with high-pressure tactics, aggressive marketing, and the kind of confidence that made customers believe they were buying the future. And nobody could sell confidence like Larry Ellison.

The early years were chaotic. The software barely worked. Crashes were routine. Customer complaints poured in. But Ellison had learned a crucial lesson from watching IBM: in enterprise software, perception mattered as much as reality. If customers believed your product was the industry standard, they'd tolerate bugs and problems they'd never accept from a smaller vendor. Oracle's marketing claimed they were the leader in relational databases, a claim that was technically true mainly because almost nobody else was in the market yet.

"We were not just competing with other database companies," Ellison later explained. "We were competing with the idea that you should build your own database. We had to convince the world that buying was smarter than building."

By 1983, the company had renamed itself Oracle Corporation and released Oracle 3 (they skipped version 2 to make customers think the product was more mature than it was, classic Ellison). Revenue was growing rapidly, doubling and tripling year over year. But the company culture that Ellison was building was as aggressive and chaotic as he was.

The Oracle Culture: Brilliant and Brutal

Working at Oracle in the 1980s was like joining a cult whose deity was market share. Ellison created a culture of extreme competitiveness, where sales teams were rewarded lavishly for wins and humiliated for losses. The company's motto might as well have been "Whatever it takes."

Sales representatives would book revenue for contracts that weren't finalized. They'd promise features that didn't exist. They'd dramatically discount deals at quarter-end to hit numbers. The product crashed regularly, but the sales force sold it as if it were bulletproof. It was aggressive, sometimes unethical, and phenomenally effective.

"Oracle wasn't just selling software," a former executive recalled. "We were selling Larry's vision of Oracle dominating the world. And if you didn't believe in the vision with religious fervor, you didn't last."

Ellison himself set the tone. He was openly contemptuous of competitors, particularly IBM, which he seemed to view as both the target to surpass and the father figure to defeat. When asked about IBM's database products, he didn't just say Oracle was better, he said IBM's technology was "obsolete" and that staying with IBM was "a career-limiting move." This wasn't marketing spin; this was Ellison's genuine personality. Subtle he was not.

But the aggression worked. By 1986, Oracle went public, and Ellison became a paper multimillionaire overnight. The company was growing at breakneck speed, adding customers, employees, and revenue at a pace that made even Silicon Valley veterans dizzy.

And then, in 1990, it all nearly came crashing down.

The Near-Death Experience

Oracle's aggressive accounting practices finally caught up with it. The company had been booking revenue prematurely, counting contracts as complete that were still being negotiated, and generally running its finances with the same reckless confidence it brought to everything else. In the spring of 1990, Oracle had to announce that its quarterly earnings were far below projections, actually the company had lost money.

The stock price collapsed, falling more than 80%. Lawsuits piled up from angry shareholders. Customers who had been suspicious of Oracle's claims felt vindicated and started looking at competitors. The company was forced to lay off 10% of its workforce, four hundred people gone in a matter of weeks. Oracle was on the verge of bankruptcy.

For Ellison, this was a crucible moment. The brash confidence that had built the company had also nearly destroyed it. He faced a choice: moderate his approach and build a stable, professionally managed company, or double down on aggression but with better execution.

In typical Ellison fashion, he chose both and neither. He brought in professional management to fix the accounting and operational chaos. He implemented proper financial controls. But he absolutely refused to back down from his competitive intensity or his vision of Oracle dominating the database world.

"The problem wasn't our ambition," he insisted. "The problem was our execution. We were driving a Formula One race car with the discipline of teenagers joyriding. We needed to grow up without losing our edge."

The turnaround took two painful years. Ellison brought in Ray Lane, a buttoned-down executive from Booz Allen Hamilton, to serve as Oracle's president and handle operations while Ellison focused on strategy and this was crucial in competing with Microsoft.

The Microsoft Obsession

By the mid-1990s, Oracle had stabilized and was again growing rapidly. Ellison had become immensely wealthy, a billionaire several times over. He could have relaxed, enjoyed his fortune, maybe even mellowed with age.

Instead, he declared war on Microsoft.

Bill Gates and Microsoft had become the dominant force in tech. Windows was everywhere. Microsoft Office was the standard. And Microsoft was moving into databases with SQL Server, directly threatening Oracle's core business. For Ellison, this was personal.

He began giving speeches attacking Microsoft's "monopolistic practices." He funded investigations into Microsoft's business tactics. He publicly mocked Bill Gates, calling Microsoft's software "buggy" and suggesting that Gates had succeeded through luck and anticompetitive behavior rather than innovation.

"Bill Gates is a genius," Ellison would say, "but not as a programmer or technologist. He's a genius at monopoly. He's brilliant at using market power to crush competitors."

The irony, that Ellison himself had built Oracle using many of the same aggressive tactics seemed lost on him. Or perhaps it wasn't lost at all; perhaps he simply enjoyed the fight.

The rivalry became legendary in Silicon Valley. Gates generally ignored Ellison's provocations, which only seemed to fuel Ellison's fire. When Microsoft's antitrust trial began in 1998, Ellison was reportedly delighted. Oracle even hired private investigators to dig through Microsoft's garbage looking for incriminating documents, a bizarre episode that became public and embarrassed even Ellison's supporters.

But beneath the theatrics was a real business competition. Oracle positioned its database as the serious, enterprise-grade solution while painting Microsoft's products as toys for small businesses. It worked. Oracle maintained its dominance in the high-end database market even as Microsoft grew its presence in the lower and middle tiers.

The Billionaire Lifestyle Kicks In

As Oracle's stock soared during the dot-com boom of the late 1990s, Ellison's wealth reached astronomical levels. At the peak in 2000, he was worth more than $47 billion, briefly making him the richest person in the world.

And unlike Bill Gates, who famously lived relatively modestly, or Warren Buffett, who stayed in the same house, Ellison spent money like a man making up for lost time or proving something to a dead adoptive father who said he'd never succeed.

He bought estates around the world. His primary residence in Woodside, California, was a twenty-three-acre Japanese-inspired compound that reportedly cost $200 million to build. Every detail was meticulously designed to his specifications, from the koi ponds to the traditional Japanese gates to the tea houses. He became obsessed with Japanese culture and aesthetics, studying Zen Buddhism and martial arts, though whether he actually absorbed the philosophy of simplicity and non-attachment is debatable given his lifestyle.

He bought yachts, not just one yacht, but multiple yachts, including the Rising Sun, one of the largest private yachts in the world at 454 feet long. It featured 82 rooms, a basketball court, a cinema, and cost approximately $200 million.

He bought aircraft. Not just a private jet, but multiple jets, and eventually a decommissioned Italian fighter jet that he learned to fly himself. Ellison had always been fascinated by aviation, perhaps a connection to the absent

Air Force pilot father he never knew and now he could indulge that passion completely.

He bought cars, Ferraris, McLarens and Acuras from his partnership with the company, and more. He bought a Hawaiian island, not a house on an island, but 98% of the entire island of Lanai, Hawaii's sixth-largest island, for approximately $300 million in 2012.

He competed in yacht racing, spending enormous sums to field America's Cup teams. Oracle Team USA won the America's Cup in 2010 and again in 2013 (after being down 8-1 in an incredible comeback), validating Ellison's competitiveness in yet another arena.

The spending was legendary even among billionaires. But it wasn't mindless consumption, it was statement-making. Every purchase seemed designed to say: "I have arrived. I am not the unwanted child. I am not the dropout. I am not the failure my father predicted."

The Personal Life Complications

Ellison's romantic life was as tumultuous as his business career. He was married and divorced four times. His marriages followed a pattern: intense courtship, lavish weddings, a few years of marriage, and then divorce when his obsessive work habits and demanding personality became unsustainable.

He had two children, David and Megan, from his third marriage to Barbara Boothe. His relationship with them was complicated, he was often absent, consumed by Oracle and his various pursuits. David Ellison eventually became a successful film producer, founding Skydance Media with his father's financial backing. It was a relationship rebuilt partly through business, as if that was the language Ellison spoke most fluently.

Romantically, Ellison seemed to be searching for something he could never quite find. His partners ranged from novelist Melanie Craft (his fourth wife) to various high-profile women in the years between marriages. But lasting intimacy seemed to elude him. How do you trust people when you're worth tens of billions? How do you know if they love you or your money? These are the problems of extreme wealth that Ellison never seemed to solve.

Friends were complicated too. His closest friendship was probably with Steve Jobs, the Apple co-founder who shared Ellison's intensity, perfectionism, and reality distortion field. They became close in the 1990s, bonding over their shared competitiveness and appreciation for Japanese aesthetics. When Jobs died in 2011, Ellison was reportedly devastated, it was perhaps the one relationship in his life that felt fully authentic because Jobs neither needed Ellison's money nor was intimidated by his personality.

"Larry and Steve understood each other," a mutual friend observed. "They were both difficult, demanding, and sometimes cruel to the people around them. But they recognized in each other a kind of relentless drive toward perfection that most people don't have."

Oracle's Evolution: Cloud Wars and Staying Relevant

As Ellison moved through his sixties and then seventies, he faced a challenge that many tech founders encounter: staying relevant as the industry transforms. The 2000s brought a new paradigm, cloud computing that threatened to make Oracle's traditional on-premise database business obsolete.

Companies like Salesforce (founded by former Oracle executive Marc Benioff, who Ellison had mentored) were building software delivered entirely through the internet. Amazon Web Services was offering computing infrastructure on demand. The future was cloud-based, and Oracle was late to the party.

For a few years, Ellison dismissed cloud computing as hype. "The computer industry is the only industry that is more fashion-driven than women's fashion," he said in 2008. "Maybe I'm an idiot, but I have no idea what anyone is talking about. What is it? It's complete gibberish."

But by 2010, Ellison realized this wasn't hype, it was the future. And being Larry Ellison, he didn't gradually ease into the cloud. He went all-in, declaring that Oracle would become a cloud company and that its future depended on it.

The transformation was expensive and difficult. Oracle had to rebuild its products for cloud delivery. It had to compete with Amazon, Microsoft, and Google companies that had head starts. It required acquiring companies like NetSuite (for $9.3 billion) to bulk up cloud offerings. The transition hurt Oracle's growth for several years as the traditional business slowed while the cloud business scaled.

But by 2020, Oracle had successfully transformed itself into a major cloud player, particularly in enterprise applications and database services. It wasn't the dominant cloud company, that title belonged to Amazon but it was a credible competitor. Once again, Ellison had managed to avoid obsolescence.

In 2014, at age seventy, Ellison stepped down as CEO, handing operational control to two lieutenants while remaining as chairman and chief technology officer. It was a partial retirement that let him focus on technology strategy while reducing the daily management burden.

The Paradox of Larry Ellison

Trying to make sense of Larry Ellison is like trying to assemble a puzzle where the pieces come from different boxes. He is simultaneously:

The wounded child seeking validation: His entire career can be read as a response to his adoptive father's prediction of failure. Every billion dollars, every yacht, every competitor crushed, they all seem to scream "See? I'm not nothing. I'm not a failure."

The brilliant technologist: Beneath the ego and the lifestyle, Ellison genuinely understood database technology and made real contributions to the field. His instinct for what customers needed was often prescient.

The ruthless competitor: His willingness to use any legal tactic to win, aggressive sales, strategic lawsuits, public attacks on competitors made him feared and sometimes hated in the industry.

The aesthete: His appreciation for Japanese art and architecture, his perfectionism about design, his love of sailing, these suggest a man seeking beauty and meaning beyond just accumulation.

The generous friend: By many accounts, Ellison was loyal and generous to his small circle of close friends, including his famous friendship with Steve Jobs.

The difficult boss: Countless Oracle employees have stories of his harsh criticism, unrealistic demands, and narcissistic behavior.

As of 2025, at age eighty, Larry Ellison remains actively involved in Oracle and is worth well over $100 billion, making him one of the ten richest people on Earth. He continues to spend lavishly, compete aggressively, and speak his mind without filters.

Lessons from the Samurai of Silicon Valley

What can we learn from Larry Ellison's remarkable and controversial life?

Chip-on-shoulder motivation is powerful: Ellison's desire to prove his adoptive father wrong fueled five decades of relentless ambition. Psychological wounds can be converted into extraordinary drive, though at what cost to one's inner peace?

Timing matters, but persistence matters more: Ellison wasn't the first programmer to understand databases. But he was persistent enough to build Oracle through multiple near-death experiences and market shifts.

Aggression can work, with limits: Oracle's cutthroat culture and sales tactics helped it dominate the database market. But the same aggression nearly bankrupted the company in 1990. Ellison learned to channel aggression more carefully without eliminating it.

You can buy yachts but not serenity: Despite wealth that lets him buy almost anything, Ellison's personal life suggests that money doesn't solve problems of intimacy, belonging, or inner peace. The unwanted child is still somewhere inside the billionaire.

Staying relevant requires humility: When cloud computing emerged, Ellison initially dismissed it and nearly missed the industry's biggest shift. His willingness to eventually admit error and embrace the cloud kept Oracle relevant.

Rivalry drives excellence: Ellison's obsessive competition with IBM, Microsoft, and others pushed Oracle to improve constantly. His competitive fire was sometimes petty, but it was also a source of innovation.

You can't escape your past: Ellison's entire life reads as an argument with his adoptive father and a search for the biological parents who gave him up. All the money in the world couldn't resolve those primal wounds.

In the end, Larry Ellison is perhaps the most purely competitive of all the tech billionaires not motivated by changing the world (like Bill Gates once claimed) or connecting people (like Mark Zuckerberg says) or solving humanity's problems (like Elon Musk declares). Ellison wanted to win. At business. At sailing. At life itself.

Whether he has actually won is a question he might still be asking himself, late at night, in one of his many palatial homes, thinking about a father who said he'd never amount to anything, a father whose prediction he's spent eighty years and $100 billion proving wrong.

Sometimes, the richest people in the world are still trying to become rich enough to fill a void that money can't touch.

Chapter 13

The Google Founders - Larry Page & Sergey Brin

In the summer of 1995, Larry Page arrived at Stanford University for a weekend campus visit, part of the orientation for prospective PhD students. Sergey Brin, already a second-year graduate student in computer science, volunteered to show him around. They argued almost immediately about nearly everything. Politics, technology, the best route to walk across campus. Where one saw opportunity, the other saw problems. Where one was enthusiastic, the other was skeptical.

"We both found each other obnoxious," Page later recalled with a smile.

Within a year, they would become inseparable collaborators. Within three years, they would launch a company that would reorganize how humanity accesses information. Within two decades, they would each be worth over $100 billion and preside over one of the most powerful corporations in human history.

But the transformation from arguing graduate students to titans of the digital age wasn't inevitable. It required insight, timing, technical brilliance, and a willingness to think impossibly big along with some lucky accidents and a few moral compromises that would complicate their legacy.

Two Immigrant Success Stories

Larry Page and Sergey Brin were the products of parents who believed in the transformative power of education and technology. Both came from academic families. Both grew up around computers at a time when that was still unusual. And both had internalized the idea that brilliant people could change the world through technology.

Larry Page was born in 1973 in East Lansing, Michigan, to Carl Victor Page and Gloria Page, both professors of computer science at Michigan State University. His house was filled with computers, science magazines, and the constant hum of intellectual curiosity. Carl Page was an early pioneer in artificial intelligence and computer science education, and young Larry absorbed his father's conviction that computers would revolutionize human capability.

"I was the first kid in my elementary school to turn in a word-processed document," Page remembered. This was in the early 1980s, when most adults had never touched a computer. He grew up assuming that building things with technology was what smart people did.

Sergey Brin was born in Moscow in 1973 to a Jewish family facing discrimination in the Soviet Union. His father, Mikhail Brin, was a mathematician who struggled to advance his career under the Soviet system's antisemitic policies. In 1979, when Sergey was six, the Brin family emigrated to the United States, settling in Maryland where Mikhail took a position as a mathematics professor at the University of Maryland.

Sergey grew up with his father's stories of Soviet oppression and censorship, lessons that would later inform his views on information freedom and the importance of open access to knowledge. "I came here to the United States when I was six years old, and I feel that I was saved," Brin said years later. "My family fought to leave, and I am very grateful that they did."

Both boys were mathematically gifted, socially awkward, and intensely curious. Both followed predictable paths for children of their backgrounds: excellent grades, admission to top universities, graduate school in computer science. Page went to the University of Michigan, then Stanford. Brin went to the University of Maryland, then Stanford.

Stanford in the mid-1990s was the epicenter of the emerging internet revolution. The web browser had just been invented. Amazon and eBay were launching. Marc Andreessen, who had created the first popular web browser while still a student, was becoming Silicon Valley royalty. The sense of possibility was electric.

Into this environment came Page and Brin, two twenty-something graduate students who initially couldn't stand each other but shared a conviction that the existing ways of doing things were inadequate.

The Birth of BackRub (Yes, Really)

Larry Page's PhD research focused on the World Wide Web's link structure. While other researchers were focused on the content of web pages, Page became fascinated by the links between pages, who linked to whom, and what that network of connections revealed.

The insight was deceptively simple but profound: links were like citations in academic papers. When one website linked to another, it was essentially saying, "This is important" or "This is authoritative." A page with many links pointing to it was probably more valuable than a page with few links. Moreover, links from important pages should count more than links from obscure ones.

This was actually inspired by Page's academic family background. In academic publishing, the importance of a paper is partially determined by how many other papers cite it. Page wondered: could you rank web pages the same way?

He started building a web crawler to download web pages and analyze their link structure. He called it BackRub, a reference to analyzing the "back links" pointing to a page. The name was awkward and slightly suggestive, and thankfully would not survive.

Sergey Brin, with his strong mathematics background, got interested in Page's project. The problem of analyzing the web's link structure was mathematically fascinating, it involved matrices, eigenvalues, and probability distributions. For a mathematician, it was beautiful.

Together, they developed PageRank (named after Larry Page, not web pages), an algorithm that treated the entire web as a massive democracy where pages "voted" for other pages through links. Pages with more votes, especially votes from other important pages ranked higher. It was elegant, mathematically sophisticated, and it worked remarkably well.

They started testing their search engine on Stanford's network in 1996. The results were noticeably better than existing search engines like AltaVista, Excite, and Yahoo. While those services often returned irrelevant results loaded with spam, BackRub/PageRank consistently surfaced useful, authoritative pages.

There was just one problem: it required enormous computing power. Page and Brin filled their dorm rooms with hard drives, building a custom computer out of Lego bricks (for the case) and cheap disk drives. They maxed out Stanford's internet connection downloading and analyzing web pages. They were causing problems for Stanford's network administrators, but they were onto something big.

The Reluctant Entrepreneurs

Here's something surprising: Larry Page and Sergey Brin didn't initially want to start a company. They were academics who wanted to publish papers and finish their PhDs. They actually tried to sell their search technology to existing companies for $1 million.

They approached Yahoo, then the dominant web portal. Yahoo's executives said no, they wanted people to stay on Yahoo's site, not use it as a gateway to leave. They approached Excite. The CEO came close to buying it for $750,000, but ultimately passed. Other companies looked at their technology and essentially shrugged. Search wasn't seen as particularly valuable. It was a feature, not a business.

In retrospect, this was one of the greatest missed opportunities in business history. But at the time, it made sense to the established players. How do you make money from search? Yahoo made money from advertising on its portal. Amazon made money from selling products. But a search engine that quickly sent people away to other sites? What was the business model?

Unable to sell their technology, and increasingly convinced it was too important to abandon, Page and Brin made a fateful decision: they would start a company themselves.

In September 1998, they officially incorporated Google Inc. The name was a play on "googol," the mathematical term for the number 1 followed by 100 zeros, a reference to their ambition to organize the vast amount of information on the web. (The misspelling was accidental but stuck.)

They raised $100,000 from Andy Bechtolsheim, one of the founders of Sun Microsystems, who wrote them a check made out to "Google Inc." before the company legally existed. They rented a garage in Menlo Park from Susan Wojcicki (who would later become YouTube's CEO). They hired their first employee, Craig Silverstein, a fellow Stanford graduate student.

They were, in classic Silicon Valley fashion, a startup.

The Early Years: Idealism Meets Reality

The early Google was infused with the idealism of its academic founders. They wrote a corporate philosophy that included principles like "Focus on the user and all else will follow" and, most famously, "Don't be evil."

That last phrase deserves attention. It wasn't just marketing fluff, it reflected a genuine belief that technology companies had been evil, or at least indifferent to user welfare. Pop-up ads, privacy violations, deliberately confusing interfaces designed to trick users, these were common practices in the late-1990s internet. Page and Brin believed they could build a different kind of company.

The early Google homepage was radically simple: a logo, a search box, and two buttons. That was it. No ads cluttering the page. No attempts to keep you on Google's site. Just a tool to help you find what you needed and move on. It was so austere it looked broken compared to Yahoo's busy portal crammed with links, news, and advertising.

But it worked beautifully. Word spread among tech-savvy users: Google was better. Much better. By 2000, Google was handling 100 million searches per day. By 2001, it was profitable.

The profitability came from a deceptively simple innovation: AdWords.

The Business Model That Prints Money

In 2000, Google faced a crisis. They had users, millions of them but they didn't have a sustainable business model. Banner ads weren't working. They needed something better.

The solution came from an unlikely source: Overture (formerly GoTo.com), a competitor that was selling ads triggered by search terms. If you searched for "digital camera," you'd see ads from camera retailers. It was called "search advertising," and it worked because the ads were actually relevant to what users wanted.

Google adapted the model but improved it significantly. Instead of just selling ads to the highest bidder, Google ranked ads based on both the bid price and the ad's relevance and quality. Better ads that users clicked on more frequently ranked higher. This meant users saw more useful ads, advertisers got better results, and Google made more money. Everybody won.

AdWords launched in 2000, and it was revolutionary. Suddenly, small businesses could advertise to customers with purchase intent, paying only when someone clicked. The system was self-service, auction-based, and measurable. You could spend $100 and see exactly how many clicks, customers, and sales you got.

The money started pouring in. Not just flowing, pouring. By 2001, Google was profitable. By 2004, it was printing money. The economics were extraordinary: once the system was built, each additional search cost Google almost nothing, but generated advertising revenue. The margins were spectacular.

"We didn't set out to build an advertising company," Page later said. "But we needed to fund this mission of organizing the world's information, and advertising turned out to be a very effective way to do that."

This statement captures both the truth and the tension in Google's evolution. They really did want to organize information. But the money from advertising was so enormous that it became increasingly hard to separate the mission from the business model.

Going Public: Billionaires in Their Thirties

On August 19, 2004, Google went public in one of the most anticipated IPOs in tech history. The company sold shares at $85 apiece, raising $1.67 billion and valuing the company at $23 billion.

Larry Page and Sergey Brin, both just thirty years old, each became worth approximately $3.8 billion overnight. They were suddenly among the richest people in the world, joining an exclusive club that included older titans like Bill Gates, Warren Buffett, and Larry Ellison.

But the Google IPO was unusual in several ways. First, they used a "Dutch auction" process designed to prevent Wall Street banks from allocating shares to favored clients. They wanted regular people to have a chance to buy shares, a democratizing impulse that annoyed investment bankers.

Second, they included a "Founder's Letter" in the IPO prospectus that was remarkably candid and unconventional. Page and Brin wrote about wanting to build a company for the long term, not to maximize quarterly earnings. They explained their "Don't be evil" philosophy. They warned potential investors that they would make decisions based on what was right for users and the long-term vision, not short-term stock price.

"Google is not a conventional company," they wrote. "We do not intend to become one."

Most remarkably, they instituted a dual-class share structure that gave them voting control even after going public. Page, Brin, and CEO Eric Schmidt (whom they'd brought in to help manage the growing company) would maintain control. Public shareholders would have economic rights but limited governance power.

Wall Street hated it. The press criticized it as anti-democratic. But it worked. Google's leaders could pursue long-term strategies without worrying about activist investors or quarterly earnings pressure. It was a structure that would inspire other tech founders, from Mark Zuckerberg to Evan Spiegel, to maintain control of their companies even after going public.

The Expansion: From Search to Everything

With billions in cash flow from AdWords, Google began expanding beyond search with remarkable ambition. The goal wasn't just to build a profitable company, it was to organize all the world's information and make it universally accessible.

In 2004, Google launched Gmail, a free email service with 1 gigabyte of storage, 500 times more than competitors offered. The catch? Google would scan your emails to show relevant ads. This sparked immediate privacy concerns, but users loved the additional storage and superior interface.

In 2005, Google launched Google Maps, which evolved into one of the most-used apps globally. They sent cars with cameras to photograph every street (Street View), raising privacy concerns but creating an incredibly useful service.

In 2006, Google bought YouTube for $1.65 billion. Many analysts thought they'd overpaid for a company that was hemorrhaging money on bandwidth costs and facing potential copyright lawsuits. In retrospect, it was one of the best acquisitions in tech history. YouTube became the world's second-largest search engine (after Google itself) and a major advertising platform.

They launched Google Chrome browser in 2008, which became the world's most popular browser. They developed Android, an open-source mobile operating system that would eventually power billions of smartphones. They launched Google Books, attempting to scan every book ever published (prompting lawsuits from publishers).

The expansion was breathtaking in scope and ambition. No company since perhaps AT&T in its heyday had attempted to build infrastructure touching so many aspects of daily life. And unlike AT&T, Google was doing it mostly by giving things away for free, subsidized by advertising.

The Cracks in the Idealism

As Google grew from a startup to a corporation with tens of thousands of employees and hundreds of billions in market value, the early idealism became complicated.

The "Don't be evil" motto began to ring hollow in various controversies:

China (2006-2010): Google launched a censored version of its search engine in China, agreeing to filter results to comply with the Chinese government's requirements. This directly contradicted Google's stated mission to make information universally accessible. Brin, whose family had fled Soviet oppression, was reportedly conflicted but argued that providing even censored information was better than providing nothing. After cyber attacks and increasing discomfort with censorship, Google withdrew from China in 2010 but the initial decision had damaged their reputation.

Privacy concerns: Google's business model depended on collecting vast amounts of data about users' searches, emails, locations, and behavior. As they grew, so did concerns about surveillance, data breaches, and the power of one company knowing so much about billions of people. The Street View cars were found to be collecting WiFi data from homes. Gmail scanning raised concerns about reading people's private messages.

Antitrust issues: Google's dominance in search (90%+ market share globally) raised questions about whether they were abusing their position. Were they favoring their own services in search results? Making it impossible for competitors to succeed? By 2010, regulators in the US and Europe were investigating.

Tax avoidance: Google employed sophisticated international tax strategies (with names like "Double Irish with a Dutch Sandwich") to minimize tax payments. It was legal, but it looked hypocritical for a company claiming to make the world better to go to such lengths to avoid contributing to public services.

Employee unrest: In 2018, thousands of Google employees walked out to protest the company's handling of sexual harassment claims and its work on military AI projects. The idealistic engineers who joined Google to "organize the world's information" were questioning whether the company still represented their values.

Page and Brin responded to these challenges inconsistently. Sometimes they made course corrections (withdrawing from China, ending certain controversial projects). Sometimes they defended their decisions. Increasingly, they seemed frustrated by the impossible expectations, they had positioned Google as a different kind of company, and now people held them to that standard.

Alphabet: The Conglomerate Play

By 2015, Google had become a sprawling conglomerate working on everything from self-driving cars to life extension research to internet-beaming balloons. This created confusion for investors and management challenges for the leadership.

Page and Brin's solution was radical: they created a new parent company called Alphabet Inc. Google would become just one subsidiary of Alphabet (though by far the largest). Other ambitious projects, self-driving cars (Waymo), life sciences (Verily), internet balloons (Loon), and so on would become separate Alphabet companies.

The reorganization let Page and Brin focus on the experimental, ambitious "moonshot" projects they found most interesting while leaving Google's day-to-day operations to professional management. Sundar Pichai, who had risen through Google's ranks, became CEO of Google. Page became CEO of Alphabet. Brin became President of Alphabet.

It was a creative solution, but it also represented a shift. Page and Brin were explicitly moving away from running Google, the search and advertising company that made all the money, to focus on the more speculative ventures that might shape the future.

Some saw this as visionary, freeing two brilliant minds to work on humanity's biggest challenges. Others saw it as bored billionaires playing with expensive toys funded by advertising dollars.

The Gradual Retreat

In December 2019, Larry Page and Sergey Brin announced they were stepping down from their roles as CEO and President of Alphabet. Sundar Pichai would become CEO of both Google and Alphabet. Page and Brin would remain on the board and retain voting control through their supervoting shares, but they were stepping back from day-to-day operations.

They were both just forty-six years old.

The announcement was striking in its brevity and lack of drama. There was no scandal forcing them out, no health crisis, no conflict with the board. They simply said that Alphabet had matured, that Pichai was ready to lead, and that they would step back.

The unspoken subtext was clear: they were bored, or frustrated, or tired of the scrutiny, or perhaps all three. Running a large public company means dealing with regulators, lawsuits, employee activism, press criticism, and congressional hearings. It means compromise and constraint. For two people who got into technology to build things and explore ideas, it had become a grind.

Since stepping down, Page and Brin have been remarkably quiet. Unlike other billionaire tech founders who remain visible through Twitter, interviews, or new ventures, Page and Brin have largely disappeared from public view. They attend board meetings. They occasionally weigh in on major decisions. But they've granted almost no interviews and made few public appearances.

This silence is itself notable. They built a company whose mission was to make information accessible, but they themselves have become inaccessible. The two men who organized the world's information have largely withdrawn from the world they helped create.

What Did They Actually Believe?

Looking back at Page and Brin's twenty-year journey from graduate students to retired billionaires, a central question emerges: did they really believe the idealistic things they said, or was it always just marketing?

The answer appears to be: both, and neither. They genuinely believed that organizing information and making it accessible was important and valuable work. They really did want to build a "different kind of company." They honestly thought that brilliant engineers could solve major problems.

But they also underestimated how difficult it would be to maintain those ideals at scale. How do you organize information neutrally when every decision about ranking affects billions of people and billions of dollars? How do you provide free services without a business model that depends on surveillance? How do you maintain a "Don't be evil" culture when your company grows to 100,000+ employees?

They were brilliant at technology but perhaps naive about the political, social, and ethical complexity of building a global information infrastructure. Their academic backgrounds hadn't prepared them for questions like: "Should you help the Chinese government censor its citizens?" or "How do you balance free speech against misinformation?" or "What do you owe society when your company essentially becomes public infrastructure?"

In fairness, nobody had good answers to these questions. But Page and Brin had claimed they would be different, that they wouldn't be evil, that they would put users first. That made the failures and compromises sting more.

The Personal Price of Building Google

Page and Brin each married and had children, but they've kept their personal lives extraordinarily private. Page married Lucy Southworth, a research scientist, in 2007; they have two children. Brin married Anne Wojcicki, co-founder of genetic testing company 23andMe, in 2007; they had two children before divorcing in 2015. Brin later married Nicole Shanahan, though that marriage also ended in divorce.

The personal cost of building Google is hard to measure from outside, but there are hints. Page developed vocal cord paralysis in 2013, which affected his voice and made speaking difficult, a condition possibly related to stress. He's given very few public speeches or interviews since.

Brin has been more visible but still extraordinarily private. He's invested in causes like Parkinson's research (his mother has the disease, and he carries a genetic variant that increases his risk) and in various technology ventures, but he rarely discusses his personal life or motivations.

Both men, now worth over $100 billion each, live in an entirely different reality than the graduate students who argued about everything in 1995. They have resources that let them pursue any interest, fund any project, go anywhere, do anything. Yet they seem, by all accounts, to be fairly reserved and private people who are happiest thinking about technology problems.

They're not flashy like Larry Ellison with his yachts and fighter jets. They're not messianic like Elon Musk with his Mars ambitions and Twitter pronouncements. They're not systematic philanthropists like Bill Gates with his foundation's detailed metrics. They're just... quiet. Wealthy beyond imagination, powerful beyond precedent, and remarkably uninterested in the spotlight.

Legacy: What Google Created

Whatever the complexities of Page and Brin's personal beliefs and decisions, Google's impact is undeniable:

Information access: Google made it possible for anyone with an internet connection to access humanity's accumulated knowledge almost instantly. This is historically unprecedented. The transformation of how we learn, research, and find information is profound.

Economic opportunity: Google's advertising platform enabled millions of small businesses to reach customers affordably. YouTube created opportunities for creators to build audiences and earn income. Android made smartphones affordable globally.

Technological advancement: Google's infrastructure innovations, search algorithms, machine learning research, and open-source contributions advanced computer science significantly.

Corporate influence: Google's workplace culture (free food, 20% time for passion projects, casual dress, stock options for everyone) influenced how tech companies operate globally.

But the negative impacts are also significant:

Privacy erosion: Google normalized surveillance capitalism, the business model of providing free services in exchange for vast data collection used for targeted advertising.

Misinformation infrastructure: YouTube's recommendation algorithm has been shown to promote increasingly extreme content, contributing to radicalization and misinformation.

Monopoly power: Google's dominance makes it nearly impossible for competitors to emerge in search, raising concerns about innovation and fairness.

Addiction by design: Google's products are deliberately designed to maximize engagement (and thus ad exposure), contributing to technology addiction and mental health concerns.

Centralized power: So much of the internet's infrastructure running through one company creates both practical vulnerabilities and concerning power concentration.

Lessons from the Accidental Empire Builders

What can we learn from Larry Page and Sergey Brin's journey?

Academic insights can create commercial empires: Page and Brin weren't trying to build a business initially. They were solving an interesting technical problem. Sometimes the best businesses come from genuine curiosity rather than business planning.

Timing is everything: They hit the perfect moment when the web was growing exponentially but search was still terrible. Five years earlier or later, Google might never have happened.

Idealism is powerful but fragile: "Don't be evil" was a genuine motivating force in Google's early days. It attracted talent and users. But maintaining ideals while navigating complexity, growth, and commercial pressures proved nearly impossible.

Control enables long-term thinking: The dual-class share structure let Page and Brin invest in ambitious projects without quarterly earnings pressure. But it also insulated them from accountability when they made controversial decisions.

Scale changes everything: The principles that work beautifully for a small idealistic startup become complicated when applied to a global infrastructure company affecting billions of people.

You can't escape politics: Page and Brin wanted to focus on technology, not politics. But when your company affects how billions of people access information, your technology becomes inherently political. You can't opt out.

Success at organizing information doesn't mean success at organizing society: Page and Brin were brilliant at information technology but perhaps naive about the social, political, and ethical implications of their work.

In the end, Larry Page and Sergey Brin created something remarkable: a tool that genuinely made humanity's information more accessible. But they also created new problems: surveillance, addiction, centralized power, and the challenge of who controls the world's information infrastructure.

They started as two idealistic graduate students who thought a better search algorithm could organize the world's information. They became billionaires presiding over one of the most powerful corporations in history. They stepped back, still relatively young, to... do what, exactly? Even now, that question remains unanswered.

Perhaps that's the ultimate lesson: even when you achieve exactly what you set out to do, organize the world's information you might still be searching for what comes next.

PART IV: THE MODERN TITANS (2000s-Present)

Chapter 14

Jeff Bezos - Everything Store to Everything Company

On July 16, 1995, a new website went live. It had a plain white background, simple blue text, and a logo that looked like it had been designed in about ten minutes. The site sold exactly one category of product: books. The name was strange and hard to spell: Amazon.com.

Wall Street analysts who bothered to notice were skeptical. Why would people buy books online when they could browse at a bookstore? How could an online retailer compete with established chains like Barnes & Noble and Borders? And books, really? Books had thin margins and required expensive warehousing. It seemed like a terrible business.

The founder, a thirty-one-year-old former hedge fund executive named Jeff Bezos, had a different vision. He wasn't really starting a bookstore. He was building the infrastructure for the future of retail, all retail. Books were just the beginning, the Trojan horse that would get customers comfortable with buying things online. Eventually, Bezos believed Amazon would sell everything.

"We want to be Earth's most customer-centric company," he told anyone who would listen, "where customers can find and discover anything they might want to buy online."

By 2025, thirty years after that modest website launch, Bezos had built exactly that. Amazon had become the everything store, and then the everything company, e-commerce, cloud computing, streaming video, grocery stores, healthcare, and more. Bezos himself had become, for a time, the richest person in human history, with a fortune exceeding $200 billion. He had also become divorced, remarried, and transformed himself from a bookish nerd into a muscular, bald, divorced-dad-energy mogul who owned newspapers, space companies, and superyachts.

The story of Jeff Bezos is the story of relentless long-term thinking, customer obsession bordering on ruthlessness, and the transformation of

American retail and internet infrastructure. It's also the story of how extreme wealth changes a person, for better and worse.

The Overachiever's Origins

Jeffrey Preston Jorgensen was born in Albuquerque, New Mexico, in 1964 to Jacklyn Gise, a seventeen-year-old high school student, and Ted Jorgensen, an eighteen-year-old bike shop owner. The marriage was troubled from the start. Ted was immature and reportedly abusive. When Jeff was seventeen months old, Jacklyn left Ted and the marriage was over.

When Jeff was four, his mother married Miguel "Mike" Bezos, a Cuban immigrant who had fled Castro's regime as a teenager, arriving in America alone and speaking no English. Mike adopted Jeff, giving him the Bezos surname and raising him as his own son. By all accounts, Mike was a devoted, supportive father, the complete opposite of Jeff's biological father, who faded from his life so completely that Ted Jorgensen later didn't even recognize the name "Jeff Bezos" when a reporter tracked him down decades later.

The Bezos family moved to Houston, where Mike worked as an engineer for Exxon. Young Jeff was brilliant, driven, and fascinated by science and technology. He spent summers at his maternal grandfather's ranch in Texas, where he learned self-reliance, problem-solving, and the value of hard work. His grandfather, Preston Gise, had been a regional director for the U.S. Atomic Energy Commission, a man who believed in the power of science and technology to shape the future.

Jeff excelled at everything he attempted. He was valedictorian of his high school class. He was a National Merit Scholar. He graduated summa cum laude from Princeton with degrees in electrical engineering and computer science. He could have pursued academia or gone to work at a prestigious tech company.

Instead, in 1986, he went to Wall Street.

The Hedge Fund Years: Learning to Think Big

Bezos spent the late 1980s and early 1990s working at several Wall Street firms, eventually landing at D.E. Shaw, a quantitative hedge fund at the cutting edge of using computers and algorithms for trading. He rose quickly, becoming one of the firm's youngest senior vice presidents at age twenty-eight.

D.E. Shaw wasn't a typical Wall Street firm. Founder David Shaw had hired physicists and computer scientists to build trading systems, and the culture rewarded analytical thinking and unconventional ideas. It was here that Bezos learned to think in terms of systems, scale, and data-driven decision-making.

It was also here, in 1994, that Bezos encountered a statistic that changed his life: web usage was growing at 2,300% per year.

Think about that number. Not 23%, not 230%, but 2,300%. Bezos had never seen anything growing that fast. "Things just don't grow that fast," he later said. "It's highly unusual, and that started me wondering, okay, what kind of business plan might make sense in the context of that growth?"

Bezos did what any good analyst would do: he made a list of products that might sell well online. He considered twenty possibilities, analyzing each for their suitability to internet retail. Books kept rising to the top. There were millions of titles in print, far more than any physical bookstore could stock. Books were standardized products that didn't need to be touched or tried on. They were easy to ship. And people who bought books often bought more books, which meant repeat customers.

Moreover, the two big bookstore chains, Barnes & Noble and Borders, were focused on superstores and malls. They weren't thinking about the internet. There was a window of opportunity.

Bezos faced a choice: stay at D.E. Shaw with a lucrative, secure career, or leap into the unknown and start an internet bookstore. He later described his decision-making process using what he called the "regret minimization framework." He imagined himself at age eighty, looking back on his life. Would he regret leaving a safe Wall Street job? Probably not. Would he regret not trying to be part of the internet revolution? Absolutely.

In 1994, at age thirty, Jeff Bezos quit his job, drove across the country to Seattle with his wife MacKenzie (whom he'd met at D.E. Shaw), and started an online bookstore in a garage. It was the most clichéd startup origin story possible and it was true.

Amazon 1.0: The Bookseller That Wouldn't Die

The early Amazon was chaotic, underfunded, and constantly on the verge of collapse. Bezos and his small team worked insane hours, packing books on their hands and knees because they couldn't afford packing tables. (Bezos later joked that he suggested using knee pads, before realizing they should just buy packing tables.)

But from the very beginning, Bezos made decisions that revealed his long-term thinking. He chose Seattle partly because of its proximity to a large book distributor in Oregon, but also because Washington state had a relatively small population, meaning Amazon wouldn't have to collect sales tax for most of its customers, giving them a price advantage.

He named the company Amazon after the world's most voluminous river, suggesting vast selection. He insisted on customer reviews, even though publishers hated the idea of negative reviews appearing on a retailer's site. He obsessed over customer service, personally answering customer emails late into the night and forwarding particularly problematic ones to executives with just a question mark, the dreaded "Jeff question mark" that meant someone had screwed up and needed to fix it immediately.

When Amazon went public in May 1997 at $18 per share, raising $54 million, Bezos was worth about $60 million on paper. But he warned investors in his first annual shareholder letter that Amazon would focus on long-term growth over short-term profitability. "We will make bold rather than timid investment decisions," he wrote. "We will make investment decisions in light of long-term market leadership considerations rather than short-term profitability considerations or short-term Wall Street reactions."

This was unusual. Most companies tried to show profits as quickly as possible. Bezos was explicitly saying Amazon would lose money for years while building market share and infrastructure. Incredibly, investors bought into the vision or at least enough of them did to keep funding the company's expansion.

True to his word, Amazon spent lavishly and lost money spectacularly. They expanded into music and DVDs. They built massive distribution centers. They spent heavily on technology. The losses mounted: $31 million in 1997, $125 million in 1999, $1.4 billion in 2000.

Wall Street analysts called it "Amazon.bomb" and predicted bankruptcy. In the dot-com crash of 2000-2001, when hundreds of internet companies collapsed, Amazon's stock plummeted from over $100 per share to $6. Bezos's net worth on paper dropped from several billion dollars to a few hundred million. The company came within weeks of running out of cash.

But Amazon survived. Barely.

The Turn to Profitability and the Third-Party Platform

The near-death experience forced discipline on Amazon. They cut costs, closed distribution centers in Europe, laid off employees. But Bezos didn't abandon his long-term vision, he just got smarter about execution.

The breakthrough came from an unlikely source: other sellers. In 2000, Amazon launched Marketplace, which allowed third-party sellers to list products on Amazon's site, competing directly with Amazon's own inventory. Traditional retailers thought this was insane, why would you let competitors sell on your platform?

But Bezos understood something profound: Amazon wasn't really a retailer. It was a platform, an infrastructure company. If third-party sellers could offer better selection or prices, that made Amazon better for customers. Amazon would take a commission on every sale, earning money without holding inventory or taking risk. It was brilliant.

By 2003, third-party sales accounted for over 20% of Amazon's unit sales. By 2018, it would be over 50%. Amazon had transformed from a retailer into an infrastructure platform, the real estate owner of the internet mall, collecting rent from thousands of tenants.

Amazon also launched Amazon Prime in 2005, a subscription service offering free two-day shipping for $79 per year. Wall Street analysts thought it was financially insane, Amazon would lose money on shipping. But Bezos understood that Prime members would shop more frequently and spend more. It was a loyalty program that made Amazon the default choice for online shopping.

He was right. Prime members spent roughly double what non-Prime members spent. As Amazon built out its logistics infrastructure, more warehouses, its own delivery trucks and even its own cargo planes it could fulfill orders faster and cheaper than anyone else. The flywheel was spinning: better selection attracted more customers, which attracted more sellers, which improved selection, which attracted more customers.

By 2015, Amazon was doing $107 billion in annual revenue. Jeff Bezos was worth over $50 billion and climbing.

But the most surprising part of Amazon's success wasn't retail at all. It was something that started as an internal project to solve Amazon's own infrastructure problems.

AWS: The Accidental Empire Within the Empire

In the early 2000s, Amazon's engineers faced a problem: every time they wanted to launch a new feature, they had to build infrastructure from scratch. It was slow and inefficient. They started building internal tools and services, standardized ways to store data, run computations, and build applications.

In 2003, someone had an idea: what if they offered these infrastructure services to outside companies? Businesses could rent computing power and storage from Amazon instead of building their own data centers. It seemed tangential to Amazon's retail mission, but Bezos approved a small team to explore it.

Amazon Web Services (AWS) launched in 2006, offering basic computing and storage services to developers. The initial reaction was skepticism. Why would serious companies trust their infrastructure to an online bookstore?

But AWS had several advantages: it was cheap, flexible, and you only paid for what you used. Startups could launch services without buying servers. Companies could scale up or down instantly. It was revolutionary.

AWS grew slowly at first, then explosively. By 2015, AWS was generating over $7 billion in annual revenue with operating margins around 25%, far higher than retail. By 2020, AWS revenue exceeded $45 billion with operating income of $13.5 billion. This "side project" was generating more profit than the entire retail operation.

AWS had transformed Amazon from an online retailer into a fundamental piece of internet infrastructure. Massive portions of the internet—Netflix, Airbnb, countless startups, even parts of the U.S. government ran on AWS. Amazon had become, almost accidentally, the landlord of the internet.

This created a strange dynamic: Amazon competed with companies like Netflix in streaming video while also providing the infrastructure Netflix ran on. It raised questions about conflicts of interest and whether Amazon was using data from AWS to gain competitive advantages. But it also made Amazon nearly impossible to dislodge. Competing with Amazon meant either building your own global infrastructure or renting from Amazon.

Bezos had built something unprecedented: a company that dominated e-commerce while also dominating the infrastructure that powered much of the internet. It was like if Walmart also owned the highways, the electrical grid, and the banking system.

The Richest Man in Modern History

As Amazon's stock soared, so did Jeff Bezos's wealth. By 2017, he was worth over $100 billion. In 2018, he briefly topped $150 billion, making him the richest person in modern history (adjusting for inflation, though not surpassing historical figures like Rockefeller or Mansa Musa).

The wealth was almost abstract, $150 billion is impossible to conceptualize. If you spent $1 million per day, it would take over 400 years to spend $150 billion. Bezos was earning more per minute than most Americans earned in a year.

But the wealth also made him a target. As wealth inequality became a central political issue, Bezos became a symbol of extreme capitalism. Amazon warehouse workers reported brutal conditions, timed bathroom breaks, injuries from repetitive motion, impossible productivity quotas. They were paid $15/hour while their boss was worth $150 billion.

Critics noted that Amazon paid minimal federal income taxes despite huge profits, using legal tax strategies to offset income. The company was accused of destroying small businesses and main street retail. Cities competed for Amazon's "HQ2" with massive tax incentives, essentially paying Amazon to bring jobs.

Bezos seemed tone-deaf to the criticism. In 2017, he asked Twitter for "philanthropy ideas," suggesting he didn't know what to do with his money. When asked about wealth inequality, he said his best contribution was building Amazon and Blue Origin (his space company). He seemed to genuinely believe that building companies was more valuable than philanthropy.

This was a stark contrast to Bill Gates, who had transitioned from ruthless Microsoft CEO to beloved philanthropist. Bezos was still in "build mode," focused on growing Amazon and Blue Origin rather than giving money away.

The Transformation: Divorce, Muscles, and Midlife Changes

On January 9, 2019, Jeff and MacKenzie Bezos announced they were divorcing after twenty-five years of marriage. The announcement came one day before the National Enquirer published a story about Jeff's affair with Lauren Sanchez, a former TV anchor and helicopter pilot.

The divorce was finalized in April 2019. MacKenzie received 25% of their Amazon shares, worth about $36 billion, making her one of the richest women in the world. Jeff retained 75% of the shares and voting control.

The divorce coincided with or perhaps catalyzed a remarkable personal transformation. The nerdy, slightly goofy Bezos of the 1990s and 2000s had been replaced by a jacked, bald, fashion-conscious billionaire who wore tight black t-shirts, aviator sunglasses, and dated a glamorous woman who piloted helicopters.

He started appearing at Hollywood events, investing in movies, hanging out with celebrities. He bought a $165 million mansion in Beverly Hills, the most expensive home ever sold in Los Angeles. He bought a $500 million superyacht so large it required a support yacht to carry the helicopter.

The transformation was remarkable and slightly ridiculous. Bezos seemed to be living out every middle-aged divorced man's fantasy, except with unlimited resources. SNL parodied him. Twitter mocked him. But he seemed unbothered, perhaps even amused by his new public image.

He also became more politically engaged. In 2013, he had purchased The Washington Post for $250 million, pocket change for him. Under his ownership, the Post experienced a digital renaissance, growing readership and winning Pulitzer Prizes. It also became a frequent target of President Trump's attacks, particularly when it published critical investigations of his administration.

Bezos generally didn't respond to Trump's attacks publicly, but in 2019, he did something unexpected: he published a blog post exposing that the National Enquirer had tried to blackmail him with intimate photos unless he stopped investigating the tabloid's connection to Trump. It was a remarkable moment, one of the world's richest and most powerful men openly fighting with a president and a tabloid using the most personal of weapons.

The old Bezos would never have published such a personal statement. The new Bezos seemed willing to fight publicly, to show emotion, to be something other than the relentlessly optimistic and customer-focused CEO.

Blue Origin: The Real Passion Project

While Amazon made Bezos wealthy, space exploration seemed to be his true passion. He had founded Blue Origin in 2000, four years before Elon Musk founded SpaceX with the goal of making space travel accessible.

Bezos's approach to Blue Origin was characteristically different from Musk's SpaceX. While Musk was loud, public, and moved fast with high-profile launches (and explosions), Bezos kept Blue Origin quiet, private, and methodical. The company motto was "Gradatim Ferociter", Latin for "Step by Step, Ferociously."

Blue Origin developed reusable rockets, successfully landing and reusing the same rocket multiple times. In 2021, Bezos himself flew to space on Blue Origin's New Shepard rocket, bringing along his brother Mark and two other passengers for an eleven-minute suborbital flight.

The flight was criticized as a billionaire joyride while Bezos underpaid his Amazon warehouse workers. But for Bezos, it represented something deeper. "I want to use my financial lottery winnings from Amazon to move the needle on space," he said. His vision was to build infrastructure in space, manufacturing, habitats and energy production eventually moving heavy industry off Earth to preserve the planet.

Critics noted that Elon Musk's SpaceX was far ahead of Blue Origin in capability, having already developed orbital rockets, won major NASA contracts, and established itself as the leading commercial space company. Blue Origin remained primarily a research and development operation with limited commercial success.

The space rivalry between Bezos and Musk became personal, with Musk occasionally mocking Blue Origin's slower progress and Bezos criticizing SpaceX's approach. It was Larry Ellison versus Bill Gates all over again, but with rockets instead of databases.

Stepping Down: The Post-CEO Phase

On February 2, 2021, Jeff Bezos announced he would step down as Amazon's CEO. After twenty-seven years leading the company he founded, he would transition to Executive Chairman while Andy Jassy, the founder of AWS, would become CEO.

Bezos was fifty-seven years old and worth approximately $190 billion, the perfect time to step back and focus on other interests: Blue Origin, the Washington Post, climate philanthropy through his Bezos Earth Fund, and whatever else captured his attention.

The transition was smooth. Jassy had been with Amazon since 1997 and had built AWS from nothing into a dominant business. Amazon's stock barely moved on the announcement, the market was confident in the succession plan.

For Bezos, stepping down meant freedom. He could focus on projects with longer time horizons, like making humanity a multiplanetary species without quarterly earnings calls and Congressional testimony about antitrust concerns.

But it also marked the end of an era. Jeff Bezos had been Amazon for nearly three decades. His annual shareholder letters were famous for their long-term thinking and customer obsession. His famous laugh, a honking, barking sound was legendary inside Amazon. His question-mark emails kept executives up at night. He was Amazon's founder, philosopher, and driving force.

Now he was stepping back, joining Bill Gates, Larry Page, Sergey Brin, and others in the club of tech founders who built empires and then partially retreated from them.

The Bezos Principles: What Actually Worked?

Jeff Bezos's success at Amazon was built on several core principles that he articulated consistently over the years:

Customer obsession over competitor obsession: Bezos always said Amazon should focus on customers, not competitors. "If you're competitor-focused, you have to wait until there is a competitor doing something. Being customer-focused allows you to be more pioneering." This sounds like marketing speak, but Amazon lived it. They pioneered features like customer reviews, one-click ordering, and Prime even when competitors thought they were crazy.

Long-term thinking: The willingness to lose money for years while building infrastructure and market share was unusual and powerful. Most companies couldn't do this because of pressure from shareholders, but Bezos convinced investors to be patient.

High standards: Amazon became famous (or infamous) for its high standards and demanding culture. Employees received feedback documents from colleagues ranking them. Meetings started with silent reading of six-page memos. Mediocrity wasn't tolerated. This created a high-performance culture, but also led to burnout and criticism about work-life balance.

Disagree and commit: Bezos encouraged healthy debate but insisted that once a decision was made, everyone had to commit fully, even if they disagreed. This allowed fast execution despite disagreements.

Day One mentality: Bezos kept a sign on his desk saying "It's still Day One," meaning Amazon should always act like a startup, paranoid, hungry, customer-focused. "Day Two is stasis. Followed by irrelevance. Followed by excruciating, painful decline. Followed by death. And that is why it is always Day One."

These principles worked spectacularly for building Amazon. Whether they worked for human flourishing is more debatable. Amazon employees often worked punishing hours. The company was accused of creating a cutthroat culture where only the toughest survived. Bezos's relentless focus on efficiency and growth left little room for considerations like worker welfare, environmental impact, or social responsibility beyond what was legally required or good for business.

The Complicated Legacy

As of 2025, Amazon is one of the most valuable companies in the world, worth over $1.5 trillion. It has fundamentally transformed retail, logistics, cloud computing, and entertainment. Over 300 million people are Amazon Prime members. Millions of businesses depend on Amazon's platform and infrastructure.

Jeff Bezos, now sixty-one, is worth over $170 billion. He splits his time between space projects, philanthropy, his various homes, and his relationship with Lauren Sanchez. He no longer runs Amazon day-to-day but remains its largest shareholder and a cultural force.

His legacy is deeply complicated:

Revolutionary achievements: Bezos proved that e-commerce could be the dominant form of retail. He built infrastructure that powers much of the internet. He pushed boundaries of what was possible in logistics, technology, and customer service.

Human cost: Amazon warehouse workers face some of the most demanding conditions in retail. The company fights unionization efforts. Small businesses have been driven out by Amazon's dominance. Main street retail has been decimated.

Economic concentration: Amazon's dominance in multiple sectors, retail, cloud computing and logistics raises serious questions about monopoly power and whether any company should control such vast infrastructure.

Innovation driver: Amazon forced traditional retailers to innovate or die. It created tools and services that benefit millions of businesses and consumers. The competitive pressure made other companies better.

Environmental impact: Amazon's delivery model generates massive carbon emissions, though the company has pledged to reach net-zero carbon by 2040. The question is whether fast, convenient delivery is worth the environmental cost.

Philanthropy lag: Unlike Gates or Buffett, Bezos has been slow to give away his wealth. He's committed $10 billion to climate change through the Bezos Earth Fund, but that's still a small percentage of his fortune. His approach to wealth is more "I'll create value through businesses" than "I'll solve problems through philanthropy."

What Drives Jeff Bezos?

After thirty years of building Amazon and accumulating more wealth than anyone needs in a hundred lifetimes, what actually drives Jeff Bezos?

The answer seems to be: legacy, curiosity, and the pleasure of building. Bezos genuinely seems to find joy in creating things, whether it's retail infrastructure, space rockets, or new ways of doing business. The money is almost beside the point; it's a way of keeping score and funding bigger projects.

He's also driven by a vision of humanity's future. His space ambitions aren't just about tourism or ego, he genuinely believes humanity needs to expand beyond Earth. "We will run out of energy on Earth," he says. "This is just arithmetic. It's going to happen. We can have a trillion humans in the solar system, which means we'd have a thousand Mozarts and a thousand Einsteins. That would be a really cool civilization."

Whether this vision is inspiring or delusional depends on your perspective. But it reveals someone thinking on civilizational timescales, not quarterly earnings.

There's also the proving instinct, the child of a teenage mother and absent father who became the richest person in the world still wants to prove he can do impossible things. The kid who was rejected by all his top-choice colleges except Princeton still wants to show he's the smartest guy in the room.

And perhaps there's simple momentum. When you've spent three decades building, it's hard to stop. When you're used to conquering one industry after another, retirement sounds boring. Why stop at retail and cloud computing when you could tackle space travel and immortality research?

Jeff Bezos built the everything store, and then he built the infrastructure for the everything economy. Now he's trying to build the infrastructure for humanity's expansion into space. It's ambitious to the point of megalomania, practical to the point of ruthlessness, and visionary to the point of delusion.

Whether history remembers him as a visionary who advanced human capability or a robber baron who exploited workers and concentrated power will depend on what happens next, with Amazon, with space exploration, and with how he chooses to use his unfathomable wealth in whatever time remains.

One thing is certain: the kid who started an online bookstore in a garage changed the world. Whether he changed it for better or worse is still being written.

Chapter 15

Elon Musk - The Real-Life Tony Stark

In December 2008, Elon Musk stood at the edge of total failure. Tesla, his electric car company, was burning through cash and weeks away from bankruptcy. SpaceX, his rocket company, had just suffered its third consecutive launch failure, one more failure and the company would be finished. His marriage was collapsing. The global financial crisis had destroyed the market for luxury electric cars. He had invested virtually all of his fortune, about $200 million from the sale of PayPal into these two companies, and both were dying.

"I thought we would fail," Musk later said. "I thought Tesla and SpaceX would both die."

Friends described him as emotionally shattered, sleeping on the floor of a friend's house, unsure where his next meal would come from. He was, by any measure, facing the most catastrophic failure possible for an entrepreneur. He had bet everything, his money, his reputation, his marriages and his mental health on two impossibly ambitious ventures, and he was losing.

And then, in the final days of 2008, two miracles happened. SpaceX's fourth launch succeeded, reaching orbit and winning a $1.6 billion NASA contract. Tesla secured a crucial investment on Christmas Eve, literally hours before the company would have run out of money. Both companies survived by the thinnest of margins.

By 2025, Tesla is worth over $800 billion, making it more valuable than most traditional automakers combined. SpaceX is worth over $150 billion and dominates commercial space launch. Elon Musk himself has been the richest person in the world, with a net worth that has exceeded $300 billion making him, briefly, richer than anyone in modern history.

The story of Elon Musk is unlike any other in this book. It's a story of impossible ambition, near-constant crisis, Twitter addiction, midnight manufacturing shifts, public breakdowns, messianic self-belief, and a relentless drive to build things that most serious people said couldn't be built. It's the story of how one man became both the most admired and most criticized figure in business, sometimes in the same week, sometimes on the same day.

The South African Childhood: Brutal and Formative

Elon Reeve Musk was born in 1971 in Pretoria, South Africa, to Maye Musk, a model and dietitian, and Errol Musk, an engineer. His childhood was, by his own account, difficult and often traumatic.

South Africa in the 1970s and 80s was under apartheid, a system of institutionalized racism that Musk later said he found "morally wrong." But his personal trauma wasn't political, it was familial. His parents divorced when he was nine, and Elon chose to live with his father, a decision he later called "a mistake."

Errol Musk was, by multiple accounts including Elon's, a difficult and psychologically abusive father. "He was such a terrible human being," Musk told Rolling Stone. "You have no idea... My dad will have a carefully thought-out plan of evil. He will plan evil." The exact nature of the abuse Musk experienced remains private, but his relationship with his father clearly left deep scars.

School was also brutal. Young Elon was small, awkward, and intellectually precocious, a perfect target for bullies. He was beaten so badly at one point that he was hospitalized and had to have his nose reconstructed. "They got my best friend to lure me out of hiding so they could beat me up," he recalled. "And that hurt."

Musk escaped into books and computers. He read constantly, science fiction, encyclopedias, anything he could find. At age ten, he taught himself computer programming. At twelve, he sold his first piece of software: a space-themed game called Blastar, for which he received $500.

The combination of an abusive father, violent bullying, and intellectual escape created a particular psychological profile: a deep need to prove himself, a conviction that he had to rely only on himself, an almost pathological work ethic, and a belief that conventional wisdom was often wrong. These traits would define his entire career.

At seventeen, Musk left South Africa for Canada (his mother was Canadian), partly to avoid mandatory military service in the apartheid regime, partly to escape his father, and partly because he believed America was where the future happened. He worked odd jobs, stayed with relatives he barely knew, and eventually enrolled at Queen's University in Ontario.

After two years, he transferred to the University of Pennsylvania, where he earned bachelor's degrees in economics and physics. His professors remember him as brilliant but not particularly social. He was already thinking about big problems: "I thought about what would most affect the future of humanity," he later said. His answer: the internet, sustainable energy, and space exploration.

Zip2 and PayPal: The First Fortunes

In 1995, Musk and his brother Kimbal started Zip2, a company that provided online city guides and maps for newspapers. It was the internet era's equivalent of the Yellow Pages, a business directory that helped newspapers enter the digital age.

The early days were classic startup chaos. The brothers worked out of a small rented office, showered at the YMCA, and slept on the floor. Elon coded during the day and tested at night. "I had to be the one who did all the programming," Musk said, "because I didn't trust anybody else to do it."

This control freak tendency would become a pattern. Musk had difficulty delegating and trusting others, a trait that made him a hands-on innovator but also a difficult boss and partner.

Zip2 grew steadily, securing contracts with newspapers like the New York Times and Chicago Tribune. But Musk clashed with the board and investors over strategy. He wanted to pursue a more ambitious vision; they wanted steady growth. In 1999, Compaq bought Zip2 for $307 million. Musk, who owned 7% of the company, walked away with $22 million at age twenty-seven.

Most people would have retired, or at least taken a break. Musk immediately started his next company.

X.com, founded in 1999, was Musk's attempt to create an online bank that would revolutionize finance. "I thought, what's the biggest, most fundamental thing you could do on the internet?" he said. "Financial services seemed like the obvious answer."

X.com merged with a company called Confinity, which had developed a money transfer system called PayPal. The merger was rocky, two companies with strong-willed founders don't combine easily. Musk became CEO but was ousted in 2000 while on his belated honeymoon, replaced by Peter Thiel in what would become Silicon Valley legend as a board coup.

Despite losing the CEO role, Musk remained the largest shareholder. When eBay bought PayPal in 2002 for $1.5 billion, Musk received $165 million for his stake. At thirty years old, he was worth close to $200 million.

Most people would have retired, or at least taken a break. Musk started planning to build rocket ships and electric cars.

SpaceX: Building Rockets in a Garage (Almost)

After the PayPal sale, Musk became obsessed with a question: why hadn't humanity colonized Mars? He believed, genuinely, messianically that becoming a multi-planetary species was essential for human survival. "I don't want us to be one of those single-planet species. One eventually goes extinct," he said.

His initial plan was modest by Musk standards: buy a rocket, send a greenhouse to Mars to inspire public interest in space exploration, revive NASA's budget. He flew to Russia to buy refurbished ICBMs. The Russians, according to Musk, treated him dismissively and quoted ridiculous prices. "I realized I could actually build a rocket myself cheaper than buying one," Musk said.

This is peak Musk logic: the rockets are too expensive, so I'll just build my own rocket company. Never mind that he'd never built rockets before. Never mind that rocket companies traditionally had government contracts and massive budgets. Never mind that the last several rocket startups had failed spectacularly.

In 2002, Musk founded Space Exploration Technologies, SpaceX in a Los Angeles suburb. He hired aerospace engineers, many from NASA and Boeing, and set an audacious goal: build a reusable rocket that would dramatically reduce the cost of space launch.

The aerospace establishment thought he was delusional. Rockets were expensive because space was hard. Decades of engineering from the smartest people in the world had produced the current costs. A dot-com millionaire with no aerospace experience wasn't going to revolutionize the industry.

SpaceX's first three launches, from 2006 to 2008, all failed. Rockets exploded on the pad, broke apart in flight, and failed to reach orbit. Each failure cost tens of millions of dollars. Musk was watching his fortune evaporate in fireballs visible from space.

The company was down to enough money for one more attempt. If the fourth launch failed, SpaceX would be finished.

On September 28, 2008, the Falcon 1 successfully reached orbit, the first privately developed liquid-fuel rocket to do so. Two months later, NASA awarded SpaceX a $1.6 billion contract to resupply the International Space Station. SpaceX had survived.

Tesla: Making Electric Cars Cool

While building rockets, Musk also became involved with Tesla Motors, an electric car startup founded by Martin Eberhard and Marc Tarpenning in 2003. Musk led Tesla's Series A investment round in 2004, investing $6.5 million and becoming chairman of the board.

Musk's involvement with Tesla quickly grew from investor to driving force. He pushed for the company to build the Roadster, a high-performance sports car that would prove electric vehicles could be sexy and fun, not just slow and practical. "We had to prove you could have an electric car that was better than a gasoline car," Musk explained.

But Tesla was plagued by problems: production delays, cost overruns, technical challenges, and management conflicts. In 2008, Musk ousted Eberhard as CEO and eventually took over as CEO himself. This would later become controversial, Musk claimed he was a co-founder of Tesla, while Eberhard insisted he and Tarpenning were the true founders. They eventually settled, with Musk and three others allowed to call themselves co-founders.

The deeper truth is that Tesla probably would have failed without Musk. He provided capital when no one else would. He drove the vision of making electric cars aspirational. He oversaw the design and engineering with obsessive attention to detail. Whether he "founded" Tesla is a semantic debate; what's clear is that he made Tesla what it became.

By late 2008, Tesla was burning through money and facing the same near-death crisis as SpaceX. The global financial crisis had destroyed demand for luxury vehicles. Musk put in his last remaining money, about $40 million to keep Tesla alive. When that wasn't enough, he had to borrow money from friends to pay his rent.

The Christmas Eve 2008 funding round, secured just hours before bankruptcy, kept Tesla alive. It was the narrowest of escapes.

The 2010s: Vindication and Expansion

The 2010s were Elon Musk's vindication decade. Both SpaceX and Tesla went from struggling startups to industry leaders, proving the skeptics wrong and making Musk into a business legend.

SpaceX's achievements were extraordinary:

- Successfully launching and landing reusable rockets, something the aerospace industry had said was impossible or impractical
- Dramatically reducing launch costs, SpaceX charges roughly $60 million per launch versus $150+ million for competitors
- Becoming the dominant commercial launch provider, launching more rockets than any other entity
- Successfully docking with the International Space Station and returning astronauts to Earth
- Beginning development of Starship, an even more ambitious fully reusable rocket designed for Mars colonization

Tesla's transformation was equally remarkable:

- Launching the Model S sedan in 2012 to critical acclaim, Motor Trend's Car of the Year
- Surviving near-bankruptcy again in 2013 and 2018 ("production hell" periods)
- Launching the Model 3, a mass-market electric vehicle that sold millions
- Building Gigafactories, massive battery and vehicle production facilities
- Forcing the entire automotive industry to accelerate electric vehicle development
- Becoming the most valuable automaker in the world by market capitalization

Musk's approach to both companies was hands-on to an almost obsessive degree. He slept on factory floors during production crises. He personally reviewed code and designs. He fired executives who couldn't keep pace. He set deadlines that employees called impossible, then pushed them to achieve them anyway.

"Nobody ever changed the world on 40 hours a week," Musk said. His Twitter bio at one point read: "Naughty by Nature." He cultivated a persona of the genius disruptor who didn't play by normal rules.

The Twitter Years: Genius or Madman?

As Musk's companies succeeded and his wealth exploded, his Twitter presence became increasingly central to his public persona and increasingly problematic.

Musk used Twitter constantly, tweeting about everything from engineering problems to memes to attacks on critics to drug jokes. His tweets moved markets, generated headlines, got him sued, and sparked endless controversy.

Some highlights (or lowlights):

2018: Musk tweeted "Am considering taking Tesla private at $420. Funding secured." The SEC sued him for securities fraud, claiming he hadn't actually secured funding. Musk settled, agreeing to pay $20 million in fines and step down as Tesla chairman (but remained CEO). The tweet cost him dearly and arguably wasn't even true.

Pedo guy incident: When a British diver criticized Musk's attempt to help rescue Thai soccer players trapped in a cave, Musk called him "pedo guy" on Twitter. He was sued for defamation and ultimately won the case, but the incident revealed Musk's thin skin and willingness to lash out viciously at critics.

COVID skepticism: Musk downplayed COVID-19, calling lockdowns "fascist," claiming children were "essentially immune," and reopening Tesla factories against local health orders. His position was controversial and arguably contributed to vaccine skepticism.

Stock price tweets: Musk repeatedly tweeted that Tesla's stock price was "too high," sending it tumbling, or made outrageous claims about Tesla's future that boosted the price. His ability to move Tesla's stock price with tweets gave him enormous power but also created liability.

The Twitter behavior revealed something fundamental about Musk: he craved attention and validation, couldn't resist responding to critics, believed his own judgment was superior to experts', and had either no filter or no desire for one.

Supporters saw this as authenticity and transparency, a billionaire who actually engaged with regular people. Critics saw it as irresponsible, narcissistic, and dangerous given his influence over markets and public opinion.

The Twitter Acquisition: $44 Billion Impulse Purchase

In April 2022, Musk made an unsolicited offer to buy Twitter for $44 billion, claiming he wanted to protect free speech and make the platform better. Twitter's board, initially resistant, accepted his offer.

Then Musk tried to back out, claiming Twitter had misrepresented the number of bot accounts on the platform. Twitter sued to force him to complete the acquisition. After months of legal battles and public drama, Musk completed the purchase in October 2022, paying $44 billion for a company that had never been particularly profitable.

He immediately fired top executives, laid off roughly half the workforce, and began making rapid changes to the platform, some sensible, many chaotic. He reinstated previously banned accounts, changed verification policies, renamed the company "X," and alienated many advertisers with his approach to content moderation.

The Twitter acquisition revealed several things about Musk:

1. **Impulsivity**: The $44 billion purchase appeared to be made without thorough planning, based largely on Musk's conviction that Twitter was important for free speech.

2. **Overconfidence:** Musk seemed to believe he could fix Twitter quickly using principles that worked at Tesla and SpaceX, not recognizing that social media platforms face different challenges than manufacturing companies.

3. **Financial strain:** To finance the purchase, Musk had to sell billions in Tesla stock and take on significant debt, putting pressure on both his personal finances and Tesla's stock price.

4. **Mission drift:** The Twitter acquisition distracted from Tesla and SpaceX at crucial moments in both companies' development.

By 2024, Twitter (now X) had lost significant value, many advertisers had reduced spending, and the platform faced growing competition from alternatives. Whether Musk could turn it around remained an open question.

The Personal Life: Marriages, Children, and Chaos

Musk's personal life has been as turbulent as his business ventures. He's been married three times (twice to the same woman), has twelve children (one died in infancy), and has had several high-profile relationships.

His first marriage, to Canadian author Justine Wilson, ended in divorce after eight years. They had six children together (twins and triplets through IVF), though their first son died of SIDS at ten weeks old. Justine later wrote about the marriage, describing Musk as emotionally unavailable and controlling, claims Musk disputed but which painted a picture of someone consumed by work and ambition.

He married British actress Talulah Riley twice, once in 2010, divorced in 2012, remarried in 2013, and divorced again in 2016. The pattern suggested someone who wanted companionship but couldn't maintain it given his work obsession and personality.

He had a high-profile relationship with actress Amber Heard after her divorce from Johnny Depp, which ended badly. He dated musician Grimes, with whom he had three children (including a son initially named X Æ A-12, later changed for legal reasons to X Æ A-Xii). Their relationship was on-and-off and ultimately ended, though they remain connected through their children.

Reports also emerged in 2022 that Musk had twins with Shivon Zilis, a director at his company Neuralink, bringing his total number of known children to eleven (ten living).

The pattern across all these relationships is consistent: intense initial connection, children (often through IVF), eventual separation as Musk's work obsession and difficult personality make sustained intimacy impossible. Friends have described him as lonely despite his wealth and fame, driven by demons he can't escape.

"I'm a fucking idiot when it comes to dating," Musk has admitted. "I'm utterly terrible at it. I don't know what to do when it comes to relationships."

The Musk Method: What Actually Works?

Despite all the chaos, drama, and questionable decisions, Elon Musk has achieved things that most serious people said were impossible. What explains his success?

First principles thinking: Musk is famous for breaking problems down to their fundamental principles and rebuilding from there. When told rockets were expensive, he asked: what are rockets made of? Aluminum, copper, carbon fiber, commodities that cost a fraction of finished rocket prices. Therefore, the cost is in the assembly and manufacturing, which could be redesigned.

Extreme work ethic: Musk regularly works 80-100+ hour weeks. He sleeps at his factories during crises. He's personally involved in engineering details that most CEOs wouldn't touch. This isn't sustainable for most people, but it allows him to push organizations harder than competitors.

High risk tolerance: Musk has repeatedly bet everything on ventures that could fail. Most people avoid such risks; Musk seems energized by them.

This tolerance for risk allows him to pursue opportunities others won't touch.

Reality distortion field: Like Steve Jobs, Musk has an ability to convince people that impossible things are possible. Employees regularly accomplish things they initially said couldn't be done, pushed by Musk's insistence and refusal to accept limitations.

Vertical integration: Both Tesla and SpaceX make most components in-house rather than relying on suppliers. This gives them more control, faster iteration, and cost advantages but requires enormous capital and expertise.

Speed of iteration: Musk's companies move fast, test quickly, learn from failures, and iterate rapidly. SpaceX blows up prototypes regularly but learns from each explosion. Traditional aerospace companies would never accept such failure rates, but SpaceX's approach leads to faster improvement.

Mission-driven narrative: Musk frames his work as solving existential problems, climate change, species extinction, human flourishing. This attracts talented people willing to work hard for lower pay than they could get elsewhere.

The Dark Side: Costs and Consequences

Musk's success has come with significant costs:

Worker exploitation: Tesla and SpaceX employees regularly report brutal hours, impossible deadlines, injuries from unsafe conditions, and retaliation for complaining. Musk's attitude seems to be that the mission justifies the sacrifice.

Management by chaos: Musk's impulsive decisions, sudden layoffs, strategy pivots, midnight tweets create instability for employees, investors, and partners.

Misinformation: Musk has spread questionable claims about COVID, AI risk, autonomous driving timelines, and other topics where his expertise is limited or his statements are self-serving.

Market manipulation concerns: His tweets have moved markets, enriching him and harming others. The line between enthusiastic promotion and manipulation is often unclear.

Failed promises: Musk has repeatedly promised things that didn't materialize: fully autonomous driving "next year" (said for multiple years), Mars missions by specific dates, production targets that were missed by months or years. Some were genuine optimism; some looked like deliberate hype.

Environmental irony: While Tesla fights climate change, Musk's private jet usage, SpaceX launches, and opposition to public transit raise questions about whether his net environmental impact is actually positive.

Authoritarian sympathies: Musk's criticisms of "woke" culture, his interactions with right-wing figures, and his approach to content moderation on X have raised concerns about his political evolution.

The Verdict: Genius, Grifter, or Both?

As of 2025, Elon Musk is worth over $200 billion (his net worth fluctuates wildly with Tesla's stock price). He's simultaneously one of the most admired and most criticized businesspeople alive. Understanding Musk requires holding multiple contradictory truths:

He has achieved genuinely impressive things: Making electric cars mainstream and reusable rockets work are historic accomplishments that advance human capability.

He exaggerates and misleads constantly: His timelines are always optimistic to the point of absurdity. His claims about capability often exceed reality.

He's a brilliant engineer and system thinker: His technical understanding is genuinely deep, and his ability to simplify complex problems is real.

He's a narcissist who craves attention: The constant tweeting, the need to be the smartest person in every room, the thin-skinned reactions to criticism, classic narcissism.

He's moved industries forward: Tesla forced automakers to take electric vehicles seriously. SpaceX revived space exploration and made it commercially viable.

He's often wrong and reckless: His COVID takes, his Twitter management, his drug use (allegedly), his treatment of employees, these show poor judgment.

He genuinely believes in his missions: The Mars obsession, the climate concern, the AI safety worry, these seem to be authentic beliefs, not just marketing.

He's also motivated by ego and status: The need to be the richest, the most followed on Twitter, the most famous, pure ego.

The truth is that Elon Musk contains multitudes. He's the abused child who still hasn't healed, the brilliant engineer who sees solutions others miss, the workaholic who can't stop or be present in relationships, the visionary who might actually help humanity become multi-planetary, the reckless promoter who misleads investors, the mission-driven entrepreneur who inspires thousands to work toward impossible goals, and the narcissistic billionaire who tweets memes while workers suffer.

The Long-Term Question

Will Elon Musk's legacy be overwhelmingly positive or negative? The answer likely depends on what happens next:

If Tesla successfully transitions to autonomous driving and sustainable energy: He'll be remembered as the entrepreneur who solved two existential challenges, climate change and transportation.

If SpaceX successfully establishes a Mars colony: He'll be remembered as the person who made humanity multi-planetary, possibly the most important achievement in human history.

If either company fails catastrophically: He might be remembered as a hype man who misled investors and wasted resources on impractical dreams.

If his Twitter behavior and misinformation continue harming public discourse: He might be remembered as someone whose brilliance was overshadowed by his need for attention and his recklessness.

The most likely outcome is a mixed legacy: real achievements in engineering and manufacturing, genuine advancement of electric vehicles and space technology, but also worker exploitation, misinformation, market manipulation, and the cautionary tale of a brilliant mind undermined by psychological wounds and unchecked ego.

Elon Musk wanted to be Iron Man, the genius billionaire playboy philanthropist who saves the world through technology. He's achieved the genius billionaire part. The playboy aspect hasn't worked out, too many failed relationships, too lonely despite fame. The philanthropist part is complicated, his philanthropy is mostly building companies, not giving money away like Gates or Buffett.

And whether he's actually saving the world or just building a fortune on government subsidies and investor hype remains the central question of his career.

What's certain is that no billionaire in this book, maybe in all of history, has been quite like Elon Musk. Part visionary, part charlatan, part genius, part madman, he remains the most fascinating and frustrating figure in modern capitalism. You either love him, hate him, or experience whiplash as you alternate between both.

And that's probably exactly how he wants it.

Chapter 16

Mark Zuckerberg - Social Network, Social Responsibility?

On February 4, 2004, a Harvard sophomore launched a website from his dorm room. It was called "TheFacebook" and it was limited to Harvard students with a harvard.edu email address. The design was simple, almost crude. The purpose was straightforward: connect with other students, see who was in your classes, check out who was dating whom.

Within twenty-four hours, 1,200 Harvard students had signed up. Within a month, over half of Harvard's undergraduate population had profiles. Within a year, TheFacebook had spread to most major universities across America. Within a decade, it would be called simply "Facebook" and would connect over a billion people worldwide.

The nineteen-year-old who built it, Mark Elliot Zuckerberg, would become the youngest self-made billionaire in history. By age twenty-three, he was worth $3 billion. By thirty, he was worth over $50 billion. By 2025, his fortune would exceed $100 billion, and he would control one of the most powerful communications platforms in human history, a platform used by over 3 billion people, influencing elections, shaping public discourse, and fundamentally transforming how humans interact.

But the story of Mark Zuckerberg and Facebook is not a simple tale of technological triumph. It's a story about unintended consequences, the corrosive effects of unchecked growth, the challenge of building tools that shape society without understanding the responsibility that entails, and the transformation of an idealistic "bring the world closer together" mission into what critics call a surveillance capitalism empire that profits from addiction, misinformation, and polarization.

It's also the story of a prodigy who built something extraordinary, then spent two decades struggling to understand what he had actually created.

The Prodigy from Dobbs Ferry

Mark Zuckerberg was born in 1984 in White Plains, New York, and grew up in the affluent suburb of Dobbs Ferry. His father, Edward Zuckerberg, was a dentist who ran his practice from the family home. His mother, Karen, was a psychiatrist. He had three sisters. It was, by all accounts, a stable, supportive, upper-middle-class childhood, quite different from the trauma and struggle that marked many other tech founders.

What marked young Zuckerberg as different was his intellectual intensity and obsessive focus. He taught himself programming as a child. At twelve, he built a messaging program called "ZuckNet" that allowed his father's dental office to communicate with the house. In high school, he built a music player called Synapse that used machine learning to predict what users wanted to hear next, Microsoft and AOL both reportedly offered to buy it and hire him before he'd even graduated high school.

He was also intensely competitive. He fenced. He studied ancient Greek and Latin (he could read Homer in the original Greek). He was captain of the fencing team. Teachers remember him as brilliant but socially awkward, more comfortable with computers than people.

"He was very energetic and very smart," a high school teacher recalled. "But he didn't have much of a filter. If he thought something, he'd just say it."

That lack of filter, an inability or unwillingness to recognize social boundaries would become a defining characteristic.

Zuckerberg was admitted to Harvard in 2002, intending to study psychology and computer science. He arrived with a reputation as a programming prodigy. Within weeks, he had built CourseMatch, a program that let students see what classes their friends were taking. Then he built Facemash, a "hot or not" style website that let users compare photos of Harvard students and vote on who was more attractive.

Facemash was controversial immediately. Zuckerberg had scraped photos from Harvard's residential halls' face books without permission. Women's groups protested, calling it misogynistic. The Harvard administration charged him with breaching security and violating privacy. He faced expulsion but was ultimately allowed to stay, though his reputation was damaged.

The incident revealed several Zuckerberg traits that would recur throughout his career: technical brilliance, a move fast and ask permission later approach, questionable judgment about privacy and consent, and a tendency to build first and consider consequences later.

Just months after the Facemash scandal, Zuckerberg launched TheFacebook.

The Facebook Creation Myth and Reality

The creation of Facebook is surrounded by controversy and competing narratives, dramatized in the 2010 film "The Social Network" and multiple lawsuits.

The basic facts: In late 2003, twin brothers Cameron and Tyler Winklevoss, along with Divya Narendra, approached Zuckerberg to work on their social networking site called Harvard Connection (later ConnectU). Zuckerberg agreed to help but worked slowly on their project while simultaneously building his own social network.

When TheFacebook launched in February 2004, the Winklevoss twins felt betrayed. They believed Zuckerberg had stolen their idea. A lawsuit followed, eventually settling in 2008 for $65 million (a combination of cash and Facebook stock that would later be worth far more).

Zuckerberg has always maintained that the ideas were different and that social networking was "in the air" in 2003-2004, with multiple sites like

Friendster and MySpace already existing. The Winklevosses claimed he stole their specific vision for a Harvard-centric network that would expand to other universities.

The truth probably lies somewhere in between. Social networking was clearly an emergent idea. Multiple people were working on similar concepts. But Zuckerberg's willingness to work on their project while building his own showed questionable ethics at best.

There's also the question of co-founders. Eduardo Saverin provided the initial funding ($15,000) and was listed as co-founder and CFO. But as Facebook grew and moved to California, the relationship with Saverin deteriorated. Sean Parker (of Napster fame) became involved and helped push Saverin out. In the restructuring, Saverin's ownership was dramatically diluted. Another lawsuit followed, resulting in a settlement that restored some of Saverin's shares.

The messy founding story, the allegations of stolen ideas, the betrayed business partner and the dubious ethics would haunt Facebook's reputation for years. It suggested that Zuckerberg, for all his brilliance, had a blindspot when it came to how his actions affected others.

But whatever the ethical complications, what's undeniable is that Zuckerberg built something that worked extraordinarily well.

The Explosive Growth: Connecting the World

TheFacebook expanded beyond Harvard rapidly. Within months, it was at Yale, Columbia, Stanford. By the end of 2004, it had one million users. Zuckerberg dropped out of Harvard to focus on the company full-time, moving to Palo Alto.

In 2005, the company raised $12.7 million from Accel Partners and dropped "The" from the name, it was now just Facebook. The venture capitalists saw what Zuckerberg had built: not just a website, but a platform with unprecedented user engagement. People weren't just visiting Facebook; they were living on it, checking constantly, sharing their lives, connecting with friends.

In 2006, Facebook opened to anyone over thirteen with an email address. This was a crucial decision. Some advisors worried that opening beyond college students would dilute the brand. But Zuckerberg believed Facebook should connect everyone, not just students. The decision proved prescient. Growth exploded.

By 2007, Facebook had 50 million users. Microsoft invested $240 million for a 1.6% stake, valuing Facebook at $15 billion and making twenty-three-year-old Mark Zuckerberg worth several billion dollars on paper. He was the youngest self-made billionaire in history.

The growth continued relentlessly: 100 million users in 2008, 500 million in 2010, 1 billion in 2012, 2 billion in 2017, and eventually over 3 billion across Facebook's family of apps (Facebook, Instagram, WhatsApp) by 2024.

Zuckerberg's vision was ambitious and, on its surface, idealistic: "Give people the power to build community and bring the world closer together." He genuinely seemed to believe that connecting people would make the world better, that transparency and communication were inherent goods.

"By giving people the power to share, we're making the world more transparent," he said in interviews. "A more transparent world creates a better-governed world and a better world overall."

This was the optimistic, almost naive vision of a young programmer who believed that technology was neutral and that more connection was inherently good. Events would severely test this belief.

The Business Model: Surveillance Capitalism

Facebook's astronomical growth created a problem: how do you make money from a free service? Zuckerberg had famously turned down a $1 billion acquisition offer from Yahoo in 2006, believing Facebook could be worth much more. But to justify that valuation, Facebook needed revenue.

The answer was advertising but not traditional advertising. Facebook developed something more powerful and more troubling: targeted advertising based on comprehensive surveillance of user behavior.

Facebook tracked everything: what you clicked, what you liked, who your friends were, what pages you visited across the internet (through Facebook pixels and tracking cookies), what you bought, where you went (if you had location services enabled), even what you typed but didn't send.

This data was used to build detailed profiles that advertisers could target with precision. Want to reach thirty-five-year-old men in Ohio who are interested in fishing and recently got engaged? Facebook could do that. Want to reach people who had visited your competitor's website in the last week? Facebook could do that too.

The business model was extraordinarily effective. Advertisers loved it, they could reach exactly who they wanted with measurable results. By 2024, Facebook was generating over $130 billion in annual advertising revenue, making it one of the most profitable companies in history.

But the model required comprehensive surveillance. Facebook needed to know everything about you to target you effectively. Privacy wasn't just compromised, it was fundamentally incompatible with the business model.

Zuckerberg repeatedly claimed that users controlled their privacy and could opt out. But the settings were deliberately complex, defaults were set to maximize sharing, and most users didn't understand how much data was being collected or how it was being used.

"If you're not paying for the product, you are the product," became the common refrain. Users weren't Facebook's customers, advertisers were. Users were the inventory being sold.

The Pivot to Mobile: Survival Through Transformation

In the early 2010s, Facebook faced an existential crisis: mobile. Smartphones were rapidly replacing desktop computers as the primary way people accessed the internet. But Facebook's mobile experience was terrible, a clunky mobile website that didn't work well and generated little revenue.

In 2012, Facebook went public in one of the most hyped IPOs in history. The stock was priced at $38 per share, valuing the company at $104 billion. But the IPO was troubled, technical glitches delayed trading, and the stock immediately fell, dropping to around $18 within months. Investors had lost faith. The mobile problem seemed insurmountable.

Zuckerberg made a radical decision: Facebook would become "mobile first." He reorganized the entire company around mobile, moved teams, changed priorities, and demanded that mobile become the primary platform, not an afterthought.

The transformation was painful but successful. Facebook rebuilt its mobile apps from scratch, made them fast and elegant, and figured out how to show ads in the mobile feed without destroying the user experience. By 2014, mobile advertising revenue exceeded desktop. By 2016, mobile accounted for over 80% of advertising revenue.

The mobile pivot saved Facebook and vindicated Zuckerberg's leadership. The stock price recovered and then soared. By 2015, Zuckerberg was worth over $40 billion. Facebook had survived what could have been a terminal threat.

But success brought new problems, problems that would prove far more difficult to solve than mobile optimization.

The Acquisitions: Building an Empire

As Facebook's stock price soared and its coffers filled with advertising revenue, Zuckerberg went on an acquisition spree, buying potential competitors before they could threaten Facebook's dominance:

Instagram (2012): Purchased for $1 billion, which seemed absurdly expensive at the time for a photo-sharing app with thirteen employees and no revenue. In retrospect, it was one of the best acquisitions in tech history. Instagram grew to over 2 billion users and became a major advertising platform in its own right.

WhatsApp (2014): Purchased for $19 billion, an even more staggering sum for a messaging app. WhatsApp's founders, Jan Koum and Brian Acton, had built a service with no ads and strong encryption, promising user privacy. After the acquisition, tensions grew as Facebook pushed to monetize WhatsApp and integrate it with Facebook's infrastructure. Both founders eventually left, with Acton publicly stating "I sold my users' privacy" and donating $50 million to fund Signal, an encrypted messaging competitor.

Oculus (2014): Purchased for $2 billion, Facebook's bet on virtual reality. This acquisition was different, not about eliminating a threat but about positioning for the next platform beyond mobile.

The acquisitions revealed Zuckerberg's strategy: identify potential threats early and either copy their features or buy them outright. Instagram Stories was a direct copy of Snapchat. Marketplace copied Craigslist. Facebook

Dating copied Tinder. If Facebook couldn't build the next big thing, it would buy it or copy it.

This strategy was effective but raised serious antitrust concerns. Was Facebook using its dominant position and massive resources to prevent competition? Critics said yes. Regulators began investigating.

The Reckoning: 2016-2020

For the first twelve years of Facebook's existence, Zuckerberg largely avoided serious scrutiny. Facebook was seen as a positive force, connecting people, enabling social movements like the Arab Spring, giving voice to the voiceless. Zuckerberg was portrayed in the media as a young genius building the future.

Then came 2016, and everything changed.

Russian interference: Russian operatives used Facebook to spread misinformation and sow discord during the 2016 U.S. presidential election. Fake accounts, targeted ads, and divisive content reached millions of Americans. Facebook initially denied the problem, then minimized its scope, and finally admitted the platform had been exploited.

Cambridge Analytica (2018): A political consulting firm had harvested data from 87 million Facebook users without their consent and used it to target political advertising. The scandal revealed how carelessly Facebook had allowed outside developers to access user data and how little oversight existed.

Myanmar genocide (2018): Facebook was used to spread hate speech and coordinate violence against the Rohingya Muslim minority in Myanmar. UN investigators concluded that Facebook had played a "determining role" in the genocide. Facebook had only two Burmese-speaking content moderators reviewing posts in a country with millions of users.

Live-streamed violence: Mass shootings in Christchurch, New Zealand, were live-streamed on Facebook, and the video was shared thousands of times before Facebook could remove it. Similar incidents occurred repeatedly.

Mental health concerns: Research increasingly showed that Facebook and Instagram use was correlated with anxiety, depression, and body image issues, particularly among teenage girls. Internal Facebook research confirmed these harms but was kept secret.

Misinformation and polarization: Facebook's algorithm, designed to maximize "engagement," was shown to promote divisive, emotional, and often false content because such content kept users on the platform longer. The company was accused of prioritizing profit over public good.

For each crisis, Zuckerberg followed a pattern: deny, minimize, apologize, promise to do better, and then continue operating largely as before. He gave congressional testimony in 2018, looking uncomfortable in a suit and tie, answering questions about privacy and Russian interference. His robotic demeanor and apparent lack of genuine contrition became fodder for memes.

"Senator, we run ads," became an infamous response when a senator asked how Facebook sustained a business model while being free to users, a response that was technically accurate but revealed how disconnected Zuckerberg was from the deeper questions about surveillance capitalism.

Critics began asking fundamental questions: Should one company control how billions of people communicate? Should a platform optimized for engagement be responsible for moderating political speech? Can any content moderation system scale to handle billions of posts per day? Was Facebook's business model fundamentally incompatible with democracy and mental health?

The Metaverse Bet: Rebranding and Refocusing

By 2021, Facebook faced existential challenges: regulatory scrutiny, platform growth stagnation, competition from TikTok, and a damaged reputation. Zuckerberg's solution was radical: pivot to a new vision entirely.

In October 2021, Facebook rebranded as Meta, with Zuckerberg declaring that the company would focus on building the metaverse, an immersive virtual world where people would work, play, socialize, and live portions of their lives in virtual reality.

"The metaverse will be the successor to the mobile internet," Zuckerberg declared. "We'll be able to feel present, like we're right there with people no matter how far apart we actually are."

He committed to investing $10 billion per year in Reality Labs, the division building metaverse technology. This meant developing VR headsets, AR glasses, haptic suits, virtual worlds, and the infrastructure to connect them all.

The reaction was mixed:

Supporters saw visionary thinking, positioning for the next computing platform before competitors could dominate it, much as Facebook had successfully pivoted to mobile.

Critics saw desperation, Zuckerberg trying to distract from Facebook's problems by betting on a speculative future that might never materialize. The metaverse demonstrations looked cartoonish and uninspiring. Adoption was slow. The losses were enormous, $13.7 billion in 2022 alone.

Employees and investors grew increasingly frustrated as the company hemorrhaged money on metaverse projects while cutting costs elsewhere, including layoffs of thousands of employees in 2022 and 2023.

By 2024, the metaverse bet looked questionable at best. VR headset sales remained niche. The virtual worlds Zuckerberg demoed looked dated. Competitors weren't rushing to build similar platforms. It began to look like Zuckerberg had bet tens of billions on a future that consumers didn't actually want.

Meanwhile, the company's core businesses, Facebook, Instagram, and WhatsApp continued generating massive revenue but faced continuing challenges from TikTok, regulation, and a young generation that saw Facebook as their parents' social network.

The Personal Transformation

Mark Zuckerberg has undergone a remarkable personal transformation over his two decades as a billionaire. The awkward, hoodie-wearing Harvard dropout has evolved into... well, it's complicated.

In his twenties, Zuckerberg was famous for wearing the same gray t-shirt every day (he reportedly owned dozens of identical shirts). He seemed awkward in interviews, robotic in presentations, and uncomfortable with attention. He married his college girlfriend, Priscilla Chan, in 2012 in a surprise ceremony in their backyard.

In recent years, Zuckerberg has transformed physically and in public presentation:

- He's become an avid mixed martial arts practitioner, training seriously and even competing in tournaments
- He's learned to surf and appears regularly posting action sports photos

- He's become more comfortable on camera, even appearing on podcasts and interviews showing more personality
- He's grown his hair out and changed his style
- He seems more relaxed, more willing to show humor and humanity

The transformation feels like a deliberate attempt to seem more relatable and less robotic. Whether it's genuine personal growth or calculated image rehabilitation is unclear, probably some of both.

With Priscilla Chan, he's had three daughters and seems to have a stable family life. The couple has committed to giving away 99% of their Facebook shares through the Chan Zuckerberg Initiative, focused on education, scientific research, and criminal justice reform. The commitment is real, they've already transferred billions in shares to the initiative.

But the Chan Zuckerberg Initiative is structured as an LLC, not a traditional foundation. This gives them more flexibility but also more control and fewer transparency requirements. Critics note that it allows Zuckerberg to maintain voting control of Facebook while claiming philanthropic intent.

The Control Obsession

One constant throughout Zuckerberg's career has been his obsession with control. Facebook's stock structure gives Zuckerberg majority voting control despite owning far less than 50% of shares. This means he effectively cannot be fired or overruled. He is, for all practical purposes, the permanent dictator of Meta.

This control allowed him to make long-term bets like the mobile pivot and metaverse investment without shareholder revolt. But it also meant there were no meaningful checks on his power. When Facebook made decisions that harmed users or democracy, Zuckerberg alone decided how to respond or whether to respond at all.

The control extends beyond corporate structure. Zuckerberg has been reluctant to empower independent oversight of Facebook's content moderation. The Oversight Board, created in 2020 as an "independent" body to review content decisions, has limited power and can only review cases Facebook allows it to review.

This need for control seems rooted in Zuckerberg's personality and perhaps his experience with the messy founding story. Having been sued by the Winklevosses and Saverin, having fought battles with investors and executives, Zuckerberg seems determined to never again be vulnerable to others' decisions.

But the cost is enormous. One person, however brilliant, cannot possibly understand all the implications of a platform used by 3 billion people across hundreds of countries and cultures. The complexity of content moderation, the nuances of political speech, the cultural sensitivities across different societies, these require diverse perspectives and genuine power-sharing.

Zuckerberg's unwillingness to cede control means Facebook's decisions reflect one person's worldview, a worldview shaped by an affluent suburban American upbringing, elite education, and two decades living in a bubble of extreme wealth and power.

The Fundamental Questions

Twenty years after launching Facebook, several fundamental questions remain unresolved:

Did connecting the world make it better? Zuckerberg's original vision assumed that connection was inherently good. The evidence suggests it's far more complicated. Facebook enabled social movements, helped people maintain relationships, and created opportunities. But it also enabled genocide, spread misinformation, and polarized societies. More connection isn't automatically better if the connections amplify our worst impulses.

Can surveillance capitalism coexist with democracy? Facebook's business model requires comprehensive data collection and algorithmic manipulation of what people see. This creates asymmetric power, Facebook knows vastly more about its users than users know about Facebook. Can democracy function when a private company has such information asymmetry and influence?

Should one person have so much power? Mark Zuckerberg controls how 3 billion people communicate. His decisions about what content is allowed, how algorithms prioritize posts, and what features exist affect elections, social movements, and individual lives. Should any private citizen have such power?

What responsibility comes with building infrastructure? Facebook started as a way to connect college students. It became fundamental infrastructure for human communication. But it's still a private, for-profit company optimized for engagement and revenue. What responsibility does it have to society? Who decides?

Can a platform scaled to billions be moderated effectively? Facebook employs tens of thousands of content moderators, uses AI to detect violations, and still struggles with harmful content. Is effective moderation even possible at this scale? Or does the scale itself create insurmountable problems?

Zuckerberg's responses to these questions have evolved but remain unsatisfying. He seems to genuinely struggle with the weight of these challenges while also being unwilling to make the fundamental changes that might address them, like changing the business model away from surveillance, sharing real power over content moderation, or breaking up the company.

The Verdict So Far

As of 2025, Mark Zuckerberg is forty years old, worth over $100 billion, and controls one of the most powerful platforms in human history. He's created something unprecedented: a private communication network used by nearly half of humanity.

His legacy is deeply complicated:

Revolutionary achievement: Connecting billions of people is a genuine accomplishment. The technology Facebook built, scalable infrastructure, photo sharing, messaging, video is impressive.

Unintended harm: The mental health impacts, the role in spreading misinformation, the enabling of genocide and violence, these are catastrophic failures that Zuckerberg didn't anticipate but is responsible for.

Business acumen: The mobile pivot, the strategic acquisitions, the development of multiple billion-user platforms, Zuckerberg is a capable business leader.

Moral blindness: The repeated scandals followed by inadequate responses suggest someone who either doesn't understand the harm caused or doesn't care enough to make necessary changes.

Philanthropic commitment: The pledge to give away 99% of wealth is meaningful, even if the structure and focus remain questionable.

Power concentration: The refusal to share control or meaningfully constrain Facebook's power raises serious concerns about democracy and accountability.

Unlike Larry Ellison's chip-on-shoulder competitiveness or Elon Musk's messianic ambition, Zuckerberg's driving motivation seems simpler: he wanted to build something people used and found valuable. He succeeded beyond anyone's imagination. But he built something he didn't fully understand, and whose consequences he still struggles to grasp.

The young programmer who wanted to connect Harvard students built a machine that reshaped human communication and society. Whether that machine makes the world better or worse may be the defining question of the twenty-first century.

And Mark Zuckerberg, hoodie-wearing billionaire turned MMA-practicing metaverse enthusiast, is still trying to figure out the answer, while maintaining absolute control over what may be the most consequential communications platform in human history.

The story isn't over. Zuckerberg is only forty. He could spend the next forty years trying to fix what he built, or doubling down on the metaverse, or building something entirely new. Or he could simply manage Facebook's decline as a new generation abandons it for whatever comes next.

What seems certain is that whatever happens, Mark Zuckerberg will remain one of the most important and controversial figures in the history of technology and wealth. The awkward teenager who wanted to see who was in his classes built a platform that now determines what 3 billion people see about the world.

He connected the world. What the world does with those connections and what we do about the unprecedented power he wields, remains to be written.

Chapter 17

Warren Buffett - The Oracle of Omaha

In 1958, a twenty-eight-year-old stockbroker named Warren Buffett bought a five-bedroom stucco house in Omaha, Nebraska, for $31,500. It wasn't fancy, just a modest gray house in a middle-class neighborhood. But it was comfortable, close to work, and suitable for his growing family.

Nearly seventy years later, Warren Buffett still lives in that same house. He's now worth over $120 billion, making him one of the ten richest people on Earth. He could buy palaces, islands, superyachts, anything money can purchase. Instead, he lives in the same house, drives himself to work (though he's upgraded from a Volkswagen to a Cadillac), and eats breakfast at McDonald's, carefully choosing between the $2.95, $3.17, or $3.85 menu options depending on how the market did the previous day.

"If the market's down, I'll go with the $2.95," he jokes.

Warren Buffett is the anti-Musk, the anti-Ellison, the anti-tech-billionaire. He doesn't tweet. He doesn't build rockets or metaverses. He doesn't buy newspapers to fight presidents or wear black turtlenecks to product launches. He sits in Omaha, reads annual reports, eats Dairy Queen Blizzards, drinks five Cokes a day, and makes investments that compound over decades.

He's also one of the most successful investors in history, turning a small textile company called Berkshire Hathaway into a $800+ billion conglomerate through patient, disciplined investing. His annual letters to shareholders are studied like sacred texts by business students worldwide. His wit, wisdom, and folksy charm have made him beloved even as he's accumulated a fortune that would make Gilded Age robber barons blush.

But the story of Warren Buffett is more than just an investing success story. It's a story about patience in an impatient world, about finding joy in work rather than consumption, about the power of compound interest applied over a lifetime, and about how someone can be brilliant at making money while being less successful at other aspects of life.

It's also a story about what we can learn from someone who did almost everything differently from the modern billionaire archetype and ended up wealthier than nearly all of them.

The Boy Who Loved Numbers

Warren Edward Buffett was born in 1930 in Omaha during the Great Depression. His father, Howard Buffett, was a stockbroker who later became a Republican congressman. His mother, Leila, struggled with mental health issues and could be emotionally volatile, a source of pain throughout Warren's childhood.

Young Warren was obsessed with numbers from early childhood. He memorized baseball statistics, calculated probabilities, and found patterns everywhere. "I was wired at birth to allocate capital," he later said. While other kids played, Warren calculated compound interest in his head.

At six, he bought six-packs of Coca-Cola for twenty-five cents and sold individual bottles for a nickel each, making a five-cent profit per pack. At eleven, he bought his first stock, three shares of Cities Service Preferred at $38 per share. The stock immediately fell to $27. Young Warren held on nervously, sold at $40 to make a small profit, and then watched it climb to $200. He learned two lessons: patience pays, and don't let short-term volatility shake you out of good investments.

At thirteen, he filed his first tax return, deducting $35 for his bicycle and watch as business expenses for his paper route. At fourteen, he used $1,200 of his savings to buy forty acres of Nebraska farmland, which he rented out to a farmer. He was already thinking about owning income-producing assets.

By the time he graduated high school, Buffett had saved $5,000 from various business ventures, paper routes, selling golf balls, pinball machine rentals. In 1930s and 40s dollars, this was substantial money for a teenager. More importantly, he had internalized lessons about business, saving, and investing that would guide him for life.

He attended the University of Pennsylvania's Wharton School, but found the coursework boring. He transferred to the University of Nebraska, graduating at nineteen. He applied to Harvard Business School and was rejected, a rejection he later called one of the luckiest things that ever happened to him, because it led him to Columbia Business School instead.

At Columbia, he studied under Benjamin Graham, the father of value investing and author of "The Intelligent Investor" and "Security Analysis." Graham taught a systematic approach to investing: buy stocks trading below their intrinsic value, maintain a margin of safety, ignore market fluctuations, and think like a business owner, not a speculator.

For Buffett, finding Graham was like a religious conversion. "It was like Paul on the road to Damascus," he said. "It really did change my life." He earned an A+ in Graham's class, the only A+ Graham gave in decades of teaching.

The Buffett Partnership: Learning the Craft

After Columbia, Buffett returned to Omaha to work in his father's brokerage firm, then went to New York to work for Benjamin Graham's investment firm. When Graham retired in 1956, Buffett moved back to Omaha and started Buffett Partnership Ltd. with $100,000 raised from family and friends (including $100 from his father).

The partnership's strategy was pure Graham: find companies trading below their intrinsic value, buy them, wait for the market to recognize their value, sell, and repeat. Buffett was disciplined, patient, and phenomenally successful. From 1957 to 1969, the partnership returned 29.5% annually, nearly tripling the market's return.

The returns compounded beautifully. An initial $10,000 investment in 1957 would have grown to $150,000 by 1969. Buffett himself went from modest savings to multi-millionaire during these years.

But by 1969, Buffett felt the market had become overvalued, prices had risen far above intrinsic values, making it hard to find good investments. In a move that showed remarkable discipline, he closed the partnership and returned money to investors, recommending they work with other managers. He was walking away at the peak, unable to find investments that met his standards.

Most investors can't do this. The pressure to keep deploying capital, to keep the fees coming, to stay relevant, it's overwhelming. Buffett simply said the opportunities weren't there and stopped. It was vintage Buffett: patient, disciplined, rational even when it meant walking away from a lucrative business.

Berkshire Hathaway: The Worst Investment That Became the Best

During the partnership years, Buffett had accumulated shares in a failing New England textile company called Berkshire Hathaway. He'd initially bought it as a classic Graham value play, the stock was trading below the company's working capital value. But he kept buying more, eventually taking control of the company.

He later called it "the biggest investment mistake" of his career. Textiles were a terrible business, commoditized, low-margin, facing foreign competition. Buffett spent years trying to make the textile operations work, finally closing them in 1985. If he'd invested the same capital elsewhere, he calculated, he'd be worth far more.

But the mistake became a triumph through an accident of tax law. Because Berkshire was a corporation, not an investment fund, Buffett could defer taxes on gains indefinitely by not selling appreciated stocks. This created a massive advantage: money that would have gone to taxes stayed invested, compounding over decades.

Buffett transformed Berkshire from a textile company into an investment vehicle and holding company. He bought insurance companies like GEICO and National Indemnity, which generated "float", premium money that wouldn't be paid out in claims for years. This float provided capital to invest. Better yet, if Buffett underwrote insurance profitably, the float was essentially free money to invest.

He bought wholly-owned businesses: See's Candies (1972), Nebraska Furniture Mart (1983), Scott Fetzer (1986), and eventually hundreds of companies. He invested in publicly traded stocks: Coca-Cola, American Express, Wells Fargo, and later Apple. Each investment was made with the same discipline: understand the business, buy at a reasonable price, hold for the long term.

The Berkshire model was brilliant in its simplicity: use insurance float and operating company profits to make investments, let the investments compound without paying taxes, reinvest the returns, and repeat for decades. The compounding was relentless. Berkshire's stock price went from $19 in 1965 to over $600,000 per share by 2024, a 3.7-million-percent return over nearly sixty years.

An investment of $10,000 in 1965 would be worth over $370 million by 2024. No other public company comes close to this long-term performance.

The Buffett Method: Simple but Not Easy

Warren Buffett's investment approach is deceptively simple. Anyone can understand the principles. Few can execute them consistently:

1. **Circle of competence:** Only invest in businesses you understand. Buffett avoided technology stocks for decades because he didn't understand them. He stuck to banks, insurance, consumer goods, and other businesses whose economics he could analyze.

2. **Economic moats:** Invest in companies with durable competitive advantages, strong brands, network effects, switching costs, cost advantages. These "moats" protect profits from competition.

3. **Management quality:** Buffett looks for honest, capable, shareholder-oriented managers. "I try to buy stock in businesses that are so wonderful that an idiot can run them," he says, "because sooner or later, one will."

4. **Buy at a reasonable price:** Even wonderful companies can be bad investments if you overpay. Buffett waits for opportunities when great businesses trade at reasonable or cheap prices.

5. **Long-term holding:** "Our favorite holding period is forever." Buffett doesn't trade actively. He buys businesses he wants to own for decades. This minimizes taxes, reduces transaction costs, and lets compounding work its magic.

6. **Ignore market noise:** Daily market fluctuations are meaningless. Buffett doesn't care if the stock market closes for years, as long as the businesses he owns keep generating profits.

7. **Be greedy when others are fearful:** Buffett makes his best investments during crises when everyone else is panicking. He bought stocks during the 1973-74 crash, the 1987 crash, the 2008 financial crisis, and the 2020 COVID crash.

8. Compound over a lifetime: Starting young and letting returns compound over sixty+ years creates staggering wealth. Buffett's net worth didn't reach $1 billion until he was fifty-six. Most of his wealth was created after age sixty-five. Longevity matters.

These principles are simple to state but psychologically difficult to follow. Patience is hard. Contrarian thinking is hard. Ignoring market volatility is hard. Waiting for opportunities instead of constantly deploying capital is hard. Buffett's genius isn't complex analysis, it's the discipline to stick to simple principles over decades.

The Simple Life of an Impossibly Rich Man

Warren Buffett's lifestyle is legendary for its ordinariness. He lives in the same house he bought in 1958. He drives himself to work (though he totaled his car in 2008 and had to upgrade). He eats at Gorat's steakhouse in Omaha and orders the same thing: T-bone steak, hash browns, and Cherry Coke.

He famously eats like a six-year-old: McDonald's breakfast sandwiches, ice cream, candy, Coke (five cans a day). "I checked the actuarial tables, and the lowest death rate is among six-year-olds," he jokes. "So I decided to eat like a six-year-old." He's ninety-four and still going strong, so maybe there's something to it.

He doesn't own a yacht, doesn't collect art, doesn't buy fancy clothes. He once bought a vacation home in Laguna Beach for $150,000 and sold it years later, deciding he preferred Omaha. His one indulgence is a private jet, which he named "The Indefensible" in recognition that it contradicted his frugal image.

Why the modesty? Partly, it's genuine, Buffett seems to derive little pleasure from material consumption. He's said repeatedly that he has everything he needs and buying more stuff wouldn't make him happier.

Partly, it's good PR, the folksy, modest billionaire is much more likeable than the yacht-buying, mansion-collecting alternative.

But there's also a deeper truth: Buffett's pleasure comes from the game itself, not the prizes. He loves investing, loves studying businesses, loves the intellectual challenge of finding value. Money is just a way of keeping score. Once you have enough for comfortable living, more consumption doesn't add much happiness but the game remains endlessly engaging.

"I get to do what I love to do every single day," Buffett says. "I tap dance to work. I work with people I love. I'm not trying to get anything done. I work with people I trust. It doesn't get any better than that."

This is a crucial insight often missed in discussions of wealth: what you do matters more than what you buy. Buffett found work he loves and structured his life to maximize time doing it. The money is almost beside the point.

The Friendship: Buffett and Munger

No account of Warren Buffett is complete without Charlie Munger, Buffett's business partner and vice chairman of Berkshire Hathaway. They met in 1959 and formed one of the most successful partnerships in business history.

Munger influenced Buffett's evolution from pure Graham value investing (buying cheap, mediocre companies) to buying wonderful companies at fair prices. "It's far better to buy a wonderful company at a fair price than a fair company at a wonderful price," became a Buffett maxim, largely due to Munger's influence.

The two men were different but complementary. Buffett was more optimistic and diplomatic; Munger was more cynical and blunt. Buffett focused on the upside; Munger focused on avoiding disasters. At Berkshire annual meetings, Buffett would give expansive, thoughtful answers; Munger would follow with terse responses like "I have nothing to add" or occasionally devastating one-liners that punctured pretension.

Their friendship was built on mutual respect, intellectual engagement, and shared values. They spoke almost daily for sixty years. When Munger died in November 2023, just weeks before his 100th birthday, Buffett was devastated. "Berkshire Hathaway could not have been built to its present status without Charlie's inspiration, wisdom, and participation," Buffett wrote.

The Buffett-Munger partnership shows the value of finding someone who both complements your skills and challenges your thinking. They made each other better investors and better thinkers.

The Giving Pledge: Redefining Billionaire Philanthropy

Despite living modestly, Warren Buffett understood he had more money than he could possibly need. In 2006, he announced he would gradually give away his entire fortune, then worth about $44 billion to philanthropic causes, with the bulk going to the Bill & Melinda Gates Foundation.

The decision was remarkable for several reasons:

Scale: $44 billion (now grown to over $100 billion in pledged giving) was the largest philanthropic commitment in history at the time.

Timing: Most wealthy people wait until death to give away their fortunes. Buffett started in his mid-seventies, ensuring he could see the impact.

Trust: Giving the bulk to the Gates Foundation rather than creating his own foundation showed unusual humility and pragmatism. "Bill and Melinda are doing a better job than I could do," Buffett explained.

Strategy: Buffett gave Berkshire stock, not cash. The stock would continue appreciating, meaning the philanthropic capital would keep growing until it was distributed.

In 2010, Buffett and Bill and Melinda Gates launched the Giving Pledge, asking billionaires to commit to giving away at least half their wealth. Over 200 billionaires have signed, including Mark Zuckerberg, Elon Musk (though his commitment is questionable), MacKenzie Scott, and many others.

The Giving Pledge reframed billionaire philanthropy. Instead of building monuments to themselves or giving token amounts, billionaires were asked to give away the majority of their wealth. Buffett was giving away 99%, setting a high bar.

Critics note that billionaire philanthropy, however generous, doesn't address structural wealth inequality. Buffett himself has said the system that allows billionaires to accumulate such wealth probably needs reform, including higher taxes on the wealthy. He advocated for higher estate taxes, higher income taxes on the rich, and reforming carried interest rules that benefit investment managers.

"There's class warfare, all right," Buffett famously said, "but it's my class, the rich class, that's making war, and we're winning."

It's a remarkable position: a billionaire arguing he should pay more taxes and that the system that made him wealthy needs reform. Whether this is genuine social conscience or sophisticated reputation management is debatable. But it's certainly effective, Buffett is beloved even by many who criticize wealth inequality.

The Personal Costs

Warren Buffett's professional success came with personal costs, particularly in his first marriage. He married Susan Thompson in 1952, and they had three children: Susie, Howard, and Peter. But Buffett was consumed by work, emotionally distant, and by his own admission, not a particularly engaged father or husband.

In 1977, Susan moved to San Francisco to pursue her own interests, particularly singing. It was essentially a separation, though they never divorced. Susan remained close to Warren, and in an unusual arrangement, she introduced him to Astrid Menks, who became his companion. Susan, Warren, and Astrid maintained a close relationship until Susan's death from cancer in 2004.

Buffett's relationship with his children was complicated. He provided modest trust funds ($90,000 each when they turned thirty) but made it clear they wouldn't inherit billions. "I want to give my kids just enough so that they would feel that they could do anything, but not so much that they would feel like doing nothing," he explained.

His son Peter Buffett wrote a book partly about growing up as the son of someone consumed by work and numbers, emotionally distant despite being physically present. Howard Buffett, now a farmer and philanthropist, has spoken about feeling pressure to live up to his father's success while forging his own path.

The pattern is familiar among ultra-successful people: the single-minded focus that builds extraordinary careers often comes at the cost of personal relationships. Buffett acknowledges this but seems to view it as an acceptable trade-off. Work brought him joy; emotional intimacy was more challenging.

After Susan's death, Buffett married Astrid Menks in 2006, a quiet ceremony with just a few witnesses. By all accounts, it's been a stable, happy marriage, with Astrid providing companionship and managing aspects of daily life Buffett finds burdensome.

The Later Years: Still Going at 94

As of 2025, Warren Buffett is ninety-four years old and still actively running Berkshire Hathaway. He arrives at the office most mornings, reads for hours (newspapers, annual reports, business documents), makes occasional investments, and writes his famous annual letter to shareholders.

His mental acuity remains sharp. His wit is still quick. His investment judgment is still sound, though he's made adjustments, notably investing heavily in Apple, finally embracing a technology company after decades of avoidance. The Apple investment, started in 2016, became one of Berkshire's most valuable holdings, validating that even in his eighties, Buffett could adapt.

Succession planning has been a concern for years. Who can replace Warren Buffett? The answer is: probably no one can fully replace him, but Berkshire has carefully planned the transition. Greg Abel, who runs Berkshire's non-insurance operations, is designated to become CEO when Buffett steps down or dies. Investment decisions will be handled by Buffett's deputies, Ted Weschler and Todd Combs, who've been managing portions of Berkshire's portfolio for years.

The transition will be tested eventually. Buffett won't live forever, though he jokes about it. "I plan to live to 100," he says, "and then we'll see." He's certainly earned the right to optimism about longevity.

When he does pass, Berkshire will continue but will inevitably change. Buffett's annual letters, his wit, his wisdom, his reputation, these are irreplaceable. The company will endure, but it will be different.

What Warren Buffett Teaches Us

Warren Buffett's life offers lessons that extend beyond investing:

1. **Compound interest is magical:** Start early, be patient, let returns compound over decades. Most of Buffett's wealth accumulated after age sixty. Time is the friend of good investments.

2. **Know what you're good at:** Buffett stuck to his circle of competence. He didn't try to be a tech entrepreneur or a global celebrity. He did what he did best and ignored pressure to be someone else.

3. **Avoid debt and financial risk:** Buffett uses almost no leverage personally. He's never been in a position where he could be forced to sell at the wrong time. Financial stability provides emotional stability and better decision-making.

4. **Find work you love:** Buffett "tap dances to work" at ninety-four. When you love what you do, it's not work, it's life. This matters more than any amount of money.

5. **Material consumption has diminishing returns:** Past a modest level of comfort, more stuff doesn't increase happiness. Buffett has essentially infinite money but lives simply because he genuinely doesn't want or need more.

6. **Reputation takes a lifetime to build and a moment to destroy:** Buffett has carefully cultivated a reputation for honesty, integrity, and putting shareholders first. This reputation has made business easier and more enjoyable.

7. **Be generous:** Giving away 99% of his wealth won't reduce Buffett's quality of life one bit. He'll still live in the same house, eat the same food, do the same work. But the money can do enormous good elsewhere.

8. Humility is strength: Buffett readily admits mistakes, acknowledges luck, and defers to others' expertise. This openness to learning has kept him relevant for seventy years.

9. Think independently: Buffett's best investments came from thinking differently than the crowd. When everyone was panicking in 2008, he was "greedy." When everyone was euphoric in the late 1990s dot-com bubble, he was cautious.

10. Optimize for happiness, not status: Buffett could live anywhere, do anything, buy anything. He chooses to live in Omaha, eat at local restaurants, and spend days reading. He optimized for what actually makes him happy, not what impresses others.

The Buffett Paradox

There's something paradoxical about Warren Buffett. He's accumulated one of the largest fortunes in history using the capitalist system, yet he's critical of wealth inequality and advocates for higher taxes on the wealthy. He lives modestly while sitting on over $100 billion. He's giving away his fortune yet continues accumulating more wealth. He's beloved as a folksy, regular guy while wielding enormous corporate power.

The contradictions are real but also revealing. Buffett seems to genuinely believe that accumulating wealth through patient, disciplined investing is valuable and legitimate. But he also believes that extreme wealth inequality is problematic and that successful people have an obligation to give back.

He loves the game of investing but doesn't particularly care about the prizes. He's competitive about returns but not about lifestyle or status. He wants to be remembered well but doesn't want to change who he is to achieve that.

In a sense, Warren Buffett represents an older model of American capitalism, one where wealth was celebrated if it was earned through skill and hard work, where modesty was valued, where giving back was expected. It's a vision that feels almost quaint in the age of Musk's Twitter rants and Zuckerberg's metaverse and Ellison's Hawaiian islands.

But it's also proven remarkably effective. Buffett is worth more than Larry Ellison despite starting with far less and living far more modestly. He's more beloved than almost any other billionaire. His investment approach has withstood decades of market changes and financial innovation.

Maybe there's something to be said for staying in Omaha, eating at McDonald's, reading annual reports, and letting compound interest do its work over seventy years.

The Oracle's Ultimate Bet

Warren Buffett's greatest investment isn't Coca-Cola or Apple or any particular stock. It's his bet on America, the belief that over the long term, the American economy will grow, businesses will innovate, and patient investors will be rewarded.

"Never bet against America," is one of his most famous sayings. Through wars, recessions, political turmoil, and market crashes, he's maintained this optimism. It's not blind faith, it's based on two centuries of evidence that America's combination of free markets, rule of law, innovation, and immigration has created unprecedented prosperity.

This optimism is his ultimate investment thesis. As long as he's right about America's long-term trajectory, his investment approach works. If he's wrong, if America enters permanent decline or if capitalism fundamentally breaks down then his entire philosophy fails.

So far, he's been right for seventy years. At ninety-four, he's still betting on America, still investing in businesses, still writing annual letters explaining why patient, rational investing in wonderful businesses will reward shareholders over time.

The Oracle of Omaha sits in his modest house, drinking Cherry Coke, reading annual reports, and continuing to prove that the simple approach, done with discipline over a lifetime, beats nearly every complex strategy and flashy alternative.

He won't live forever. But his lessons about patience, compounding, living below your means, doing work you love, and giving generously will endure long after the last Berkshire Hathaway annual meeting.

And somewhere, a young person is reading "The Intelligent Investor," calculating compound interest, and dreaming of tap-dancing to work for seventy years. If they follow Buffett's example, the discipline, not just the strategy they might not become billionaires.

But they'll probably be a lot happier than most people who do.

Chapter 18

The Fashion and Luxury Billionaires

In October 2021, Bernard Arnault briefly overtook Jeff Bezos to become the richest person in the world. His fortune, estimated at over $200 billion, came not from technology or oil or finance, but from handbags, perfume, champagne, and haute couture.

While tech billionaires dominated headlines with their rockets, electric cars, and social networks, Arnault had quietly built the world's largest luxury goods empire. His company, LVMH (Moët Hennessy Louis Vuitton), controlled over seventy of the world's most prestigious brands: Louis Vuitton, Dior, Fendi, Givenchy, Dom Pérignon, Hennessy cognac, Bulgari, Tiffany & Co., and dozens more.

Arnault wasn't alone. Across Europe, a small group of fashion and luxury billionaires had built enormous fortunes by understanding something profound: people will always pay premium prices for products that make them feel special, sophisticated, or superior. While tech companies fought over efficiency and disruption, luxury companies sold aspiration and exclusivity. And it turned out to be extraordinarily profitable.

The fashion and luxury billionaires operate differently from their tech counterparts. They're more private, more European, more focused on heritage and craftsmanship than innovation and disruption. They've built empires that have lasted for generations by understanding timeless human desires for status, beauty, and belonging.

This is the story of how selling dreams became one of the most lucrative businesses in history.

Bernard Arnault: The Wolf in Cashmere

Bernard Arnault was born in 1949 in Roubaix, France, to an industrial family. His father owned a construction company, and young Bernard was expected to join the family business. He graduated from the prestigious École Polytechnique, where France's elite engineers and executives are trained, and worked in the family construction business through the 1970s.

Nothing about his background suggested he would revolutionize the luxury industry. He wasn't a designer, didn't come from fashion, had no particular aesthetic vision. What he had was something more valuable: he understood business, he understood acquisition strategy, and he was ruthlessly ambitious.

His entry into luxury goods came through an unlikely route: real estate. In 1984, Arnault acquired Financière Agache, a bankrupt textile company, for its real estate holdings. Included in the deal was Christian Dior, the storied fashion house that had dressed European royalty and Hollywood stars but had fallen on hard times.

Most people would have sold off Dior to focus on real estate. Arnault saw something else: a luxury brand that could be revitalized and used as a platform to build an empire. He kept Dior and began a decades-long campaign to acquire the world's most prestigious luxury brands.

In 1987, Arnault began acquiring shares of LVMH, a company formed from the merger of Louis Vuitton (leather goods and luggage) and Moët Hennessy (champagne and cognac). Through a combination of stock purchases, strategic alliances, and ruthless maneuvering, Arnault gained control of LVMH in 1989, becoming chairman and CEO.

What followed was one of the most successful acquisition campaigns in business history. Arnault bought Givenchy, Fendi, Céline, Kenzo, Marc Jacobs, Loro Piana, and dozens of other brands. Each acquisition followed a pattern: identify prestigious but underperforming brands, acquire them, install talented designers, invest in quality and marketing, and watch profits soar.

The strategy was simple but brilliant: luxury goods have incredible economics. High prices, high margins, low price sensitivity, repeat customers, and the perception of exclusivity that makes people want them more, not less. A Louis Vuitton handbag might cost $200 to make but sell for $2,000. If you could create or acquire brands that commanded such pricing power, the profits were extraordinary.

By 2024, LVMH generated over $90 billion in annual revenue with operating margins around 27%, margins that would make even tech companies envious. Bernard Arnault's personal fortune exceeded $200 billion, making him one of the three richest people on Earth, wealthier than Warren Buffett, Larry Ellison, or Mark Zuckerberg.

But Arnault remained largely unknown outside business and fashion circles. He rarely gave interviews. He avoided social media entirely. He worked from LVMH's elegant Paris headquarters, far from Silicon Valley's tech campuses. While Elon Musk tweeted and Jeff Bezos built rockets, Arnault acquired jewelry brands and champagne houses.

"I like to be discreet," Arnault has said. "Luxury goods are a discreet business. We don't need to be ostentatious."

The LVMH Machine: How Luxury Conglomerates Work

Bernard Arnault's genius wasn't in designing handbags, he employed brilliant designers for that. His genius was in understanding how to build and manage a luxury conglomerate, a business model that seems counterintuitive but works brilliantly.

The conventional wisdom is that luxury brands need independence and autonomy to maintain their creative integrity. Conglomerates are bureaucratic, corporate, soul-crushing. How could LVMH own seventy brands without destroying what made them special?

Arnault's answer was a hybrid model: centralized business functions with decentralized creative control. LVMH provided each brand with shared services, supply chain, logistics, real estate, finance, and legal. This created enormous efficiencies. But each brand maintained its own creative director, its own identity, its own aesthetic vision.

More importantly, LVMH brands didn't compete with each other, they served different customer segments and occasions. Louis Vuitton was aspirational luxury for the global upper-middle class. Dior was haute couture and high fashion. Bulgari was Italian jewelry. Hennessy was cognac for celebrations. A customer might buy from multiple LVMH brands depending on context and life stage.

The model created a luxury ecosystem with several advantages:

Brand portfolio protection: If one brand fell out of favor, it didn't threaten the whole company. LVMH could weather fashion trends and economic cycles.

Talent development: LVMH could move talented executives and designers between brands, developing deep expertise in luxury management.

Purchasing power: LVMH could negotiate better deals with suppliers, landlords, and media companies than individual brands.

Financial stability: The steady profits from established brands like Louis Vuitton funded investments in younger brands and acquisitions.

Cultural preservation: By acquiring struggling heritage brands, LVMH arguably saved them from bankruptcy or acquisition by companies that might have destroyed their essence.

The model worked spectacularly. LVMH's stock price increased over 1000% between 2000 and 2024, making early investors extraordinarily wealthy. The Arnault family controlled LVMH through a holding company structure that gave them voting control despite owning less than 50% of the shares, a familiar structure among billionaire-controlled companies.

Amancio Ortega: The Opposite Approach

While Bernard Arnault built his empire through acquisitions of heritage brands, Amancio Ortega took the opposite path: he built a fast-fashion empire from scratch that made luxury aesthetics accessible to the masses.

Ortega was born in 1936 in rural Spain during the Spanish Civil War. His father was a railway worker, his mother a housemaid. The family was poor, genuinely poor, not middle-class-calling-itself-poor. Young Amancio left school at thirteen to work as a delivery boy for a shirt maker in La Coruña.

He watched the garment business from the inside: how clothes were designed, manufactured, distributed, and sold. He noticed the enormous markups between wholesale and retail. He saw how traditional fashion worked: designers created collections months in advance, manufacturers produced them, wholesalers distributed them, retailers sold them. Each step added costs and time.

In 1963, Ortega and his then-wife Rosalía Mera started making bathrobes and lingerie in their living room, selling them to local stores. The business grew slowly. In 1975, Ortega opened the first Zara store in La Coruña, selling affordable versions of popular fashions.

The Zara model was revolutionary: vertical integration combined with rapid response to trends. Zara would design, manufacture, distribute, and retail its own clothes. No wholesalers, no department stores, no middlemen. This gave Zara control over the entire process and allowed it to move fast.

Speed was Zara's secret weapon. Traditional fashion brands designed collections six to nine months in advance. Zara could see what was trending, design a new item, manufacture it, and have it in stores within two to three weeks. If something sold well, they'd make more. If it didn't, they'd stop production quickly. Very little inventory sat unsold.

Zara could also respond to high fashion trends. When luxury brands showed collections at Paris Fashion Week, Zara designers would watch, identify popular elements, and create affordable interpretations within weeks. This made Zara simultaneously trendy and affordable, a powerful combination.

Ortega expanded Zara across Spain, then Europe, then globally. He created additional brands, Massimo Dutti, Pull&Bear, Bershka and Stradivarius each targeting different demographics. The parent company became Inditex (Industria de Diseño Textil), one of the world's largest fashion retailers with over 7,000 stores across 96 countries.

By 2011, when Inditex went public, Ortega was one of the richest people in Europe. At his peak, he was worth over $70 billion, briefly becoming the richest person in the world in 2015. He remained remarkably private, rarely giving interviews, never appearing at fashion shows or industry events.

Ortega's approach was opposite to Arnault's in almost every way:

- **Mass market vs. luxury**: Zara was for everyone; LVMH was for the affluent
- **Speed vs. heritage**: Zara responded to trends in weeks; LVMH cultivated brand legacies over decades
- **Efficiency vs. exclusivity**: Zara optimized for volume and turnover; LVMH optimized for margins and prestige

- **New vs. acquired:** Ortega built brands from scratch; Arnault bought established names

Yet both became wildly successful, proving there were multiple paths to fortune in fashion. Arnault sold aspiration to the wealthy. Ortega sold accessible style to everyone else. Both understood that fashion is about identity and belonging, whether you're buying a $3,000 Louis Vuitton bag or a $40 Zara dress.

The Luxury Paradox: Selling Exclusivity to the Masses

The success of both luxury and fast-fashion empires reveals a paradox at the heart of the fashion business: how do you sell exclusivity when your goal is to sell to as many people as possible?

Luxury brands face this challenge acutely. A Louis Vuitton bag is supposed to signal elite status. But if everyone has one, does it still signal status? How do you grow revenue without destroying the exclusivity that justifies the price?

Luxury companies have developed sophisticated strategies:

1. Tiered product lines: Entry-level items (small leather goods, perfume, accessories) at $200-$500 allow aspirational customers to buy into the brand. High-end items (handbags, clothing, jewelry) at $2,000-$50,000+ maintain exclusivity. Most customers buy entry-level; the brand image is built on high-end.

2. Limited editions and artificial scarcity: Creating "limited edition" items or restricting supply creates waiting lists and secondary markets. Hermès Birkin bags famously require years-long waits, making them even more desirable.

3. Experience and service: Luxury isn't just the product; it's the store experience, the packaging, the customer service, the feeling of being treated specially. This can't be easily replicated even if someone buys a counterfeit product.

4. Constantly moving the goalposts: As entry-level items become too common, introduce new products at higher price points. Keep the true elite always one step ahead of the aspirational masses.

5. Geographic expansion: A Louis Vuitton bag might be common in Paris or New York but still signals status in Shanghai or São Paulo. Luxury brands can grow by expanding to new markets where they still carry prestige.

6. Brand architecture: Within a single company, create multiple brands at different price points. LVMH's portfolio serves everyone from mass affluent (Sephora cosmetics) to ultra-wealthy (Chaumet jewelry).

The paradox is that luxury brands simultaneously need to be exclusive (to justify prices) and accessible (to grow revenue). They've solved this through careful brand management, tiered product strategies, and global expansion.

Fast fashion faces a different challenge: how do you create desire for products that change every few weeks and cost very little? The answer is speed and volume. If something sells out quickly, customers feel urgency to buy the next thing. If items are affordable, customers can buy multiple times per season. The business model depends on constant consumption.

Both models, luxury and fast fashion have significant environmental and ethical concerns. Luxury brands have been criticized for destroying unsold inventory rather than discounting (to maintain exclusivity). Fast fashion creates enormous waste and poor labor conditions. The fashion industry is one of the most polluting and exploitative globally.

Yet both models continue to be immensely profitable, suggesting that consumers' desire for new clothes and status signaling remains powerful despite growing awareness of the costs.

The Other Fashion Billionaires: A Global Phenomenon

Arnault and Ortega are the most prominent, but fashion has created many billionaires:

François Pinault (France): Built Kering (formerly PPR), which owns Gucci, Yves Saint Laurent, Bottega Veneta, Balenciaga, and other luxury brands. Pinault's fortune exceeds $30 billion. Like Arnault, he's an acquisitive businessman rather than a designer, proving the luxury conglomerate model works across companies.

Giorgio Armani (Italy): One of the few fashion billionaires who is actually a designer. Armani built his eponymous brand through elegant, understated designs and maintained control by never taking the company public. Worth over $10 billion, he's a reminder that creative talent combined with business acumen can build lasting wealth.

Miuccia Prada (Italy): Inherited her family's leather goods company and transformed it into a global luxury powerhouse. Prada combined intellectual fashion with commercial success, proving luxury could be both artistic and profitable. She's worth over $4 billion.

Ralph Lauren (USA): Created the American dream personified in clothing, preppy, aspirational, all-American style. Lauren built a brand worth billions despite never formally training as a designer. He understood that he was selling a lifestyle and identity, not just clothes.

Stefan Persson (Sweden): Inherited H&M from his father and expanded it into a global fast-fashion giant second only to Inditex. Worth over $15 billion, Persson represents the dynasty approach, inheriting and successfully growing a family business.

The Wertheimer brothers (France): Alain and Gérard Wertheimer own Chanel, perhaps the most prestigious fashion brand in the world. Worth over $40 billion each, they're famously private, almost never appearing in public or giving interviews. Chanel remains privately held, allowing the Wertheimers to focus on long-term brand management rather than quarterly earnings.

Each fashion billionaire has a slightly different story, but common themes emerge: understanding that fashion is about identity and aspiration, building or acquiring strong brands, maintaining quality and mystique, expanding globally, and (for luxury) resisting the temptation to over-commercialize.

Why Fashion Creates Such Durable Fortunes

Fashion and luxury might seem like an odd place to find some of the world's largest fortunes. These aren't innovative technologies or scarce natural resources. They're just... clothes and accessories. Why are they so valuable?

Several factors explain fashion's wealth-creating power:

1. High margins: Luxury goods often cost 10-20% of their retail price to produce. The rest is brand value, which has virtually no marginal cost once established.

2. Repeat purchases: Unlike a car or house, fashion is consumable. People buy new clothes regularly. Luxury customers often own multiple items from favorite brands.

3. Low capital requirements: Once established, fashion brands don't require massive capital investment. No factories to build (they outsource manufacturing), no R&D departments, no infrastructure. Just design, marketing, and distribution.

4. Global scalability: A handbag design that works in Paris works in Tokyo, New York, and Dubai. Fashion brands can expand globally without significant adaptation.

5. Timeless human desires: The desire for status, belonging, beauty, and self-expression are universal and unchanging. Fashion taps into fundamental human psychology.

6. Recession resilience: Wealthy customers keep buying luxury goods even during economic downturns. The "lipstick effect" suggests people buy small luxuries even during hard times. Fashion proves more recession-resistant than many industries.

7. Demographic tailwinds: The growth of the global middle class, particularly in Asia, created millions of new luxury customers. Chinese consumers alone account for over 30% of global luxury purchases.

8. Family control: Many fashion companies remain family-controlled, allowing long-term thinking and brand stewardship. They can resist short-term pressures that destroy brand value.

9. Heritage value: Fashion brands accumulate value over time. A 100-year-old brand has stories, heritage, and cultural meaning that can't be replicated. This creates a moat around established brands.

These factors combine to create extraordinary economics. LVMH's operating margins (around 27%) exceed those of most tech companies. The return on invested capital is exceptional. And the business is sustainable over generations, people were buying luxury goods in ancient Rome and will be buying them in 2100.

The Criticisms: Exploitation, Waste, and Vanity

Despite their success, fashion billionaires face substantial criticisms:

Labor exploitation: Fast fashion particularly depends on low-wage workers in developing countries, often working in unsafe conditions. The 2013 Rana Plaza factory collapse in Bangladesh, which killed over 1,100 garment workers, highlighted the human cost of cheap fashion.

Environmental destruction: Fashion is one of the most polluting industries. Textile production consumes enormous water and energy. Fast fashion's business model encourages consumption and waste, clothes worn a few times then discarded. Luxury brands have been caught burning unsold inventory rather than discounting.

Promoting materialism: Critics argue fashion billionaires have built fortunes by encouraging materialism, status anxiety, and the mistaken belief that buying things creates happiness or worth.

Counterfeiting and gray markets: The luxury industry spends billions fighting counterfeits, which some see as a waste of resources on protecting artificial scarcity.

Tax avoidance: Like other billionaires, fashion moguls have been accused of sophisticated tax avoidance strategies, paying minimal taxes despite enormous wealth.

Income inequality: Fashion billionaires symbolize extreme wealth inequality, individuals worth $100+ billion built on products that cost relatively little to make.

Fashion billionaires have responded to these criticisms with varying degrees of seriousness. Some have made genuine sustainability commitments, though critics note these often don't address the fundamental business model. Some have improved factory conditions and worker pay. Others have largely ignored criticism, assuming that consumers will keep buying regardless.

The industry is slowly changing, driven by consumer pressure, regulation, and genuine concern among some leaders. But fundamental tensions remain between profit-seeking and sustainability, between growth and environmental limits, between exclusivity and accessibility.

The Next Generation: Will Fashion Fortunes Last?

Many fashion empires face succession challenges. Bernard Arnault is seventy-five; he's carefully positioned his five children in various LVMH businesses, but which will ultimately lead is unclear. Amancio Ortega has largely stepped back, though he remains Inditex's largest shareholder. Giorgio Armani is ninety and has no clear successor for his private company.

The fashion industry also faces structural challenges:

Changing consumer values: Younger consumers increasingly value sustainability, authenticity, and experience over material possessions. The showing-off-luxury culture may be waning.

Resale and rental markets: ThredUp, The RealReal, Rent the Runway, these platforms challenge the traditional fashion business model by extending product life and reducing new purchases.

Digital disruption: Social media influencers and direct-to-consumer brands can build audiences without traditional retail. The power of established brands may be weakening.

Economic uncertainty: Luxury depends on having customers with disposable income. Growing inequality, climate change, and political instability could reduce the customer base.

Authenticity demand: Consumers increasingly question whether expensive luxury goods represent genuine quality or just clever marketing. Some younger consumers prefer understated indie brands.

Yet reports of luxury's death seem premature. Demand for luxury goods continues growing, particularly in Asia. Humans still care about status and belonging. The desire to signal identity through consumption remains powerful.

Fashion billionaires have proven adaptable. They've survived world wars, economic crises, and massive social changes. Luxury existed in ancient Rome and thrives today. The brands may change, the business models may evolve, but the fundamental human desires fashion serves are likely permanent.

What Fashion Teaches Us About Wealth

The fashion billionaires offer lessons distinct from tech titans or industrial magnates:

1. Timeless beats trendy (at the high end): Luxury brands succeed by being classic and enduring, not by chasing every trend. Heritage and history create value.

2. Scarcity creates value: Luxury's power comes partly from exclusivity. What everyone can have, nobody wants. Artificial scarcity, carefully managed, drives desire.

3. Emotion beats logic: Fashion purchases are emotional, not rational. The best businesses often tap into emotion, aspiration, and identity rather than functional needs.

4. Privacy works: Unlike tech billionaires who court publicity, fashion billionaires largely avoid it. You can build enormous wealth without being famous.

5. Vertical integration pays: Controlling the entire value chain, from design to manufacturing to retail provides control and margin power.

6. Geography matters differently: Fashion fortunes are distinctly European, built on Old World concepts of luxury, craftsmanship, and heritage. Different cultures create different kinds of wealth.

7. Business skill matters as much as creative talent: The most successful fashion billionaires (Arnault, Ortega) weren't designers, they were businesspeople who understood brand-building and acquisition strategy.

8. Patience builds dynasties: Fashion fortunes often span generations. Quick flips and exits are rare. Building lasting brand value takes decades.

Bernard Arnault and his peers prove that in a world obsessed with technological disruption, there's still enormous money in selling beautiful things to people who want to feel special. While Elon Musk promises to colonize Mars and Mark Zuckerberg builds metaverses, Arnault quietly became as wealthy as either by selling handbags and champagne.

There's something wonderfully old-fashioned about it and something that suggests that whatever new technologies emerge, humans will always want to adorn themselves beautifully and signal their status to others.

The fashion billionaires are betting that desire is permanent. Given their fortunes, it's a bet that's paid off spectacularly.

PART V: THE CAUTIONARY TALES - FORTUNES LOST

Chapter 19

Elizabeth Holmes - Theranos and the Fake-It-Till-You-Make-It Disaster

In 2014, Elizabeth Holmes appeared on the cover of Fortune magazine under the headline "This CEO Is Out For Blood." At thirty years old, she was being hailed as the next Steve Jobs, a Stanford dropout who had founded a revolutionary healthcare company called Theranos that would transform medical testing. She wore black turtlenecks like Jobs, spoke in an unnaturally deep voice about changing the world, and was worth $4.5 billion on paper.

Major investors believed in her vision: the Walton family, Rupert Murdoch, Betsy DeVos, and legendary venture capital firms. Her board of directors read like a who's who of American power: Henry Kissinger, George Shultz, James Mattis, William Perry. Theranos was valued at $9 billion. Elizabeth Holmes was the world's youngest self-made female billionaire, a feminist icon, and a Silicon Valley darling.

There was just one problem: the technology didn't work. It had never worked. And Elizabeth Holmes knew it.

By 2018, Theranos had collapsed completely. Holmes was charged with massive fraud. Patients had received false medical results. Investors had lost hundreds of millions. In 2022, Holmes was convicted on four counts of fraud and sentenced to over eleven years in federal prison.

The story of Elizabeth Holmes and Theranos is the story of Silicon Valley's hype machine gone catastrophically wrong. It's about how charisma, connections, and narrative can substitute for substance but only for so long. It's about the dangers of "fake it till you make it" culture when lives are at stake. And it's a cautionary tale about what happens when the hunger for the next unicorn blinds smart people to obvious warning signs.

This is the story of the most spectacular fraud in Silicon Valley history, and the young woman who almost got away with it.

The Overachiever's Ambition

Elizabeth Anne Holmes was born in 1984 in Washington, D.C., to a family steeped in public service and entrepreneurship. Her father, Christian Holmes IV, worked for government agencies including USAID. Her mother, Noel, worked as a Congressional committee staffer. Elizabeth grew up hearing stories about her great-great-great-grandfather, Christian Holmes, who founded Cincinnati General Hospital.

From childhood, Elizabeth was intensely driven and ambitious. She taught herself Mandarin. She started her own business selling C++ compilers to Chinese universities while still in high school. She told relatives she wanted to be a billionaire. She wasn't interested in normal teenage social activities, she was focused on achievement and success.

"Elizabeth was extremely ambitious from a very young age," a childhood friend recalled. "She wasn't just competitive, she was obsessed with being the best, with making a mark on history."

In 2002, Holmes enrolled at Stanford to study chemical engineering. She was brilliant, hardworking, and determined to do something significant. During her freshman year, she worked in a lab that tested SARS virus samples. The work required drawing blood samples, a process she found painful and inefficient.

An idea took hold: what if you could run comprehensive medical tests on just a few drops of blood from a finger prick, rather than vials drawn from a vein? It would be cheaper, faster, less painful, and more accessible. People could get tested regularly, catching diseases early. It would revolutionize healthcare.

Holmes became obsessed with this vision. In 2003, at nineteen, she dropped out of Stanford to found Real-Time Cures (later renamed Theranos, a combination of "therapy" and "diagnosis"). She used the money her parents had saved for her education as seed funding.

Dropping out of Stanford to start a company was following a well-worn Silicon Valley path, Bill Gates, Steve Jobs, Mark Zuckerberg had all dropped out of elite schools. Holmes consciously modeled herself after Jobs, adopting his black turtleneck uniform, his messianic communication style, and his reality distortion field.

But there was a crucial difference: Jobs actually built products that worked.

The Vision vs. The Reality

The Theranos vision was compelling: a small, proprietary device called the Edison (named after Thomas Edison, naturally) that could run hundreds of medical tests on a single drop of blood from a finger prick. No more needles, no more lab technicians, no more sending samples to distant facilities. Just a quick finger prick, and within hours, you'd have comprehensive results.

If it worked, it would be revolutionary. Blood testing is a $75 billion global industry. Making it faster, cheaper, and more accessible would save lives and money. The vision attracted investors, partners, and enormous media attention.

The problem was the technology was impossible or at least, impossible with current technology. Medical experts knew this, but Holmes and Theranos dismissed skepticism as the kind of resistance all revolutionary ideas face.

The reality behind Theranos was very different from the public image:

The Edison devices didn't work: They produced wildly inaccurate results. Tests would show someone was pregnant when they weren't, or diabetic when they weren't, or having a heart attack when they weren't. When problems arose, Theranos didn't fix the technology, they started running tests on traditional blood testing machines from Siemens and other manufacturers, while claiming to use their revolutionary technology.

The finger-prick samples were insufficient: You simply cannot run hundreds of tests on a few drops of blood. The samples had to be diluted, which introduced errors. Or they collected more blood than claimed, using traditional venous draws.

The science was never validated: Theranos never published peer-reviewed research. They never opened their technology to independent scientific review. When scientists or journalists asked questions, Theranos responded with legal threats and non-disclosure agreements.

The secrecy was a feature, not a bug: Holmes claimed Theranos operated in "stealth mode" to protect trade secrets from competitors. In reality, secrecy hid the fact that the technology didn't work.

Employees who raised concerns were fired: Theranos had a culture of fear. Employees who questioned results or raised safety concerns were threatened, fired, or intimidated with lawsuits. Many signed strict NDAs preventing them from speaking about their time at the company.

The Reality Distortion Field

How did Elizabeth Holmes convince so many smart, experienced people to invest hundreds of millions in technology that didn't work? The answer reveals how Silicon Valley's hype machine can overcome due diligence, skepticism, and common sense.

The narrative: Holmes was a brilliant young woman solving a major healthcare problem. She was the female Steve Jobs, the exception proving that women could found transformative tech companies. The story was irresistible to investors, media, and anyone who wanted to believe.

The pedigree: Stanford dropout, connections to Silicon Valley elite, prestigious early investors, these signaled legitimacy. If smart people at top firms had invested, surely they'd done due diligence.

The board: Henry Kissinger, George Shultz, James Mattis, these weren't technology or healthcare experts, but their names carried weight. The board was designed to impress, not to provide relevant expertise.

The media hype: Glowing profiles in Fortune, Forbes, Inc., and other publications created a feedback loop. Each article made the next investor less skeptical. "I read about Theranos in Fortune" became its own form of validation.

The charisma: Holmes cultivated an intense, Jobs-like presence. She rarely blinked during conversations. She spoke in a deep voice (many have speculated was artificially lowered). She talked about changing the world with messianic conviction. People found her either hypnotic or unsettling, rarely neutral.

The fake-it-till-you-make-it culture: Silicon Valley celebrates "reality distortion fields" and "bold visions." The line between visionary optimism and fraud can seem fuzzy. Holmes presented Theranos failures as temporary obstacles on the path to inevitable success.

FOMO (fear of missing out): When prestigious investors like Don Lucas (early Apple investor) and luminaries like Rupert Murdoch invested, others wanted in. Nobody wanted to be the skeptic who missed "the next Apple."

Exploitation of ignorance: Most investors knew nothing about blood testing or medical diagnostics. They were tech investors or wealthy individuals who didn't know enough to ask the right questions and Theranos exploited this.

Legal intimidation: Theranos had a famously aggressive legal team led by David Boies, one of America's most prominent lawyers. They sent threatening letters to journalists, whistleblowers, and anyone who questioned the company. Many people stayed silent out of fear.

The combination was powerful enough to overcome red flags that, in retrospect, seem obvious. No peer-reviewed publications. No independent validation. Extreme secrecy. Defensiveness about questions. High employee turnover. These should have triggered alarm bells. Instead, they were explained away as the natural challenges of a revolutionary company.

The House of Cards Begins to Crumble

For over a decade, Theranos maintained its façade. But several factors began to unravel the fraud:

Walgreens partnership (2013): Theranos partnered with Walgreens to offer blood testing in stores. This put the technology in front of real patients with real medical needs. When results came back wrong, misdiagnosing conditions, missing diseases and showing false positives people started complaining.

Whistleblowers: Tyler Shultz, grandson of board member George Shultz, worked at Theranos and discovered the technology didn't work. He tried to raise concerns internally, was dismissed and threatened, and eventually became a whistleblower. Erika Cheung, another Theranos employee, also came forward. Both faced legal threats and personal costs for speaking up.

John Carreyrou: A Wall Street Journal investigative reporter named John Carreyrou started investigating Theranos in 2015. Despite legal threats and intimidation from Theranos's lawyers, Carreyrou published a series of articles exposing the fraud. His reporting, later compiled in the book "Bad Blood," revealed that Theranos was using commercially available machines for most tests and that results were often inaccurate.

Regulatory investigation: The Centers for Medicare and Medicaid Services (CMS) inspected Theranos facilities in 2015 and found serious deficiencies that posed "immediate jeopardy to patient health and safety."

Scientific skepticism: As Theranos sought more partnerships, actual medical and scientific experts began examining their claims and finding them implausible. The medical community grew increasingly vocal about Theranos's refusal to publish peer-reviewed research.

Once Carreyrou's articles appeared in October 2015, the house of cards collapsed quickly. Walgreens terminated the partnership. Forbes revised Holmes's net worth from $4.5 billion to zero (since her wealth was entirely based on her Theranos shares, which were now worthless). Partners abandoned ship. Investors sued. Regulators investigated.

In 2016, CMS banned Holmes from owning or operating a medical laboratory for two years. In 2018, the SEC charged Holmes and Theranos president Ramesh "Sunny" Balwani with massive fraud. Holmes settled with the SEC, agreeing to pay a $500,000 penalty, return her shares, and give up voting control of Theranos. She was also barred from serving as an officer or director of a public company for ten years.

But criminal charges were more serious. In June 2018, Holmes and Balwani were indicted on multiple counts of wire fraud and conspiracy to commit wire fraud. The case went to trial in 2021.

The Trial: Confronting Reality

Elizabeth Holmes's trial was one of the most closely watched fraud cases in decades. It began in September 2021 and lasted months, featuring dramatic testimony, celebrity appearances, and intense public interest.

The prosecution's case was straightforward: Holmes knowingly lied to investors, partners, and patients about Theranos's capabilities. She claimed the technology worked when it didn't. She claimed Theranos was being used by the military when it wasn't. She created fake reports with pharmaceutical company logos to imply endorsements. She knew people were receiving false medical results and continued operating anyway. This wasn't entrepreneurial optimism, it was fraud.

Holmes's defense was more complex: She believed in the technology and thought it would eventually work. Investors are sophisticated and knew startup investing was risky. She relied on experts and scientists who assured her the technology was sound. And most controversially, she had been in an abusive relationship with Sunny Balwani, who controlled and manipulated her, affecting her judgment.

The abuse allegations were particularly contentious. Holmes testified that Balwani (nearly twenty years older and her secret boyfriend, then business partner) had been emotionally and sexually abusive, controlling what she ate, how she spent her time, and how she ran the company. The defense suggested this explained some of her actions.

Prosecutors countered that even if the abuse occurred, Holmes was still responsible for fraud. She was the CEO, the public face, the person who made false statements to investors and partners. Personal difficulties don't excuse defrauding investors of hundreds of millions or putting patients' health at risk.

The jury deliberated for seven days. In January 2022, they returned a mixed verdict: Holmes was convicted on four counts of fraud related to deceiving investors, but acquitted on charges related to defrauding patients. The jury believed she'd lied to investors but found the patient fraud charges less clear.

In November 2022, Holmes was sentenced to 11 years and 3 months in federal prison, far less than the maximum possible but still a substantial sentence. She was ordered to pay $452 million in restitution to victims. She reported to prison in May 2023.

By then, she had married Billy Evans, a hotel heir, and had two children. She was pregnant during the trial and gave birth to her second child while awaiting sentencing. Some saw this as a calculated attempt to generate sympathy. Others saw it as a young woman trying to build a life even as her past collapsed around her.

Why Did So Many Smart People Fall For It?

The Theranos story raises an uncomfortable question: how did Elizabeth Holmes fool so many intelligent, experienced people? The answer reveals troubling dynamics in Silicon Valley and beyond.

Pattern matching over substance: Investors saw "Stanford dropout" + "revolutionary technology" + "black turtleneck" and pattern-matched to Steve Jobs. They invested in the narrative rather than verifying the technology.

Star power over expertise: Theranos's board was full of famous names, but they were military and political figures who knew nothing about blood testing. Their presence signaled prestige, not relevant oversight.

FOMO-driven investing: Once prestigious names invested, others didn't want to miss out. Each investment validated the next. Due diligence was replaced by assuming others had done due diligence.

Gender dynamics: Some investors and media wanted to believe in a young female founder who could be "the next Steve Jobs." This created a reluctance to scrutinize her claims too aggressively for fear of seeming sexist.

Medical expertise gap: Most tech investors don't understand medical technology. They couldn't evaluate whether Theranos's claims were plausible. They relied on Holmes's credentials and confidence rather than scientific validation.

Culture of optimism: Silicon Valley celebrates "reality distortion fields" and "fake it till you make it." The line between visionary confidence and fraud can seem ambiguous. Holmes exploited this ambiguity.

Legal intimidation worked: Theranos's aggressive lawyers successfully silenced whistleblowers and journalists for years. Fear of lawsuits prevented many from speaking up.

Confirmation bias: Once people invested or committed to Theranos, they had incentive to believe it would succeed. Cognitive dissonance made it easier to explain away red flags than admit they'd been fooled.

Failure of gatekeepers: Media published glowing profiles without verifying claims. Investors didn't insist on independent technical audits. Board members didn't provide meaningful oversight. Partners like Walgreens didn't adequately validate the technology before rolling it out to patients.

The Theranos debacle wasn't just Elizabeth Holmes's fraud, it was a systemic failure of due diligence, oversight, and critical thinking.

The Bigger Questions About Silicon Valley Culture

Theranos exposed troubling aspects of Silicon Valley culture that extend beyond one fraudulent company:

"Fake it till you make it" taken too far: Silicon Valley celebrates confident founders who sell a vision before its reality. But there's a difference between being optimistic about solving hard problems and lying about whether your technology works.

Narrative over substance: The best story often wins funding, not necessarily the best technology. Holmes was brilliant at crafting narrative but terrible at building actual products.

Celebrity boards as window dressing: Boards should provide governance and expertise. Filling boards with famous but irrelevant names creates prestige without accountability.

Inadequate due diligence: Investors should verify claims, especially for medical technology. Too many invested based on reputation and narrative rather than rigorous technical evaluation.

Culture of secrecy: Theranos claimed secrecy was necessary to protect intellectual property. In reality, secrecy hid fraud. Real breakthroughs can withstand peer review and external validation.

Founder worship: Silicon Valley's tendency to treat certain founders as visionaries above questioning creates conditions for abuse. Holmes was treated as untouchable for years.

Regulatory gaps: Medical technology faces less rigorous oversight than pharmaceuticals, creating opportunities for companies to operate with unproven technology for years.

Consequences gap: When tech companies fail, investors lose money but rarely face serious consequences. When medical technology fails, people receive false diagnoses and potentially die. The stakes are higher, but the oversight wasn't commensurate.

The Victims: Beyond the Headlines

While Elizabeth Holmes became the face of the scandal, it's important to remember the victims:

Patients: People received false test results showing they had cancer when they didn't, or didn't have cancer when they did. False HIV diagnoses. Incorrect pregnancy test results. These weren't just numbers, they were people whose lives were affected by bad medical information.

Investors: Betsy DeVos, Rupert Murdoch, the Walton family, and many others lost hundreds of millions. While it's hard to feel sorry for wealthy investors, fraud is fraud. Their money could have funded legitimate medical research or companies.

Employees: Thousands of people worked at Theranos, many genuinely believing they were changing the world. When the fraud was exposed, their resumes were tarnished and their belief in their work shattered.

Whistleblowers: Tyler Shultz spent hundreds of thousands on legal fees defending himself against Theranos's lawsuits. His relationship with his grandfather George Shultz (a Theranos board member) was destroyed. Erika Cheung faced similar legal threats. Speaking the truth cost them dearly.

The medical testing industry: Legitimate companies trying to innovate in blood testing face increased skepticism and regulatory scrutiny because of Theranos.

Women in tech: Holmes was held up as proof that women could found transformative tech companies. Her fraud has been used to justify skepticism toward female founders, unfairly tarring others with her actions.

The Cautionary Lessons

Elizabeth Holmes and Theranos offer crucial lessons:

1. **Charisma is not competence:** A compelling vision and confident presentation don't mean the underlying technology works. Verify independently.

2. **Red flags matter:** Extreme secrecy, refusal to publish research, aggressive legal threats, high employee turnover, these should trigger skepticism, not be explained away.

3. **Domain expertise matters:** Medical technology should be evaluated by medical experts, not just tech investors impressed by the founder's pedigree.

4. **"Fake it till you make it" has limits:** There's a difference between being optimistic about solving hard problems and lying about whether your technology works, especially when health is at stake.

5. **Celebrity boards can be red flags:** If a board is full of famous names with no relevant expertise, be suspicious. Good boards provide governance and expertise, not just prestige.

6. **Trust but verify:** Even if prestigious people have invested, do your own due diligence. Their investment doesn't mean they did proper technical validation.

7. **Whistleblowers should be protected:** Tyler Shultz and Erika Cheung paid heavy costs for speaking the truth. Society needs better protections for people who expose fraud.

8. **Consequences matter:** Holmes is serving eleven years in prison. This sends a message that fraud has consequences, even for charismatic founders with powerful connections.

9. Gender shouldn't shield accountability: Some argued that scrutiny of Holmes was sexist. But holding fraudsters accountable regardless of gender is equality. Women founders deserve the same scrutiny and same opportunities as men.

10. Lives are at stake: In healthcare technology, fraud isn't just about money, people's health and lives are at risk. The stakes require higher standards.

The Aftermath: A Changed Landscape?

Has Silicon Valley learned from Theranos? The answer is mixed.

On one hand, there's increased awareness of the dangers of hype over substance. Investors claim to be more skeptical. Media outlets are more careful about glowing profiles of unproven companies. Healthcare technology faces more scrutiny.

On the other hand, the fundamental dynamics that enabled Theranos persist: FOMO-driven investing, pattern matching over substance, celebrity founder worship, and resistance to skepticism being dismissed as lack of vision.

Within months of Theranos's collapse, other questionable startups were raising massive funding on compelling narratives and unproven technology. WeWork's Adam Neumann raised billions for a real estate company he called a "tech platform." FTX's Sam Bankman-Fried built a cryptocurrency empire that collapsed in fraud. The lessons of Theranos didn't prevent similar dynamics from playing out.

Perhaps the real lesson is that as long as there's money chasing the next big thing, there will be people willing to fake it until they're caught. The incentive structures of venture capital, the pressure to find the next unicorn, the fear of missing out, the need to deploy capital quickly create conditions where fraud can flourish.

Theranos wasn't an aberration. It was an extreme example of dynamics present throughout Silicon Valley. Until those dynamics change, there will be more Elizabeth Holmeses, charismatic founders with compelling stories and technology that doesn't quite work the way they claim.

The Human Element: Who Was Elizabeth Holmes?

Trying to understand Elizabeth Holmes as a person is difficult. Was she a con artist from the beginning, knowing the technology didn't work? Was she delusional, genuinely believing she could make it work despite all evidence? Was she a victim of Sunny Balwani's abuse who lost control of her company? Was she simply young, ambitious, and in over her head?

The truth is probably some combination. Holmes seems to have genuinely believed in the vision initially. But at some point, perhaps gradually, perhaps suddenly she knew the technology didn't work. Instead of admitting failure, she doubled down, lying to preserve her image, her company, and her status as a visionary founder.

This is the tragedy of Elizabeth Holmes. She had intelligence, ambition, and work ethic. If she'd focused on realistic goals, accepted failure when appropriate, and built something more modest, she might have had a successful career. Instead, she became obsessed with being the next Steve Jobs, with changing the world, with proving she was special.

The obsession with significance led to fraud. The inability to admit failure led to putting patients at risk. The reality distortion field she created eventually collided with actual reality, and reality won.

Now Elizabeth Holmes is in federal prison, her reputation destroyed, her wealth gone. She's a cautionary tale and a punchline. The youngest self-made female billionaire became the face of Silicon Valley fraud.

She was thirty years old when she appeared on magazine covers as a visionary. She was thirty-eight when she reported to prison. In between, she built and destroyed a $9 billion company, fooled some of the smartest people in business, and became a symbol of everything wrong with Silicon Valley's worship of charismatic founders and reality distortion fields.

The story of Elizabeth Holmes is ultimately a very human story about ambition, deception, and the dangers of believing your own mythology. She wanted to change the world. She changed it, just not in the way she imagined. Now her legacy is a warning: charisma without competence, narrative without substance, and vision without reality are a recipe for disaster.

The woman who wanted to be remembered as the next Steve Jobs will instead be remembered as Silicon Valley's greatest fraud. Sometimes, fake it till you make it doesn't make it at all. Sometimes, reality wins.

Chapter 20

The Bankruptcy Files - When Billions Disappear

In 2008, Eike Batista was the seventh richest person in the world. The Brazilian mining and energy magnate was worth $34.5 billion and climbing. He owned a fleet of private jets, a $20 million Mercedes-Benz McLaren SLR, a luxury yacht, and multiple mansions. He dated supermodels and actresses. He predicted he would soon become the world's richest person, surpassing Bill Gates.

By 2013, just five years later Eike Batista wasn't just broke. He had a negative net worth. His companies had collapsed. His assets were seized. He owed creditors over $1 billion more than he owned. It was one of the fastest and most spectacular wealth destructions in history, $34.5 billion to less than zero in sixty months.

"I still haven't figured out what happened," Batista said in a rare interview after his collapse. But everyone else had: overconfidence, excessive leverage, fraudulent claims, and the fundamental instability of building an empire on promises rather than profits.

Batista's story is extreme but not unique. Throughout history, billionaires have lost everything through bad bets, fraud, economic crashes, hubris, and simple bad luck. For every Warren Buffett who compounds wealth over decades, there are cautionary tales of fortunes built and demolished within years.

This chapter examines the billionaires who had it all and lost it, the patterns in wealth destruction, the psychological factors that turn success into catastrophe, and the lessons about how fragile extreme wealth can be.

Eike Batista: The Man Who Would Be King

Eike Batista seemed destined for success. His father was a Brazilian mining executive and politician. Eike studied in Europe, married a Playboy model, and entered the mining business in the 1980s. He was smart, charismatic, and wildly ambitious.

His strategy was simple: identify Brazil's untapped natural resources, create companies to exploit them, take those companies public on hype and promises, use the inflated stock prices as currency to acquire more assets, and repeat. He created a group of companies all beginning with the letter X (for multiplication of wealth): OGX (oil and gas), MMX (mining), LLX (logistics), OSX (shipbuilding), MPX (energy), and more.

The pitch was compelling: Brazil was booming, commodity prices were soaring, and Batista's companies would unlock vast natural wealth. OGX claimed to have discovered massive oil reserves off Brazil's coast that would make it a major oil producer. MMX would mine iron ore. LLX would build ports to export the resources. It was a vertically integrated empire of the future.

Investors loved it. Money poured in. Batista took his companies public, raising billions. His personal wealth exploded. By 2012, he was worth over $30 billion and making increasingly bold predictions: he would surpass Carlos Slim to become the richest person in the world. Brazil would become an economic superpower. His companies would dominate South American industry.

He spent money with corresponding boldness. He bought a gold-plated Mercedes McLaren supercar and parked it in his living room as art. He owned multiple private jets and a yacht. He built lavish homes in Rio de Janeiro. He dated famous women and appeared constantly in Brazilian media as a symbol of the country's rising prosperity.

But behind the glamorous facade, Batista's empire was built on sand:

The oil reserves didn't exist: OGX's claims about massive offshore oil discoveries were wildly exaggerated. When they actually drilled, they found far less oil than promised, and what they found was expensive to extract.

The business model required constant cash: Batista's companies were burning cash faster than they generated revenue. They needed constantly rising stock prices to raise more money. When prices fell, the model collapsed.

Excessive debt: Batista had borrowed billions against future production that never materialized. When revenues didn't appear, debt became crushing.

Interconnected companies: All of Batista's X companies were interconnected, doing business with each other. When one failed, it cascaded through the entire structure.

Commodity price collapse: Global commodity prices fell, making marginal projects unprofitable and destroying the narrative of Brazil as a resource superpower.

The collapse came swiftly. In 2012, OGX announced that oil production would be far below projections. The stock price plummeted. Investors panicked. Other X companies' stocks collapsed. Batista tried to prop things up with his personal fortune, but it was mostly paper wealth that evaporated as stock prices fell.

By 2013, OGX declared bankruptcy, the largest corporate bankruptcy in Latin American history. Other X companies followed. Batista's personal wealth disappeared. He faced criminal charges for fraud and insider trading. His assets were seized to pay creditors.

The man who would be the world's richest person couldn't make bail without help. His gold Mercedes was auctioned off. His mansions were sold. His yacht was seized. In 2018, he was convicted of paying $16.5 million in bribes and sentenced to thirty years in prison (later reduced on appeal).

Eike Batista's fall was so complete and so rapid that it became a global cautionary tale about hubris, leverage, and building empires on hype rather than fundamentals.

Allen Stanford: Antigua's Knight and America's Fraudster

Allen Stanford's story reads like a bad spy novel, except it was real. A Texas-raised financier who became a billionaire running a massive Ponzi scheme from the Caribbean island of Antigua, was knighted by the island's government, sponsored international cricket tournaments, and lived a life of spectacular luxury before being arrested by the FBI, convicted of fraud, and sentenced to 110 years in federal prison.

Stanford grew up in Mexia, Texas, the son of a barber. He was an insurance salesman and gym owner before moving into banking. In the 1980s, he acquired a bank in Montserrat, a tiny Caribbean island. He later moved operations to Antigua and built Stanford International Bank.

The bank's pitch was simple: extraordinarily high interest rates on certificates of deposit, far higher than available at traditional banks. Stanford claimed these returns came from savvy investments and the bank's Caribbean location with lower overhead costs.

In reality, it was a Ponzi scheme. Stanford International Bank didn't make legitimate investments generating those returns. Instead, like Bernie Madoff (whom we'll examine next chapter), Stanford used money from new investors to pay returns to existing investors. As long as new money kept flowing in, the scheme worked. When it stopped, it would collapse.

But Stanford lived as if the wealth were real. He owned a fleet of private jets including a former airliner reconfigured for luxury travel. He bought a 112-foot yacht. He purchased a private island. He built a sprawling compound in Antigua. He financed Stanford 20/20 cricket tournaments, becoming a major figure in international cricket. The Antiguan government knighted him, Sir Allen Stanford.

He cultivated relationships with politicians, celebrities, and wealthy individuals worldwide. His bank managed over $7 billion in assets. He was charismatic, generous with donations, and presented himself as a successful businessman bringing prosperity to the Caribbean.

The scheme unraveled in 2009 when the SEC investigated Stanford International Bank and discovered it was essentially a $7 billion fraud. Stanford had been running a Ponzi scheme for decades, falsifying financial statements and lying to investors about the safety and performance of their investments.

When authorities closed in, Stanford fled. He was eventually arrested in Virginia, assaulted in jail (suffering injuries that affected his mental state during trial), and convicted on thirteen counts of fraud, conspiracy, and obstruction. In 2012, he was sentenced to 110 years in federal prison.

Investors lost over $7 billion. Many were retirees who had invested their life savings based on Stanford's promises of safe, high returns. The Antiguan economy, which had become dependent on Stanford's operations, suffered significantly. The cricket tournaments ended. The private jets were seized and sold.

Allen Stanford sits in federal prison, maintaining his innocence, claiming he was a legitimate businessman who made bad investments rather than a deliberate fraudster. Victims and prosecutors see it differently: Stanford was a con man who lived like royalty on other people's money and destroyed thousands of lives in the process.

Sean Quinn: Ireland's Richest Man Falls to Earth

Sean Quinn's story is different from Batista's hype or Stanford's fraud. Quinn built a legitimate business empire in Ireland over decades, became the country's richest person with a fortune exceeding $6 billion, then lost it all through a single catastrophically bad investment decision combined with pride, stubbornness, and the 2008 financial crisis.

Quinn grew up in rural Ireland near the border with Northern Ireland. He started his business career in the 1970s extracting gravel and sand from his family's land. From this humble beginning, he built Quinn Group into a conglomerate spanning cement, manufacturing, insurance, hotels, and real estate. By the 2000s, Quinn Group was one of Ireland's largest private companies, employing 5,500 people.

Quinn was beloved in Ireland, particularly in the border region where his businesses provided employment and prosperity. He was seen as a self-made man who stayed loyal to his roots, living modestly despite immense wealth. He eschewed publicity and built his businesses through hard work rather than financial engineering.

But in 2005, Quinn made a decision that would destroy everything he'd built: he began secretly accumulating shares in Anglo Irish Bank through contracts for difference (CFDs), essentially leveraged bets on the bank's stock price. CFDs allowed him to control large positions with relatively little cash by borrowing heavily.

Quinn's position in Anglo Irish Bank eventually reached 25% of the company, an enormous, undisclosed and leveraged bet. When the financial crisis hit in 2008 and Irish banks collapsed, Anglo Irish Bank's stock price plummeted. Quinn's CFD positions were suddenly worth far less than what he owed on them.

The Irish government nationalized Anglo Irish Bank to prevent broader financial contagion. Quinn's borrowings from Anglo exceeded the value of his entire business empire. To pay back the loans, Quinn had to surrender control of Quinn Group, which was broken up and sold. His insurance company became independent. His real estate and manufacturing assets were sold to pay creditors.

By 2011, Sean Quinn was bankrupt. The man who had been worth $6 billion in 2008 had lost everything. His family's assets were seized. He faced contempt of court charges for attempting to hide assets overseas. He eventually spent several months in prison for violating court orders.

Quinn's fall devastated not just his family but the entire border region of Ireland that depended on his businesses for employment. When Quinn Group was broken up, thousands lost their jobs. Communities that had prospered from Quinn's success suffered economic decline.

What makes Quinn's story particularly tragic is that it was avoidable. He had built legitimate, profitable businesses over decades. If he had simply continued running those businesses, he would have remained wealthy. Instead, a single overleveraged bet on Anglo Irish Bank destroyed everything.

In interviews after his bankruptcy, Quinn expressed regret but also maintained that he was unfairly treated by the Irish government and Anglo Irish Bank. He believed he'd been forced into bankruptcy unnecessarily. Critics noted that he'd made an extraordinarily reckless bet with borrowed money and paid the predictable consequences.

Sean Quinn's story is a cautionary tale about leverage, about putting all your eggs in one basket, and about how even legitimate business empires can be destroyed by a single bad decision.

Adolf Merckle: The Volkswagen Short Squeeze Tragedy

Adolf Merckle's story is perhaps the most tragic in this chapter because it ended not just in bankruptcy but in suicide. Merckle was one of Germany's richest men, worth an estimated $12.8 billion in 2007, when a series of bad bets, particularly a short position on Volkswagen stock destroyed his fortune and led him to take his own life.

Merckle inherited a pharmaceutical business from his family and expanded it into a massive conglomerate spanning pharmaceuticals, cement, financial services, and more. He was famously private, almost unknown publicly despite being one of Germany's wealthiest individuals. He lived modestly, worked from an unassuming office, and avoided publicity.

In 2008, Merckle's investment firm held a large short position on Volkswagen stock, betting that the price would fall. This was a reasonable bet in late 2008 as the global financial crisis was causing most stock prices to plummet. Shorting involves borrowing shares, selling them, hoping to buy them back cheaper, and pocketing the difference.

But something unexpected happened: Porsche announced it had been secretly accumulating Volkswagen shares and now controlled over 74% of the company. This created a "short squeeze." Short sellers like Merckle needed to buy VW shares to cover their positions, but very few shares were available because Porsche controlled most of them. The law of supply and demand went into overdrive.

VW's stock price exploded, briefly making it the world's most valuable company, more valuable than ExxonMobil or General Electric, which made no economic sense for a car manufacturer but reflected the short squeeze dynamics. The stock went from €200 to over €1,000 in two days.

Merckle's short position lost billions. He had borrowed heavily to fund the position, and now faced margin calls he couldn't meet. His business empire, which had been worth over €30 billion, was suddenly deeply in debt. Creditors demanded repayment. His lifetime of work was disappearing.

On January 5, 2009, Adolf Merckle walked to a railway track near his home in Blaubeuren, Germany, and lay down in front of an oncoming train. He was seventy-four years old. His family released a statement saying he'd been "broken by the financial crisis" and the threat to his life's work.

Merckle's death shocked Germany. It humanized the financial crisis in a way that abstract discussions of billions lost couldn't. Here was a brilliant businessman who had built a legitimate empire over decades, destroyed not by fraud or incompetence but by a leveraged bet that went catastrophically wrong during unprecedented market conditions.

His family managed to restructure the business empire and save most of it by selling some assets and negotiating with creditors. But Adolf Merckle himself didn't live to see it. The pressure of losing everything proved unbearable.

Jocelyn Wildenstein: Spending Your Way to Bankruptcy

Most of the stories in this chapter are about businesspeople who lost fortunes through bad investments or fraud. Jocelyn Wildenstein's story is different, she lost hundreds of millions through pure spending, becoming a cautionary tale about how even enormous wealth can be depleted through extravagant lifestyle and poor financial management.

Jocelyn Wildenstein became known as "Catwoman" due to extensive plastic surgery that gave her a feline appearance. She was married to Alec Wildenstein, heir to a prominent art dealing family, from 1978 to 1999. Their divorce was one of the most expensive in history, with Jocelyn reportedly receiving a $2.5 billion settlement plus $100 million annual alimony for thirteen years.

With that kind of money, most people would be set for multiple lifetimes. Jocelyn managed to spend it all and more, filing for bankruptcy in 2018.

Her spending was legendary:

- $5,000 per month on phone bills
- $60,000 per month on clothing
- Hundreds of thousands on plastic surgery
- Millions on maintaining multiple luxury residences
- Extravagant gifts and purchases

She reportedly spent over $1 million per month maintaining her lifestyle. Even with $100 million annual income, this was unsustainable, especially after the alimony payments ended in 2015.

By 2018, Wildenstein claimed to have only $0 in her bank accounts and filed for Chapter 11 bankruptcy, owing millions to creditors. She blamed her financial advisors and ex-husband's family for cutting off her access to trusts.

The bankruptcy filing was disputed, some creditors claimed she was hiding assets and spending continued even during bankruptcy proceedings. The case revealed a life of almost incomprehensible spending detached from any normal concept of budgeting or financial planning.

Jocelyn Wildenstein's story is less dramatic than Batista's business collapse or Stanford's fraud, but it illustrates an important point: no amount of money is infinite. Spending can exceed even enormous income if there's no discipline or planning. The wealth she received in divorce could have sustained generations if managed prudently. Instead, it was gone within two decades.

Common Patterns in Wealth Destruction

Examining these and other cases of lost fortunes reveals common patterns:

1. **Excessive leverage**: Batista, Quinn, and Merckle all used massive amounts of borrowed money to amplify their positions. When bets went wrong, leverage magnified losses catastrophically. As Warren Buffett says: "When you combine ignorance and leverage, you get some pretty interesting results."

2. **Concentration risk**: Quinn put 25% of his wealth into a single stock. Merckle made an enormous bet on one short position. Diversification is boring but essential. Concentration can create wealth quickly but destroy it even faster.

3. **Hubris and overconfidence**: Batista predicted he'd become the world's richest person while his companies were failing. Overconfidence leads to taking excessive risks and ignoring warning signs.

4. **Fraudulent exaggeration**: Batista exaggerated oil reserves. Stanford ran a Ponzi scheme. Holmes lied about technology. When you lie about fundamentals, the truth eventually emerges catastrophically.

5. **Economic cycle timing**: Many fortunes were lost during the 2008 financial crisis. Leverage and risky strategies work during good times but become fatal during downturns.

6. **Pride and stubbornness**: Quinn refused to accept losses on Anglo Irish Bank, doubling down instead of cutting losses. Merckle couldn't face the prospect of losing his life's work. Pride prevents rational decision-making.

7. **Lifestyle inflation**: Wildenstein's spending increased to match (and exceed) her income. When income disappeared, the lifestyle remained until everything was gone.

8. Interconnected assets: Batista's companies all depended on each other. When one failed, all failed. Lack of true diversification meant localized problems became systemic collapse.

9. Legal consequences: Stanford and Batista both faced criminal charges. Sometimes losing money is just the beginning, prison can follow.

10. Psychological breaking points: Merckle's suicide reminds us that losing a fortune isn't just financial, it's deeply psychological. Some people can't survive the transition from billionaire to broke.

The Psychology of Losing Everything

Financial loss at this scale is traumatic in ways that go beyond money. Identity, self-worth, social status, life purpose, all are threatened when extreme wealth disappears.

Identity collapse: Being a billionaire becomes central to identity. When the wealth disappears, "who am I?" becomes an existential crisis. Batista went from predicting he'd be the world's richest man to having negative net worth. That identity whiplash is psychologically devastating.

Social isolation: Billionaires often socialize with other wealthy people. When the money disappears, so do many relationships. It's unclear whether people liked you or your money and the answer is often uncomfortable.

Shame and embarrassment: Public failure is humiliating. Everyone knows you lost billions. The media covers your fall. Former friends avoid you. The shame can be overwhelming.

Sense of injustice: Many who lose fortunes feel victimized by the government (Quinn), by market manipulation (Merckle), by subordinates

(Batista blamed others). Accepting personal responsibility is difficult when your identity is tied to success.

Loss of purpose: Building and managing wealth provided purpose and structure. When it's gone, what do you do with your days? The loss of purpose can be as devastating as financial loss.

Family consequences: Spouses divorce. Children resent you. Extended family who depended on your wealth struggle. The social fabric surrounding wealth unravels.

Adolf Merckle's suicide is the extreme outcome, but psychological distress is common among those who lose massive fortunes. Some recover and rebuild. Others never do. The psychological resilience required to lose billions and continue living normally is rare.

Can You Lose It All and Come Back?

Some people who've lost fortunes have rebuilt:

Elon Musk was nearly broke in 2008 when both Tesla and SpaceX faced bankruptcy. He borrowed money for rent. A decade later, he was the richest person in the world. His comeback required both luck (SpaceX's fourth launch succeeded) and stubbornness.

Donald Trump declared bankruptcy multiple times in the 1990s, losing his father's fortune through bad casino investments. He rebuilt through branding and licensing, then became President. Whether he's actually wealthy now is debated, but he recovered from near-total loss.

Henry Ford failed at his first two automobile companies before Ford Motor Company succeeded. Early failures didn't prevent later success.

But these comebacks are rare. Most people who lose billions don't rebuild. Age matters, Musk was thirty-seven in 2008 with time to recover. Merckle was seventy-four. Skills matter, if you built wealth through legitimate business skill versus luck or fraud, rebuilding is more plausible. Network matters, connections survive financial loss and can help recovery.

The harder truth is that many people who build massive fortunes do so through a combination of skill, luck, timing, and specific historical circumstances that can't be replicated. Batista benefited from the commodity supercycle and Brazil's boom. When both ended, rebuilding was impossible. Quinn built his empire in a specific time and place in Irish history that no longer exists.

Lessons for the Rest of Us

Most people reading this won't face the specific challenge of losing billions because they'll never have billions to lose. But the lessons translate to more modest scales:

1. Avoid excessive leverage: Borrowing to invest amplifies gains but also losses. If you can't afford to lose the investment without borrowed money, you can't afford the borrowed money either.

2. Diversify: Don't put all your wealth in one investment, one company, one asset class, or one country. Spread risk.

3. Live below your means: No matter how much you make, spending more means eventual financial crisis. Build buffers and savings.

4. Don't believe your own hype: Success can create overconfidence. Stay humble. Remember that luck plays a bigger role than we typically admit.

5. Cut losses quickly: When an investment goes wrong, accept it and move on. Doubling down to avoid admitting failure usually makes things worse.

6. Separate identity from net worth: Your worth as a person isn't your net worth. Building identity around wealth makes losing it psychologically unbearable.

7. Understand what you're investing in: Quinn didn't fully understand CFDs and leverage. Merckle didn't anticipate the short squeeze. Invest in what you understand.

8. Plan for downturns: Bull markets don't last forever. Strategies that work during good times can be fatal during crashes.

9. Get independent advice: Many people who lost fortunes were surrounded by yes-men and advisors with conflicts of interest. Seek objective counsel.

10. Remember that wealth is temporary: Even enormous fortunes can disappear. Don't assume current wealth is permanent.

The Cautionary Tale Continues

The stories in this chapter are from different eras, countries, and industries, but they share a common thread: wealth is far more fragile than it appears. The billions that took decades to build can vanish in months. The business empires that seemed invincible can collapse overnight. The fortunes that appeared permanent can prove temporary.

Eike Batista sits in Brazil, his gold Mercedes long gone, facing legal consequences for fraud and bribery. Allen Stanford is in federal prison, maintaining his innocence as he serves his 110-year sentence. Sean Quinn lives in Ireland, no longer the country's richest man but rather a cautionary tale about leverage and pride. Adolf Merckle died on railway tracks, unable to face losing his life's work. Jocelyn Wildenstein filed for bankruptcy despite receiving one of history's largest divorce settlements.

These stories serve as a counterweight to the success narratives that dominate discussions of wealth. For every Warren Buffett who compounds wealth over seventy years, there are dozens of people who built fortunes and lost them. The survivors and wealth-builders get the magazine covers. The bankruptcies get a footnote.

But perhaps the bankruptcies are more instructive. Success can come from skill plus luck. Failure teaches clearer lessons: avoid leverage, diversify, control spending, manage risk, stay humble, and remember that no amount of wealth is guaranteed to last.

As the saying goes: "It takes a lifetime to build a reputation and five minutes to destroy it." The same is true of fortunes. The billions may seem solid, but they're built on confidence, market prices, and leverage that can evaporate faster than they accumulated.

The lesson isn't to avoid building wealth. The lesson is to build it carefully, manage it prudently, and never forget that losing it all is always possible, even when you're worth billions.

Chapter 21

Bernie Madoff - The $65 Billion Lie

The phone call came on December 10, 2008, just as the world was reeling from the worst financial crisis since the Great Depression. Mark Madoff, sitting in his father's Manhattan apartment, listened in disbelief as Bernie Madoff confessed what would become the largest financial fraud in American history. "It's all just one big lie," Bernie told his sons. "Basically, a giant Ponzi scheme." Mark and his brother Andrew would call the FBI within hours. Their father would be arrested the next morning. And the mythology of Bernie Madoff, respected Wall Street statesman, philanthropist, and financial genius would shatter into a thousand pieces, revealing something far more sinister underneath.

For decades, Bernard Lawrence Madoff had occupied a unique position in American finance. He wasn't just wealthy; he was *trusted*. He had served as chairman of the NASDAQ stock exchange. He sat on the board of the Securities Industry Association. He advised the SEC on trading regulations. His investment firm, Bernard L. Madoff Investment Securities LLC, was one of the most respected on Wall Street. When you invested with Bernie Madoff, you weren't taking a risk, you were joining an exclusive club. Getting access to his fund was considered a privilege, something to brag about at country club dinners and charity galas.

That exclusivity was, of course, entirely by design. It was the cornerstone of the greatest con in financial history.

The Rise of a Respected Figure

Bernie Madoff's story began far from the marble lobbies of Manhattan's financial district. Born in 1938 in Queens, New York, to Ralph and Sylvia Madoff, Bernie grew up solidly middle-class in a Jewish family that valued education and hard work. His father worked as a plumber before trying his hand at various small businesses. His mother briefly registered an investment firm in the 1960s, though it was eventually shut down for failing to file reports with the SEC, a darkly ironic prelude to her son's future.

Bernie showed entrepreneurial spirit early. As a teenager, he worked as a lifeguard and sprinkler installer, saving $5,000 that he would use to start his investment firm in 1960. He was twenty-two years old, newly married to his high school sweetheart Ruth, and ambitious. In those early days, Bernard L. Madoff Investment Securities was a legitimate operation. Bernie worked as a market maker, buying and selling stocks for customers and earning the spread between the bid and ask prices.

He was good at it. More importantly, he was an innovator. In the 1970s and 1980s, as computers began transforming Wall Street, Madoff was at the forefront of electronic trading. He pioneered the use of computer technology to disseminate stock quotes and helped develop the NASDAQ exchange into a viable competitor to the New York Stock Exchange. This wasn't smoke and mirrors; this was genuine innovation that earned him legitimate respect.

His firm grew steadily. He hired his brother Peter as chief compliance officer. Eventually, his sons Mark and Andrew would join the trading side of the business. By the 1990s, Bernard L. Madoff Investment Securities was handling up to five percent of the trading volume on the New York Stock Exchange. The firm's legitimate market-making operation was successful and profitable.

But running parallel to this legitimate business was something else entirely: the investment advisory service that would become the Ponzi scheme. This side of the operation was run from a separate floor, the 17th floor of the Lipstick Building in Manhattan and operated with remarkable secrecy even within Madoff's own firm. The legitimate trading operation run by his sons was on the 18th and 19th floors. They believed their father's investment advisory service was small and separate. They had no idea it would eventually claim $65 billion in fictitious account balances.

The Mechanics of the Lie

A Ponzi scheme is elegantly simple in concept, devastatingly complex in execution. Named after Charles Ponzi, who became infamous for such a scheme in 1920, the fraud works like this: you promise investors high returns, but instead of actually investing their money, you simply use new investors' money to pay the "returns" to earlier investors. As long as more money keeps coming in than going out, the scheme can continue. The moment withdrawals exceed deposits, the house of cards collapses.

Madoff's version had several sophisticated twists that allowed it to survive for an estimated 17 years, possibly longer. Some investigators believe the fraud may have begun as early as the 1970s, though Madoff himself claimed it started in the 1990s during a recession when his legitimate business was struggling.

The investment strategy Madoff claimed to employ was called a "split-strike conversion." This involved buying a basket of stocks, usually blue-chip stocks from the S&P 100 and then buying and selling options to protect against market downturns. On paper, it was a conservative strategy that would generate steady, moderate returns while limiting risk. The beauty of this approach, from a fraudster's perspective, was that it was complex enough that most investors didn't fully understand it, but plausible enough that it seemed legitimate.

The returns Madoff reported were remarkable not for being outrageously high, but for being impossibly *consistent*. Year after year, his fund reported returns between 10 and 12 percent. In good markets and bad, through boom and bust, through the dot-com crash and the 2008 financial crisis, Bernie Madoff's fund just kept delivering. For investors, it seemed like financial magic. For anyone paying close attention, those consistent returns were a massive red flag.

Harry Markopolos, a financial analyst and portfolio manager, certainly noticed. Beginning in 1999, Markopolos repeatedly tried to alert the Securities and Exchange Commission that Madoff's returns were mathematically impossible. He submitted detailed reports in 2000, 2001, 2005, 2007, and 2008, providing extensive evidence that Madoff was running a Ponzi scheme. His analysis showed that the options markets weren't large enough to accommodate the trading Madoff claimed to be doing. The returns were too consistent, too smooth, defying every principle of market volatility.

The SEC investigated Madoff multiple times and found nothing. Or rather, they failed to find what was hiding in plain sight. In a devastating failure of regulatory oversight, the SEC conducted examinations of Madoff's firm in 1992, 2004, 2005, and 2007. Each time, Madoff's charm, reputation, and the complexity of his operation allowed him to deflect serious scrutiny. Investigators would later discover that Madoff had been extraordinarily lucky at times, in one case an SEC examiner failed to verify account statements with the Depository Trust Company, which would have immediately revealed the fraud. In another instance, examiners accepted Madoff's explanations without demanding to see the actual trading records.

The reasons for these failures were manifold. Madoff's reputation insulated him; investigators couldn't believe that a former NASDAQ chairman would be running a Ponzi scheme. The SEC was understaffed and under-resourced, particularly when it came to investigating complex financial products. And Madoff was a masterful manipulator who knew exactly how to talk to regulators, after all he had helped write some of their rules.

The Architecture of Trust

What made Madoff's scheme different from typical Ponzi schemes was the sophisticated social engineering that kept it running for so long. He didn't advertise. He didn't cold-call prospects. Instead, he cultivated an aura of exclusivity that made people desperate to invest with him. Getting into Madoff's fund wasn't about having money, it was about having connections.

Madoff targeted a specific demographic with laser precision: wealthy Jews, particularly within the Boca Raton, Florida, and New York social circuits. He was active in Jewish charities and organizations. He served on boards of nonprofits. He was a generous philanthropist, though of course, he was being generous with other people's money. This wasn't random; it was strategic. By embedding himself in tight-knit communities where trust and personal relationships mattered, Madoff created networks of investors who vouched for each other and for him.

The social dynamics he exploited were powerful. In these communities, investing with Madoff became a status symbol. People didn't just invest their own money; they brought in their friends and family, earning "finder's fees" that made them complicit in recruiting new investors. This created a multi-level marketing structure where victims became unwitting accomplices, each one with a vested interest in believing the fund was legitimate.

Madoff also understood the psychology of his investors. He deliberately kept his operation mysterious. He didn't provide detailed explanations of his strategy. He didn't welcome questions. If investors pushed too hard for information, he would sometimes threaten to return their money, a reverse psychology masterpiece that made people even more eager to stay invested. After all, if he's willing to turn away money, the thinking went, he must be the real deal.

The account statements that Madoff's firm sent out were works of fiction, fabricated on the 17th floor by a small team that included Frank DiPascali, Madoff's chief lieutenant, and a handful of other employees who helped generate fake trade confirmations and statements. These documents showed steady profits, consistent returns, and a level of detail that seemed to confirm actual trading activity. Investors who checked their statements saw their wealth growing year after year. What they didn't know was that there were no actual securities in their accounts. There was no trading. There were simply numbers in a computer and paper statements that meant nothing.

The Victims: From Hollywood to Holocaust Survivors

When the scheme finally collapsed, the breadth of Madoff's victim pool was staggering. He had destroyed lives across a spectrum of wealth and fame. Film director Steven Spielberg lost millions through his charity, the Wunderkinder Foundation. Actor Kevin Bacon and his wife Kyra Sedgwick were victims. Hall of Fame pitcher Sandy Koufax lost a significant portion of his retirement savings. Mort Zuckerman, real estate billionaire and publisher of the New York Daily News, had invested heavily with Madoff.

But the most heartbreaking victims weren't celebrities. They were ordinary people who had entrusted their life savings to Madoff, often through feeder funds or charities that invested with him. Retirees who had worked their entire lives saw their nest eggs vanish overnight. Charities that had grown their endowments through Madoff's "steady returns" suddenly discovered they were bankrupt.

Particularly tragic were the Holocaust survivors who lost everything. The Elie Wiesel Foundation for Humanity, headed by Nobel laureate and Holocaust survivor Elie Wiesel, lost $15.2 million, essentially its entire endowment. Wiesel, who had survived Auschwitz and dedicated his life to bearing witness to the Holocaust, called Madoff "a thief, a scoundrel, a criminal" who had committed "financial murder." The bitter irony that Madoff, himself Jewish, had specifically targeted and destroyed Jewish individuals and institutions added another layer of betrayal to the crime.

The Shapiro family lost everything. Carl Shapiro, a Boston philanthropist who had been friends with Madoff for decades, lost nearly half a billion dollars. Jeffry Picower, a philanthropist and investor, had billions in his Madoff accounts when the fraud was revealed; his widow would later settle with the bankruptcy trustee for $7.2 billion, the largest single forfeiture in American legal history, though her lawyers maintained the Picowers had no knowledge of the fraud.

Then there were the financial institutions that had funneled money to Madoff, acting as "feeder funds" that collected fees for delivering wealthy clients to Bernie's operation. Fairfield Greenwich Group had invested $7.5 billion with Madoff. Banco Santander had invested $3.1 billion of its clients' money. The Tremont Group, Kingate Management, Ascot Partners these funds had performed little to no due diligence, seduced by Madoff's reputation and the steady fees they collected for access to his fund.

Some institutions were complicit; others were merely negligent. But the result was the same: the fraud metastasized through the financial system like cancer, touching far more people than Madoff ever dealt with directly.

The Unraveling

By the fall of 2008, the global financial system was in freefall. Lehman Brothers had collapsed in September. The stock market was plunging. Credit markets were frozen. And wealthy investors, suddenly worried about their portfolios and needing cash to meet margin calls in other investments, began withdrawing money from Madoff's fund.

This is the inevitable crisis point for every Ponzi scheme. Madoff needed new deposits to pay out withdrawals, but in the midst of the financial crisis, new money had stopped coming in. By early December, investors had requested approximately $7 billion in redemptions. Madoff had only a few hundred million dollars available.

The end came quickly. On December 9, 2008, Madoff told his employees he was going to pay out several million dollars in bonuses early, before the end of the year. His sons, suspicious of this unusual move during a financial crisis, confronted him. That's when Madoff confessed to Mark and Andrew that the investment advisory business was a fraud, that he was "finished," that he had "absolutely nothing," and that "it's all just one big lie."

His sons were devastated. They immediately consulted a lawyer, who advised them to report their father to the authorities. On December 11, 2008, FBI agents arrested Bernie Madoff at his Manhattan apartment. His alleged first words to them: "There is no innocent explanation."

The scope of the fraud slowly came into focus. Madoff had reported approximately $65 billion in account balances to his investors. The actual amount of money that had flowed into the scheme over the years was estimated at around $20 billion. The difference represented fictitious gains that had never existed. Of the $20 billion in actual principal, about $11 billion had been paid out to investors over the years as "returns" or withdrawals, leaving a shortfall of roughly $9 billion in actual cash losses.

But the human losses couldn't be measured in dollars alone. At least four people directly connected to the scandal took their own lives. Mark Madoff, Bernie's older son, hanged himself in his Manhattan apartment on December 11, 2010, exactly two years after his father's arrest. He left behind a wife and four children. Andrew Madoff, the younger son, died of cancer in 2014; those close to him believed the stress of the scandal had contributed to his illness. Thierry Magon de la Villehuchet, a French aristocrat and money manager who had lost $1.4 billion of his clients' money in the Madoff fraud, took his own life a month after the scheme's exposure. William Foxton, a British soldier and filmmaker who lost his life savings, also died by suicide.

Justice and Reckoning

Bernie Madoff's trial was brief because there was no trial. He pleaded guilty to eleven federal felonies, including securities fraud, wire fraud, mail fraud, money laundering, and perjury. On June 29, 2009, Judge Denny Chin sentenced him to 150 years in prison, the maximum possible sentence. In his statement, Judge Chin called Madoff's crimes "extraordinarily evil" and noted that the breach of trust was "massive."

Madoff showed little genuine remorse. In his allocution before sentencing, he offered what many felt was a hollow apology: "I am responsible for a great deal of suffering and pain. I understand that." But in later interviews from prison, he would attempt to justify his actions, minimize his guilt, and even blame his victims for being greedy. In a 2011 interview, he claimed that banks and feeder funds "had to know" about the fraud because the returns were too good to be true, an astounding argument that essentially blamed others for not catching him.

His wife Ruth maintained she had known nothing of the fraud, though she agreed to forfeit $80 million in assets, leaving her with $2.5 million. She became estranged from much of her family and lived a quiet, reclusive life after the scandal. Peter Madoff, Bernie's brother and the firm's chief compliance officer, pleaded guilty to conspiracy and falsifying records and was sentenced to 10 years in prison. Frank DiPascali, Madoff's right-hand man who helped execute the fraud for decades, cooperated with prosecutors and pleaded guilty, but died of cancer before sentencing.

Five former Madoff employees, known as the "back office five" were convicted in 2014 of helping to perpetuate the fraud by creating false documents and account statements. They received sentences ranging from 2.5 to 10 years.

The bankruptcy trustee, Irving Picard, began the monumental task of recovering funds for victims. Over the following years, he would recover approximately $14 billion through settlements with feeder funds, clawbacks from investors who had withdrawn more than they had invested (taking out fictitious profits), and deals with financial institutions that had facilitated the fraud. It was one of the most successful asset recovery efforts in history, though many victims would never be made whole.

The Psychology of a Con Man

What kind of person runs a $65 billion fraud for nearly two decades, stealing from friends, family, charities, and Holocaust survivors? The psychological profile of Bernie Madoff has fascinated criminologists and psychologists since his arrest.

Madoff himself alternately presented as remorseful and defiant in prison interviews. He claimed he had been trapped by the fraud, that once he started, he couldn't figure out how to stop without destroying everything he had built. This narrative painted him as a victim of his own success, a rationalization that ignored the daily choice he made to continue stealing.

Some psychologists have suggested Madoff exhibited traits of narcissistic personality disorder which include grandiosity, the sense of entitlement, and the lack of genuine empathy for his victims. Others have noted sociopathic characteristics: the ability to lie convincingly, the charm and charisma he deployed to manipulate people, the complete absence of guilt despite the massive suffering he caused.

What's particularly striking about Madoff is how he compartmentalized his life. He maintained close relationships with his family while destroying their futures. He served on charity boards while stealing from those very organizations. He advised regulators on market integrity while running the largest fraud in financial history. This ability to hold contradictory realities simultaneously, to live a double life without apparent internal conflict, suggests a profound disconnection from normal moral reasoning.

In the end, Bernie Madoff died in federal prison on April 14, 2021, at age 82, from chronic kidney disease. He had served less than 12 years of his 150-year sentence. His death brought a measure of closure for some victims, though many expressed that no punishment could truly address the harm he had caused.

Lessons from the Lie

The Madoff scandal revealed systemic failures that went far beyond one man's criminality. The SEC's repeated inability to uncover the fraud despite numerous warnings exposed deep problems in financial regulation. The willingness of sophisticated financial institutions to invest billions without proper due diligence revealed an industry more interested in fees than fiduciary responsibility. The ease with which Madoff exploited social networks and ethnic communities demonstrated how trust, that most valuable of human bonds, could be weaponized.

Perhaps most troubling was how long the fraud lasted simply because people couldn't believe someone in Madoff's position would be capable of such deception. His reputation became his shield. The legitimacy he had earned through his market-making business and his service to the industry allowed him to steal for decades. It was a master class in how accomplishment in one area can provide cover for criminality in another.

The scandal also illuminated uncomfortable truths about wealth and investing. Many of Madoff's victims weren't naive; they were highly educated, financially sophisticated individuals who should have recognized the warning signs. But greed and the desire for exclusive access clouded judgment. The consistent returns that should have raised red flags were instead points of pride, proof that they were smarter than other investors, that they had access others didn't.

In the cautionary tale of Bernie Madoff, we see what happens when trust is systematically exploited, when regulators fail in their duties, when communities become insular and stop asking hard questions, when the appearance of legitimacy matters more than actual verification. His story is a reminder that in finance, as in life, if something seems too good to be true, it almost certainly is.

The $65 billion lie wasn't just about money. It was about the betrayal of every relationship Madoff had, the destruction of institutions built over generations, and the revelation that even in the highest echelons of finance, fraud can hide in plain sight if the fraudster is charming enough, connected enough, and audacious enough to believe he'll never get caught.

Bernie Madoff proved that fortunes built on lies eventually collapse. The only question is how much damage they'll do before the truth emerges.

Chapter 22

The Crypto Crash - Sam Bankman-Fried and FTX

On November 11, 2022, Sam Bankman-Fried sat in his penthouse apartment in the Bahamas, watching his empire disintegrate in real time. Just days earlier, he had been worth $26 billion on paper, hailed as the savior of cryptocurrency, the industry's most effective ambassador to regulators and the public. He had appeared on magazine covers, testified before Congress, and rubbed shoulders with presidents and prime ministers. His company, FTX, had been valued at $32 billion, making it one of the most successful startups in history, achieving in three years what takes most companies decades.

Now, his exchange was facing a bank run it couldn't survive. Customers were trying to withdraw $6 billion in a single day. FTX didn't have the money. It had never had the money. And in a matter of hours, the world would discover that Sam Bankman-Fried, known universally as SBF had built his cryptocurrency empire on a foundation of fraud that made it functionally indistinguishable from a massive Ponzi scheme.

The collapse of FTX would wipe out $8 billion in customer funds, trigger a cascade of bankruptcies across the crypto industry, destroy the life savings of millions of retail investors, and ultimately send SBF to prison for 25 years. It was the fastest rise and fall of a billionaire in modern history, and a cautionary tale about hype, hubris, and the dangerous intersection of idealism and greed.

The Effective Altruist Who Wanted to Save the World

To understand how Sam Bankman-Fried became both a billionaire and a fraud, you have to start with the philosophy that supposedly motivated everything he did: effective altruism.

Born in 1992 to two Stanford Law School professors, Sam grew up in the rarefied air of academic excellence. His parents, Joseph Bankman and Barbara Fried, were successful legal scholars who emphasized intellectual rigor and social responsibility. Sam was brilliant from an early age, the kind of kid who could solve complex math problems for fun and debate philosophy with graduate students while still in high school.

He attended MIT, studying physics and mathematics, and it was there that he discovered effective altruism, a philosophical movement that would shape his public persona and, ironically, provide cover for his eventual crimes. Effective altruism, popularized by philosopher Peter Singer and others, argues that we have a moral obligation to do the most good possible with our resources. Rather than following our emotional impulses about what feels good to support, we should calculate which interventions save the most lives or reduce the most suffering per dollar spent.

A subset of this philosophy, called "earning to give," suggested that talented individuals could do more good by pursuing high-paying careers in finance and donating large portions of their earnings than by working directly for nonprofits. This idea appealed to Sam. He could make vast amounts of money and be morally righteous about it. Wealth accumulation wasn't greed, it was altruism with a longer time horizon.

After graduating from MIT in 2014, Sam took a job at Jane Street Capital, a quantitative trading firm known for recruiting the brightest mathematical minds. He was good at it, making money by finding small inefficiencies in markets and exploiting them with sophisticated algorithms. But he grew restless. Jane Street was making him wealthy, but not world-changingly wealthy. And for someone who believed he had a moral duty to accumulate as much money as possible to give away, merely being successful wasn't enough.

In 2017, Sam quit Jane Street and founded Alameda Research, a cryptocurrency trading firm, with a small group of fellow effective altruists. The timing was perfect. Cryptocurrency was entering a massive bull market, and the nascent industry was riddled with inefficiencies that a smart quantitative trader could exploit.

Arbitrage, Ambition, and the Birth of an Empire

The trade that made Sam Bankman-Fried his first fortune has become legendary in crypto circles. It was called the "kimchi premium", a pricing inefficiency where Bitcoin traded at significantly higher prices on South Korean exchanges than on American ones, sometimes a difference of 30 percent or more due to capital controls and regulatory barriers.

Sam and his team at Alameda Research would buy Bitcoin in the United States and sell it in South Korea, pocketing the difference. It was arbitrage at its purest, risk-free profit from market inefficiency. At the peak, Alameda was reportedly making $25 million per day from this single trade. Sam's personal wealth exploded. Within months, he had gone from comfortable to genuinely wealthy.

But the kimchi premium eventually closed as markets became more efficient. Sam needed a new edge. In 2019, he founded FTX, a cryptocurrency derivatives exchange that would allow traders to bet on the future price of Bitcoin and other digital assets with enormous leverage. The name stood for "Futures Exchange," though Sam would later joke it sounded like the phonetic spelling of someone saying "fucked."

FTX was designed to be everything the existing crypto exchanges weren't: professional, user-friendly, and appealing to both retail investors and sophisticated institutional traders. While competitors like Binance operated in regulatory gray zones, Sam positioned FTX as the responsible player that would work with regulators rather than against them. He moved the company to Hong Kong, then to the Bahamas, where crypto-friendly regulations made it easier to operate.

The exchange grew explosively. By 2021, FTX was processing billions of dollars in daily trading volume. Sam recruited top engineering talent, offering generous compensation and the chance to work on cutting-edge financial technology. He signed celebrity endorsers, NFL star Tom Brady and his then-wife Gisele Bündchen became investors and ambassadors. Comedian Larry David appeared in a Super Bowl commercial mocking people who doubted crypto, with the tagline "Don't be like Larry." FTX Arena, home of the NBA's Miami Heat, became a gleaming advertisement for the exchange.

Venture capital firms lined up to invest. Sequoia Capital, one of Silicon Valley's most prestigious firms, published a breathless profile of Sam titled "The Next Warren Buffett?" that described him as "a kid in cargo shorts playing video games while on a call" who might "become the world's first trillionaire." SoftBank, Temasek, and BlackRock, the biggest names in finance all wanted a piece of FTX.

By January 2022, FTX was valued at $32 billion. Sam Bankman-Fried, just 29 years old, was worth $26 billion personally. He was the face of cryptocurrency's mainstream acceptance, the genius who would bring digital assets into the traditional financial system. He testified before Congress about crypto regulation. He met with regulators at the SEC and CFTC. He donated tens of millions to political candidates, becoming the second-largest Democratic donor in the 2022 election cycle. He pledged to give away his entire fortune, embodying the effective altruist ideal.

It was all built on fraud.

The House of Cards: How FTX Really Worked

The collapse of FTX revealed a stunning truth: Sam Bankman-Fried had been using customer deposits from FTX to fund risky bets at his trading firm, Alameda Research. This wasn't a one-time mistake or a temporary liquidity issue. It was systematic theft that had been happening from the very beginning, facilitated by code Sam himself had written into FTX's systems.

Here's how the scheme worked: When customers deposited money into FTX, whether dollars, Bitcoin, or other cryptocurrencies, those assets were supposed to remain in their accounts, available for withdrawal at any time. FTX was supposed to be an exchange, a neutral platform that matched buyers and sellers and took a small fee. The company should never have been gambling with customer money.

But Sam had granted Alameda Research special privileges in FTX's code. Alameda had what amounted to an unlimited line of credit. It could borrow customer funds without those customers' knowledge or consent, and these loans didn't show up in the normal risk management systems. While regular users had strict limits on how much they could borrow, Alameda could take billions.

Sam used these customer funds to make increasingly risky bets. Alameda invested in hundreds of startups, many of them dubious crypto projects that would later become worthless. Sam bought a stake in Robinhood, the trading app, for $648 million. He funded political campaigns, donated to pandemic prevention research, and invested in artificial intelligence companies. None of this was done with Alameda's own money or FTX's corporate funds, it was customer money, billions of dollars that customers thought were safely held in their accounts.

The scheme bore an eerie resemblance to Bernie Madoff's fraud, though with a cryptocurrency twist. As long as withdrawals remained manageable and the crypto market kept going up, FTX could maintain the illusion that everything was fine. But the whole structure depended on most customers leaving their money on the exchange most of the time.

Making matters worse, much of Alameda's supposed collateral consisted of FTT, FTX's own exchange token. Sam had created this token out of thin air, given billions of them to Alameda, and then used them as collateral to borrow real assets like Bitcoin and dollars. It was the equivalent of a bank using its own stock as collateral for loans, a circular arrangement that created the illusion of assets backing liabilities when there was nothing solid underneath.

The internal controls at FTX were virtually nonexistent. There was no real board of directors, Sam controlled everything. There was no chief financial officer until late in the company's life, and when one was finally hired, they had little actual authority. Financial records were kept in disarray, sometimes on QuickBooks. The company had no accounting department to speak of. And everyone involved, the executives, the engineers and the lawyers lived together in a penthouse complex in the Bahamas, creating an insular culture where Sam's word was law and questioning the boss was unthinkable.

Life in the Bahamas: Playing Video Games While Rome Burns

The FTX crew lived like a bizarre cross between a startup accelerator and a college dorm. About 30 employees shared a $30 million penthouse complex in the Bahamas, sleeping in bedrooms that opened onto shared living spaces. Sam and his girlfriend, Caroline Ellison, who also happened to be the CEO of Alameda Research, lived there along with engineers, traders, and executives.

The culture was aggressively casual. Sam wore cargo shorts and ratty t-shirts to meetings with billionaires and senators. He was famous for playing League of Legends during important calls and meetings, claiming he could multitask better while gaming. He slept on a beanbag chair in his office. He drove a Toyota Corolla, ate vegan food, and maintained he cared nothing about personal luxury, all the money was for giving away eventually.

This image, the ascetic genius who lived modestly while building an empire was carefully cultivated. In reality, Sam was spending customer money on a $300 million real estate empire in the Bahamas, luxury condos for his executives, and a lifestyle that, while not ostentatiously luxurious, was certainly comfortable. He gave millions to his parents, who used FTX funds to buy a vacation home in the Bahamas.

The effective altruism branding served multiple purposes. It made Sam attractive to idealistic young recruits who wanted to believe they were working for a higher purpose. It provided cover for the extreme wealth accumulation, he wasn't getting rich, he was earning to give. And it gave him credibility with politicians, regulators, and journalists who saw him as different from other crypto entrepreneurs, a responsible actor in a Wild West industry.

Caroline Ellison, the CEO of Alameda, was herself a Stanford math graduate and committed effective altruist. She had worked at Jane Street before joining Alameda. Her relationship with Sam was complicated, romantic at times, professional at others, with power dynamics that made clear boundaries impossible. She would later testify that Sam had directed her to commit fraud, that she had known Alameda was using FTX customer funds, and that she had lied to lenders and investors about Alameda's financial condition at Sam's instruction.

The inner circle also included Gary Wang, a childhood friend of Sam's and FTX's chief technology officer, who had written the code that gave Alameda special privileges. Nishad Singh, the director of engineering, managed much of the FTX codebase and political donations. Ryan Salame ran FTX's Bahamas operations and was the company's primary Republican donor. All of them would eventually plead guilty to fraud charges and cooperate with prosecutors.

The Unraveling: A Twitter Thread Brings Down an Empire

The beginning of the end came from an unlikely source: a Twitter thread. On November 2, 2022, Ian Allison, a reporter for CoinDesk, published an article revealing the contents of Alameda Research's balance sheet. The numbers were shocking. Of Alameda's $14.6 billion in assets, $5.8 billion consisted of FTT tokens, FTX's own cryptocurrency. The revelation suggested that Alameda, and by extension Sam's entire empire, was built on a circular foundation of made-up tokens rather than real assets.

The crypto world erupted. Changpeng Zhao, known as CZ, the CEO of Binance and FTX's primary competitor, announced on Twitter that his exchange would sell its holdings of FTT tokens, worth about $530 million. "Liquidating our FTT," he wrote, due to "recent revelations that have come to light."

The announcement triggered a death spiral. FTT's price began to plummet. As the price fell, Alameda's balance sheet deteriorated, which caused more concern, which caused more people to try to withdraw funds from FTX. Within 24 hours, customers were attempting to withdraw $6 billion, more than FTX had in actual assets.

Sam frantically tried to stop the collapse. He claimed on Twitter that FTX was "fine" and had enough assets to cover all customer withdrawals. He announced that Binance had agreed to acquire FTX, which briefly stemmed the panic. But when Binance's due diligence team actually looked at FTX's books, they found an $8 billion hole in the balance sheet. Binance walked away within 24 hours.

"As a result of corporate due diligence, as well as the latest news reports regarding mishandled customer funds and alleged US agency investigations," Binance announced, "we have decided that we will not pursue the potential acquisition of FTX.com."

Sam was finished. On November 11, 2022, FTX filed for bankruptcy. In the filing, the new CEO, John J. Ray III, who had overseen the liquidation of Enron described FTX as having a "complete failure of corporate controls" and a "complete absence of trustworthy financial information." In 40 years of dealing with corporate bankruptcies, he had "never seen such a complete failure."

From Billionaire to Defendant: The Fall

After FTX's collapse, Sam gave a series of disastrous media interviews where he claimed the whole thing was an accident, that he hadn't realized how much customer money Alameda had borrowed, that he had made mistakes but hadn't committed fraud. He apologized to employees and customers while simultaneously claiming he had done nothing wrong.

It was a baffling PR strategy that only made things worse. Financial records would later show that Sam had known exactly what was happening. He had directed the fraud. He had written the code that enabled it. When Alameda couldn't pay back its loans, Sam had simply taken more customer money to cover the losses.

On December 12, 2022, Sam was arrested in the Bahamas at the request of U.S. prosecutors. He initially fought extradition, then changed his mind and agreed to return to the United States. He was charged with wire fraud, securities fraud, money laundering, and campaign finance violations eight criminal counts that could result in over 100 years in prison.

Released on a $250 million bond secured by his parents' home, Sam spent the next months before trial living with his parents in California. He continued to give interviews, violating his lawyers' advice and potentially undermining his own defense. He contacted potential witnesses, including

Caroline Ellison, in what prosecutors described as an attempt to influence their testimony.

The trial began in October 2023 in Manhattan federal court. Prosecutors presented a devastating case built on testimony from Sam's closest associates. Caroline Ellison, Gary Wang, and Nishad Singh all testified against him, describing in detail how Sam had directed them to use customer funds, lie to lenders and investors, and maintain the fraud even as it spiraled out of control.

Caroline's testimony was particularly damaging. She described Sam as the mastermind who made all major decisions, who had known exactly where the money was going, and who had created the special privileges in FTX's code that allowed Alameda to loot customer funds. She presented spreadsheets showing how they had tried to calculate how much they could borrow before the exchange would collapse. She described Sam's increasing recklessness as the crypto market turned south in 2022, his insistence on making bigger bets to try to recover losses, his assurances that everything would work out.

Sam's defense was that he had made mistakes but hadn't committed fraud, that he had acted in good faith, that the failure was due to poor risk management rather than criminal intent. He took the stand in his own defense, a risky move that allowed prosecutors to cross-examine him. He performed poorly, coming across as evasive and unconvincing when pressed on specific decisions.

The jury deliberated for less than five hours before returning guilty verdicts on all seven counts. On March 28, 2024, Judge Lewis Kaplan sentenced Sam Bankman-Fried to 25 years in federal prison, far less than the 110 years prosecutors had requested but still a devastating sentence for a 32-year-old man.

"There is a risk that this man will be in a position to do something very bad in the future, and it's not a trivial risk," Judge Kaplan said in explaining the sentence. The judge also dismissed Sam's expressions of remorse as insincere, noting that he had shown no genuine acceptance of responsibility.

The Victims: Billions in Losses, Lives Destroyed

The FTX collapse wiped out approximately $8 billion in customer funds. The victims ranged from sophisticated crypto traders to ordinary people who had seen ads during the Super Bowl and thought FTX was a safe place to buy Bitcoin.

Unlike the Madoff scandal where some investors had made money over the years through fictitious returns, most FTX customers were simply out their entire deposits. There had been no fake profits, no steady returns, just immediate and total loss when the exchange collapsed.

Particularly heartbreaking were stories of people who had put their life savings into FTX, trusting the celebrity endorsements and Sam's carefully constructed image as a responsible operator. Teachers, nurses, truck drivers, people who couldn't afford to lose anything but had been seduced by promises of financial freedom through cryptocurrency.

The ripple effects extended throughout the crypto industry. BlockFi, a cryptocurrency lender that had significant exposure to FTX and Alameda, filed for bankruptcy. Genesis Global Capital, another major lender, also collapsed. Voyager Digital, which FTX had been in the process of acquiring, saw its bankruptcy proceedings complicated by FTX's failure. The total damage to the crypto ecosystem was estimated at over $20 billion when accounting for all the cascading bankruptcies.

Celebrities who had endorsed FTX faced lawsuits from investors who claimed they had been deceived. Tom Brady, Gisele Bündchen, Stephen

Curry, Shaquille O'Neal, and others settled with plaintiffs or saw their cases dismissed, but the reputational damage was significant. Larry David's FTX Super Bowl commercial, which had cost $30 million to produce and air, became a symbol of crypto excess and misplaced trust.

Lessons from the Fastest Collapse

The FTX debacle offers multiple lessons about wealth, fraud, and the dangers of hype-driven markets.

First, it demonstrates how quickly fortunes can evaporate in the modern age. Sam went from a net worth of $26 billion to negative wealth, owing billions to victims in less than a week. The speed of the collapse was unprecedented, facilitated by digital systems where bank runs happen at the speed of Twitter rather than the speed of people lining up outside banks.

Second, it shows the danger of ideological cover for greed. The effective altruism branding gave Sam credibility and attracted true believers who wanted to think they were working for a noble cause. The philosophy of "earning to give" provided moral justification for accumulating wealth through any means necessary. But altruistic intentions don't make fraud less fraudulent. Sam wasn't earning to give; he was stealing to spend, and the charitable donations were largely made with stolen money, making them another aspect of the crime rather than a mitigating factor.

Third, the FTX collapse revealed profound regulatory failures. The company had operated in a legal gray zone, conducting billions in transactions with minimal oversight. Regulators at the SEC and CFTC had met with Sam, listened to his proposals for crypto regulation, and treated him as a legitimate industry leader even as he was committing massive fraud. The failure to establish clear rules for cryptocurrency exchanges before they grew to FTX's size allowed the fraud to reach catastrophic proportions.

Fourth, it demonstrated the continued power of celebrity endorsements and social proof in driving investment decisions. Millions of people trusted FTX because Tom Brady and Larry David were in the commercials, because Sequoia Capital had invested, because Sam was testifying before Congress. The appearance of legitimacy mattered more than actual due diligence.

Finally, the case showed how leverage and circular collateral can create financial weapons of mass destruction. FTX and Alameda had used borrowed customer funds to invest in assets including FTT tokens whose value depended on confidence in FTX itself. When confidence evaporated, the whole structure collapsed instantly. It was a reminder that in finance, complex interconnections can turn small problems into existential crises.

The Future of Fraud

The bankruptcy trustee has managed to recover a significant portion of the lost funds by mid-2024, estimates suggested customers might eventually recover 50 to 70 cents on the dollar, far better than many feared initially. This was possible partly because much of the stolen money had been invested in assets that still had some value, and partly because prosecutors had been aggressive in clawing back funds.

But the human costs remain. People lost not just money but faith in an entire asset class. The crypto industry, which had been moving toward mainstream acceptance, suffered a devastating blow to its credibility. And the effective altruism movement had to reckon with how its philosophy had been twisted to justify fraud.

Sam Bankman-Fried now sits in federal prison, his carefully constructed image as a genius philanthropist revealed as a fraud. He went from being compared to Warren Buffett to being mentioned in the same breath as Bernie Madoff in less than a year. His parents, both respected law professors, saw their son become a convicted felon and lost their home to his bond.

The story of SBF and FTX is a very modern cautionary tale about the intersection of technology, finance, and ideology. It shows how quickly fortunes can be built in emerging industries, and how those same fortunes can vanish even faster when they're built on lies. It demonstrates that fraud doesn't require decades of careful deception à la Madoff, in the age of cryptocurrency and social media, you can build a $32 billion company, steal $8 billion, and collapse in spectacular fashion all within three years.

Most importantly, it's a reminder that fundamental principles of finance don't change just because the technology does. Customer funds should be segregated. Companies need real financial controls. Leverage is dangerous. Circular collateral is suicidal. And no amount of idealistic philosophy can transform theft into altruism.

Sam Bankman-Fried wanted to earn billions to give away and do immense good in the world. Instead, he stole billions, destroyed lives, and became a symbol of everything wrong with the crypto boom. His story is less about the technology of cryptocurrency and more about the timeless human capacity for self-deception, hubris, and fraud when billions of dollars are at stake and oversight is absent.

The king of crypto is dead. Long live the lesson.

PART VI: PATTERNS, PRINCIPLES, AND PERSPECTIVES

Chapter 23

The Common Threads of Wealth Creation

After examining the lives of history's most remarkable billionaires, from Mansa Musa's golden caravans crossing the Sahara to Sam Bankman-Fried's cryptocurrency empire collapsing in real time on Twitter, certain patterns emerge with striking clarity. While each fortune has its unique origin story, its particular innovations and circumstances, the paths to extraordinary wealth share common elements that transcend centuries, industries, and continents.

These patterns aren't foolproof formulas. For every Rockefeller who executed them perfectly, there are thousands of equally smart, equally hardworking people who never came close to his wealth. But understanding these common threads helps explain how some individuals accumulate fortunes that dwarf the GDP of entire nations while others, despite talent and effort, remain comfortably middle class or even poor.

What follows isn't a how-to guide for becoming a billionaire, if it were that simple, there would be far more billionaires but rather an analysis of the recurring dynamics that appear again and again in the stories we've explored. Some of these factors are within an individual's control; others are pure chance. Some are admirable; others are morally troubling. Together, they form a complex tapestry that reveals as much about economic systems and historical accidents as it does about individual genius.

Timing and Luck: The Invisible Hand of History

Perhaps the most humbling realization when studying billionaires is how much their success depended on factors completely beyond their control. John D. Rockefeller didn't invent oil, but he was the right age at exactly the right moment when oil was transitioning from a curiosity to the most important commodity on Earth. Born twenty years earlier, he would have been too old to capitalize on the industry's explosive growth. Born twenty years later, he would have faced established competition too entrenched to overcome.

Bill Gates has acknowledged this repeatedly. He was born in 1955, which made him thirteen years old in 1968, the precise moment when access to computers was transitioning from impossible to merely very difficult. His wealthy private school happened to have a computer terminal. His mother happened to serve on a board with IBM's chairman, which helped Microsoft get the meeting that led to the DOS deal. Remove any of these factors, and Gates might have been a successful programmer, but not the world's richest person.

Steve Jobs and Bill Gates were born within months of each other. So were Larry Page and Sergey Brin. The Google founders were the perfect age to be graduate students just as the internet was exploding but before the search engine problem had been solved. Five years earlier, the internet wouldn't have been ready. Five years later, someone else would have already dominated search.

Jeff Bezos started Amazon in 1994, during the narrow window when the internet was becoming accessible to ordinary consumers but before e-commerce was established. His background in quantitative finance gave him the skills to understand the opportunity; his timing gave him the chance to seize it before competitors could react.

Elon Musk's fortune came from being the right age to catch three successive waves: the internet boom (Zip2 and PayPal), the transition to electric vehicles (Tesla), and the commercialization of space (SpaceX). He had the technical background, the risk tolerance, and the timing to ride all three.

Warren Buffett, asked what the biggest factor in his success was, responded: "I won the ovarian lottery." He was born in the United States in

1930, male, white, and wired in a way that made him exceptional at capital allocation in an era when compound interest could work for decades without major disruptions. Change any of those variables, born in a different country, a different era, a different gender in a time when women faced massive barriers and Buffett would have been a different person with different opportunities.

The timing factor extends beyond individual births to broader historical moments. The Rothschild banking empire emerged during an era of constant European wars that required enormous financing. Cornelius Vanderbilt built his fortune during the explosion of American transportation infrastructure. Sam Walton's discount retail model worked because American suburbs were expanding rapidly just as logistics and computing were making sophisticated supply chain management possible.

Even the frauds depended on timing. Bernie Madoff's Ponzi scheme lasted as long as it did partly because it operated during an unprecedented period of economic stability and growth from the 1990s to 2008. Sam Bankman-Fried's fraud was only possible during the cryptocurrency mania when normal due diligence was suspended in favor of hype and speculation.

Timing isn't everything, thousands of people had the same advantages and didn't become billionaires but it's far more important than we usually acknowledge. The right person in the wrong era stays middle class. The wrong person in the right era might stumble into millions. The right person in the right era can build a fortune for the ages.

Monopolistic Tendencies: Winner Takes Most

If there's one pattern that appears in virtually every billionaire's story, it's the drive toward monopoly or near-monopoly. These fortunes weren't built in competitive markets where dozens of roughly equal competitors fought for modest profits. They were built in markets where one player dominated so thoroughly that they could extract extraordinary value.

John D. Rockefeller understood this better than perhaps anyone in history. His famous quote captures it perfectly: "Competition is a sin." He didn't want to compete; he wanted to control. Through Standard Oil, he came to control approximately 90 percent of oil refining in America. This wasn't accidental, it was the explicit goal, achieved through ruthless tactics including predatory pricing, exclusive contracts with railroads, and the systematic acquisition or destruction of competitors.

Andrew Carnegie similarly pursued vertical integration in steel, controlling everything from the iron ore mines to the railroad cars that transported the finished products. By eliminating competition at each stage of production, he could maximize efficiency and minimize costs in ways that competitors couldn't match.

Modern tech billionaires have achieved monopolies through different means but with similar results. Bill Gates built Microsoft into a near-total monopoly in operating systems, which the Department of Justice literally determined was an illegal monopoly in a landmark antitrust case. The company's dominance was so complete that it could dictate terms to hardware manufacturers and software developers alike.

Google controls approximately 90 percent of internet search in most markets. This monopoly isn't maintained through the tactics Rockefeller used, there's no Standard Search buying up competitors and undercutting prices. Instead, it's maintained through network effects: Google's search gets better as more people use it, which makes more people use it, which makes it better, in a self-reinforcing cycle that's nearly impossible for competitors to break.

Facebook (Meta) achieved similar dominance in social networking. When competitors emerged such as Instagram and WhatsApp Mark Zuckerberg simply bought them for billions of dollars, eliminating potential rivals before they could threaten Facebook's core business. When TikTok emerged as a genuine competitor, Zuckerberg couldn't buy it, and Facebook's dominance began to crack.

Amazon pursued a different path to market dominance: accepting losses for years while building infrastructure that competitors couldn't match. By the time Amazon became profitable, it had achieved such scale and efficiency that competing became nearly impossible for most retailers. Jeff Bezos explicitly embraced this strategy, famously saying "your margin is my opportunity", he would sacrifice profit margins to gain market share, knowing that eventual dominance would deliver far greater returns than competing in a fragmented market.

Even in fashion and luxury goods, Bernard Arnault built LVMH into a conglomerate that controls an extraordinary portfolio of the world's most prestigious brands. By owning Louis Vuitton, Christian Dior, Moët & Chandon, and dozens of other luxury brands, LVMH can dominate multiple segments of the luxury market while preventing competitors from gaining scale.

The pattern reveals an uncomfortable truth: extreme wealth is rarely created in truly competitive markets. It's created when competition is eliminated, minimized, or prevented from emerging. This can happen through better products and innovation. Google really did have a better search engine but it's maintained through network effects, strategic acquisitions, and barriers to entry that prevent competitors from catching up.

Society has a complex relationship with this reality. We celebrate entrepreneurship and innovation, but the most successful entrepreneurs are often those who most effectively eliminate competition. We have antitrust laws designed to prevent monopolies, but we also have patent systems designed to grant temporary monopolies to encourage innovation. The tension between competition and monopoly lies at the heart of how billionaire fortunes are created.

Innovation Versus Execution: What Really Matters?

The mythology of billionaire wealth often emphasizes innovation, the brilliant inventor who creates something the world has never seen. The reality is more complex. Some billionaires were genuinely revolutionary innovators. Others were exceptional executors who took existing ideas and implemented them better than anyone else. Most were some combination of both.

Henry Ford didn't invent the automobile or even the assembly line. But he understood better than anyone how to apply assembly line principles to automobile manufacturing at scale, and he had the vision to realize that making cars affordable would create a mass market. His innovation was in execution and business model design rather than pure invention.

Steve Jobs is celebrated as an innovator, but he rarely invented anything from scratch. The graphical user interface was developed at Xerox PARC; Jobs saw it, understood its potential, and executed it brilliantly with the Macintosh. The iPod wasn't the first MP3 player, the iPhone wasn't the first smartphone, and the iPad wasn't the first tablet. Jobs's genius was in understanding what customers wanted before they knew they wanted it, and executing those visions with obsessive attention to design and user experience.

Sam Walton didn't invent discount retail. Competitors like Kmart existed before Walmart. Walton's innovation was in execution: supply chain management, distribution center locations, data-driven inventory control, and a fanatical focus on cost reduction. He took the discount retail concept and executed it better than anyone else, particularly in small-town markets that competitors had ignored.

Jeff Bezos didn't invent online retail, other internet bookstores existed when Amazon launched. His innovation was in scale, customer obsession, and long-term thinking. He was willing to lose money for years to build infrastructure and customer loyalty, betting that dominance would eventually deliver massive returns. He was right.

Conversely, some genuine inventors never became wealthy because they couldn't execute. Nikola Tesla invented revolutionary electrical systems but died in poverty because he lacked business acumen and the ability to commercialize his inventions. Xerox PARC invented much of modern computing, the graphical interface, the mouse, ethernet networking but Xerox failed to commercialize these inventions, allowing Apple, Microsoft, and others to build fortunes on PARC's innovations.

The pattern suggests that execution matters more than pure innovation in wealth creation. The person who takes an existing idea and implements it at scale, with better design, better marketing, better operations, or better business model innovation, often captures more value than the original inventor.

This creates a troubling dynamic in how we allocate credit and rewards. Society grants patents to inventors but often the real wealth goes to executors and scalers. We celebrate innovation in the abstract but the market rewards execution in practice.

Leverage: Multiplying Individual Effort

No one becomes a billionaire through their own labor alone. The math doesn't work. Even at $10,000 per hour, working every hour of every day would take over a century to earn a billion dollars. Billionaire fortunes come from leverage, using other people's money, other people's time, other people's ideas, or other people's infrastructure to multiply the impact of individual effort.

The Rothschild banking dynasty understood financial leverage: using depositors' money to fund large loans, collecting interest on the spread between what they paid depositors and what borrowers paid them. They didn't lend their own wealth; they intermediated other people's wealth and took a cut of every transaction.

Rockefeller leveraged capital by borrowing extensively to build Standard Oil. His genius was in understanding that controlling the infrastructure of oil, the refineries, the pipelines, the distribution was worth going deeply into debt. Once he controlled that infrastructure, it generated so much cash that the debt was irrelevant.

Carnegie mastered labor leverage. His steel mills employed thousands of workers. He captured the value they created while paying them wages. By constantly improving efficiency and pushing workers harder, he extracted more value from the same labor force. The massive steel fortunes came not from Carnegie's personal work but from his ability to organize and extract value from thousands of workers' efforts.

Modern tech billionaires leverage technology and network effects in ways that previous generations couldn't imagine. Mark Zuckerberg didn't become wealthy by personally connecting people, he created a platform where billions of people connect themselves. His wealth comes from capturing a tiny fraction of the value generated by billions of users who create content, view ads, and generate data that Facebook monetizes.

Jeff Bezos leveraged infrastructure investment in ways that multiplied its value. Amazon Web Services started as internal infrastructure to support Amazon's e-commerce operation. By opening it to other companies, Bezos leveraged the same servers, the same data centers, the same engineering effort across thousands of customers. The infrastructure investment got reused and monetized in multiple ways simultaneously.

Warren Buffett's entire fortune comes from financial leverage. He uses float from Berkshire Hathaway's insurance operations, money that's been paid in premiums but not yet paid out in claims to invest in stocks and businesses. He's essentially investing other people's money while keeping the returns. Over decades, with compound interest, this leverage creates exponential wealth growth.

Even fraudsters like Madoff and Bankman-Fried understood leverage, though they used it criminally. Madoff leveraged his reputation to attract deposits he could steal. SBF leveraged customer deposits at FTX to make risky bets at Alameda Research. Both understood that controlling other people's money was the path to extraordinary wealth, though they crossed the line from legitimate leverage to criminal theft.

The leverage principle reveals why working harder or being smarter individually doesn't create billionaire wealth. A brilliant lawyer or doctor might earn millions annually, but they're selling their own time and expertise. They're linearly constrained by hours in the day. Billionaires build systems that work while they sleep, that employ thousands, that leverage millions of customers or users, that compound value over time through ownership rather than labor.

Network Effects and Winner-Take-All Economics

Some markets naturally tend toward monopoly through network effects, dynamics where a product or service becomes more valuable as more people use it. These markets produce winner-take-all or winner-take-most outcomes where one or two players capture extraordinary value while everyone else struggles.

The telephone network was an early example. One phone is useless; two phones have limited value; but each additional phone makes the entire network more valuable to every user. This dynamic meant the first company to build a large network had an almost insurmountable advantage. New competitors couldn't offer the same value unless they already had a large network, but they couldn't build a large network unless they could offer value. It's a chicken-and-egg problem that creates natural monopolies.

Modern tech platforms have taken network effects to unprecedented levels. Facebook is valuable because your friends are there. Each additional user makes the platform more valuable to existing users, which attracts more users, which makes it more valuable, in a self-reinforcing cycle. Competitors face the challenge that even with a superior product, they can't offer the same value without the network of users and users won't switch without their friends switching, creating inertia that protects the incumbent.

Google's search engine benefited from a different kind of network effect. Each search query and click provides data that helps Google improve its algorithms. More users mean more data, which means better search results, which attracts more users. Competitors face the problem that even if they build a technically equivalent search engine, they lack the data to make it as good as Google's.

Amazon's marketplace exhibits network effects between buyers and sellers. More buyers attract more sellers, and more sellers attract more buyers. Each side makes the platform more valuable to the other side. This dynamic has allowed Amazon to dominate online retail in a way that would be impossible in a traditional retail environment.

These dynamics explain why tech billionaires' fortunes have grown so enormous in recent decades. Winner-take-all markets, combined with global scale through the internet, mean that the winner can capture value from billions of users. Zuckerberg doesn't just dominate social networking in America; Facebook operates globally, connecting over three billion users. That scale, combined with network effects that prevent competitors from emerging, creates wealth on a level that Rockefeller could never have imagined.

The network effects principle also explains why timing matters so much in tech. The first company to build a critical mass of users in a network effects business can become nearly unassailable. Google wasn't the first search engine, but it was the first to achieve a dominant scale just as internet usage was exploding. Facebook wasn't the first social network, but it was first to achieve global scale with a design that maximized network effects.

Understanding network effects also reveals why some industries produce billionaires while others don't. Restaurants, haircuts, and many service businesses have limited network effects. Each additional customer doesn't make the service more valuable to existing customers. These businesses can be successful and profitable, but they rarely produce billionaire founders because they lack the winner-take-all dynamics that create extreme wealth concentration.

The Role of Government: Contracts, Regulations, and Protection

Behind nearly every great fortune lies a complex relationship with government power. Sometimes it's through contracts that direct public funds to private hands. Sometimes it's through regulations that create barriers to entry protecting incumbents. Sometimes it's through intellectual property protections that grant monopolies. Sometimes it's through the absence of regulation allowing practices that would later be prohibited.

The Rothschild fortune was built on government financing. European governments needed massive loans to fund wars, and the Rothschilds became the preferred lenders, extracting wealth from public treasuries through interest payments. Their banking network, which transcended national boundaries, made them uniquely positioned to finance governments that couldn't trust banks in rival nations.

Cornelius Vanderbilt built his shipping empire partly through government mail contracts that guaranteed revenue. His railroad empire benefited from government land grants and subsidies that made railroad construction financially viable. Without government support, many of these railroads would never have been built, or would have been built by competitors who received the subsidies.

John D. Rockefeller's Standard Oil benefited from favorable railroad rebate arrangements that were technically legal but gave him systematic advantages over competitors. When the government eventually moved against him through antitrust action, the breakup of Standard Oil actually increased his wealth, the separate companies were worth more than the whole.

Howard Hughes built much of his fortune on defense contracts. His aircraft companies received massive government funding during World War II and the Cold War. The lines between his business interests and government spending became so blurred that it was difficult to determine where one ended and the other began.

Modern tech companies have complex relationships with government power. Amazon built AWS partly on CIA contracts. Google's founders received government research grants that funded their early search engine development. SpaceX exists largely because NASA needed alternatives to Russian rockets and provided contracts that kept the company alive during its near-bankruptcy period.

Intellectual property protection, patents, copyrights and trademarks represent government-granted monopolies that create enormous wealth. Pharmaceutical billionaires' fortunes rest on patent protections that prevent competitors from copying their drugs. Software billionaires benefit from copyright protections. Brand-based luxury goods empires depend on trademark protections.

Sometimes the government role is through the absence of regulation. The robber barons of the Gilded Age accumulated wealth partly because labor laws, environmental regulations, and workplace safety requirements didn't exist. They could work children in dangerous conditions, pollute freely, and crush unions without legal consequences. When these regulations were eventually imposed, they reduced profitability and made it harder for new robber barons to emerge.

The cryptocurrency boom that created Sam Bankman-Fried's fortune happened partly in a regulatory gap. Cryptocurrencies weren't clearly securities, commodities, or currencies, and this ambiguity allowed exchanges like FTX to operate with minimal oversight. When regulation eventually catches up, as it inevitably will, the era of crypto billionaires built on regulatory arbitrage will likely end.

The relationship between government and wealth creation is complex and often uncomfortable. We celebrate private sector innovation and entrepreneurship, but most great fortunes have been built with significant government support, protection, or advantageous regulation. The completely self-made billionaire, succeeding purely through private sector activity without any government involvement, is largely mythological.

This doesn't diminish the achievement, building a fortune still requires exceptional execution but it should temper the narrative that billionaires succeeded entirely through their own efforts without public support or favorable policy environments.

The Synthesis: Why These Patterns Matter

Understanding these common threads doesn't provide a formula for creating billionaire wealth, if it did, we'd have far more billionaires. The patterns are necessary but not sufficient conditions. Thousands of people have the right timing, work in potentially monopolistic industries, understand leverage, and operate in favorable regulatory environments without ever becoming wealthy.

What separates billionaires from the merely successful is usually some combination of exceptional execution, risk tolerance, obsessiveness, and luck. But the patterns reveal important truths about how wealth is created in capitalist economies.

First, they show that extreme wealth accumulation isn't primarily about working harder or being smarter. It's about being in the right place at the right time with the right product in an industry with the right economic dynamics. Individual characteristics matter, but context and structure matter more.

Second, they reveal that billionaire wealth is often created by dynamics that are socially or economically problematic, monopolies, exploitation of labor or resources, regulatory capture, or timing luck. This doesn't make all billionaires bad people, but it complicates the narrative that their wealth represents pure merit or social contribution.

Third, they explain why wealth inequality has increased so dramatically in recent decades. Network effects, global scale, and winner-take-all economics mean that modern billionaires can accumulate wealth on a scale that previous generations couldn't approach. When one company can serve billions of customers with minimal additional cost, the owner can capture value in ways that a 19th-century industrialist, constrained by physical geography and manufacturing costs, never could.

Finally, these patterns suggest that if we want different outcomes, less wealth concentration, more broadly shared prosperity we need to think structurally about economic dynamics rather than focusing solely on individual behavior. Changing tax rates might redistribute some wealth, but it doesn't change the underlying dynamics that create extreme wealth concentration in the first place.

The common threads of billionaire wealth creation reveal as much about our economic systems and historical moments as they do about individual billionaires. They show us that extreme wealth is created at the intersection of individual agency and structural forces far beyond any individual's control. Understanding these patterns doesn't tell us how to become billionaires, but it does help us understand the world we live in and potentially how to reshape it.

Chapter 24

What Money Can and Cannot Buy

When J. Paul Getty died in 1976, he was worth approximately $6 billion, one of the richest men in the world. He died alone in his mansion at Sutton Place in England, estranged from most of his family, having outlived four of his five sons. His legacy was a bitter mix of artistic patronage through the Getty Museum and family dysfunction so severe that it became legendary. One of his grandsons had been kidnapped and Getty had refused to pay the ransom until the kidnappers cut off the boy's ear and mailed it to a newspaper. His explanation for this decision was that paying one ransom would encourage the kidnapping of his other grandchildren. His life was a stark illustration of a fundamental truth: money can buy almost anything, but the things it cannot buy are often the things that matter most.

The relationship between wealth and wellbeing is one of the most studied and least understood aspects of human psychology. Billionaires themselves often express confusion about what their wealth has actually delivered. Some claim money bought them freedom and opportunity; others describe it as a burden or a curse. The truth, as revealed through examining the lives we've explored, is complex and often paradoxical.

The Happiness Plateau: Money and Wellbeing

For decades, researchers have tried to quantify the relationship between income and happiness. The results consistently show a pattern that billionaires exemplify in extreme form: money dramatically improves quality of life up to a certain point, then additional wealth produces diminishing and eventually negligible returns on happiness.

The famous "happiness plateau" research, popularized by Daniel Kahneman's work showing that emotional wellbeing stops increasing around $75,000 in annual income (in 2010 dollars), has been both confirmed and challenged by subsequent studies. More recent research suggests the picture is more nuanced, life satisfaction continues to increase with income even at high levels, but emotional wellbeing and day-to-day happiness plateau much earlier.

What this means in practical terms: the difference in quality of life between someone making $30,000 and someone making $300,000 is enormous. Access to healthcare, housing security, ability to handle emergencies, reduction in daily stress, these improvements are dramatic and life-changing. But the difference in quality of life between someone worth $300 million and someone worth $30 billion is far less significant than the thousand-fold difference in wealth would suggest.

Warren Buffett has lived in the same modest house in Omaha, Nebraska, since 1958. He bought it for $31,500. Today he's worth over $100 billion. His daily life, the activities he enjoys, the food he eats and the relationships he values wouldn't meaningfully improve if his wealth doubled or tripled. The additional billions literally don't matter to his quality of life.

Sam Walton, founder of Walmart and one of the richest men in America at his death, famously drove a pickup truck and cut his own hair at the local barbershop. When asked why he didn't live more lavishly, he said he already had everything he wanted. More money wouldn't have improved his life because he'd already exceeded the point where additional consumption added value.

Conversely, some billionaires pursue lavish lifestyles that seem designed to find uses for their wealth rather than emerging from genuine preferences. Larry Ellison's collection of mansions, yachts, and even Hawaiian islands represents spending that seems motivated more by competition with other billionaires than by actual utility. Does owning 98% of the island of Lanai make him happier than owning a very nice estate? The research suggests probably not, at least not proportionally to the cost difference.

The pattern reveals that beyond a certain threshold, wealth accumulation becomes divorced from wellbeing improvement. Yet many billionaires continue accumulating wealth long after reaching this threshold. They're not pursuing happiness through consumption, they're pursuing something else entirely. For some, it's keeping score in a competitive game where wealth is the metric. For others, it's about power, legacy, or simply the enjoyment of the game itself. The money becomes an abstraction, points on a scoreboard, rather than something connected to lived experience.

Health Money Can Buy Versus Health It Cannot

If money could buy health and longevity proportional to wealth, billionaires would live decades longer than everyone else. The reality is more limited. Money can buy excellent healthcare, but it cannot buy immunity from disease, accidents, or mortality.

Steve Jobs was worth approximately $10 billion when he was diagnosed with pancreatic cancer in 2003. He had access to the best oncologists in the world, experimental treatments, cutting-edge medicine. He lived eight years after diagnosis, longer than many pancreatic cancer patients. But the disease still killed him at age 56. His billions bought him additional time and comfort, but they couldn't save his life.

Paul Allen, Microsoft co-founder and billionaire, died from complications of non-Hodgkin's lymphoma in 2018 despite access to unlimited medical resources. David Koch, the billionaire industrialist, died from prostate cancer in 2019 after a decades-long battle that his fortune couldn't win. Mortality remains the ultimate equalizer.

Money can buy better healthcare, early detection, experimental treatments, and the time to focus on health without financial stress. Studies show that wealthy individuals do live longer on average in the United States, the richest 1% live approximately 10-15 years longer than the poorest 1%. But within the wealthy category, the difference between being very rich and ultra-rich has minimal impact on longevity.

Howard Hughes, one of the richest men in the world, descended into severe mental illness and obsessive-compulsive disorder that his wealth couldn't prevent or cure. He spent his final years isolated in hotel rooms, paranoid, consuming only specific foods, refusing medical treatment from anyone he didn't trust. His billions bought him the ability to indulge his compulsions and avoid forced treatment, but they couldn't buy mental health.

The psychological aspects of health are particularly resistant to money's influence. Depression, anxiety, addiction, and personality disorders affect billionaires at rates that don't appear dramatically different from the general population. If anything, the isolation and pressure that can come with extreme wealth may worsen some mental health conditions.

Bernie Madoff's sons both suffered enormously from their father's crimes. Mark Madoff struggled with depression and anxiety before taking his own life. Andrew Madoff developed cancer that family members believed was stress-related. Their family's wealth, legitimate before Bernie's fraud was revealed, couldn't protect them from these tragedies.

What money does buy in health is peace of mind about medical costs, access to convenience and comfort in treatment, and the ability to try every available option without financial constraint. A billionaire with cancer doesn't worry about medical bankruptcy, can travel to any specialist, can try experimental treatments. But the fundamental vulnerability of the human body to disease and the inevitability of death remain unchanged regardless of net worth.

Relationships and the Wealth Barrier

Perhaps nothing reveals the limits of money more clearly than its impact on personal relationships. Extreme wealth creates power imbalances, trust issues, and social isolation that make authentic relationships extraordinarily difficult.

J. Paul Getty's five marriages all ended in divorce. His relationships with his sons were strained or broken. When his grandson was kidnapped, Getty's first instinct was suspicion that it might be a hoax designed to extract money from him. This wasn't paranoia, it was the learned response of someone who knew that his wealth made him a target and that people's motivations around him were inevitably complicated by his fortune.

Larry Ellison has been married and divorced four times. His wealth and personality made lasting partnership difficult. When relationships are complicated by enormous wealth disparities, it's nearly impossible to know whether affection is genuine or influenced by financial considerations.

Elon Musk has had multiple high-profile relationships that ended badly, often played out in public view. His wealth and fame make normal relationship development nearly impossible. Every potential partner comes with questions: Are they attracted to him or his fortune? Would this relationship exist without the billions?

The trust problem cuts both ways. Billionaires must constantly wonder whether people like them for themselves or for their money. But the people in relationships with billionaires face their own challenges, power imbalances can make genuine partnership difficult. When one person can solve any problem with money while the other cannot, traditional relationship dynamics become distorted.

Warren Buffett's first marriage, to Susan Buffett, was by many accounts successful but unconventional. Susan eventually moved out of their shared home, and Warren lived with another woman, Astrid Menks, while remaining married to Susan. After Susan's death, Warren married Astrid. The arrangement worked for them, but it illustrated how wealth can enable unconventional relationship structures that might not be possible for people with normal financial constraints.

The children of billionaires face their own relationship challenges. They grow up knowing that their wealth makes them targets for opportunists and that they can never be entirely sure whether friends like them for themselves. Andrew Carnegie recognized this problem and wrote extensively about how inherited wealth could corrupt character and work ethic. Many billionaires struggle with how much wealth to pass to children and how much to give away, trying to balance providing for the family with the concern that too much money will harm their children's development.

Mark Zuckerberg married Priscilla Chan before Facebook made him fabulously wealthy, which likely contributed to the relationship's stability. They met in college and married in 2012, when Facebook was successful but before Zuckerberg reached his current level of wealth. Having a partnership that predates extreme wealth can provide a foundation of trust that's difficult to establish afterward.

The isolation that comes with extreme wealth can be profound. Bill Gates described the loneliness of being ultra-wealthy, noting that there are only a few dozen people in the world who truly understand what it's like to operate at that level of wealth and visibility. Ordinary social connections become complicated by fame and fortune. Even well-meaning interactions carry undercurrents of the wealth differential.

The Isolation of Extreme Wealth

Beyond romantic relationships, billionaires often describe a fundamental isolation that comes with their position. Their daily lives are so different from normal human experience that shared understanding becomes difficult.

Howard Hughes's final years represent the extreme end of wealth-induced isolation. He spent years in darkened hotel rooms, communicating with the outside world primarily through a small circle of handlers, paranoid about germs and increasingly disconnected from reality. His wealth enabled this isolation, he could afford to recreate his environment exactly as he wanted, to avoid people, to control his surroundings completely. A person without money facing similar mental health challenges would have been forced into treatment or into contact with the real world. Hughes's billions gave him the ability to descend into complete isolation.

Even billionaires who remain socially connected describe challenges. They move in different circles than they did before wealth. Their concerns, philanthropy strategy, wealth management, and legacy planning have little in common with the concerns of ordinary people dealing with mortgages, car payments, and saving for retirement. The shared experiences that form the basis of friendship become harder to find.

Security concerns create another layer of isolation. Billionaires often require security details that change the nature of public interaction. Spontaneity becomes difficult. Going to a restaurant, attending an event, or traveling requires planning and creates a barrier between the billionaire and normal social experience.

Their time becomes a scarce resource that people want access to, which makes every interaction potentially transactional. Jeff Bezos can't just grab coffee with someone without wondering whether they want something from him. Every conversation with a new person comes with the question of what they're really after.

The children of billionaires often grow up isolated in ways that can damage their development. They attend exclusive schools, live in gated communities, and interact primarily with other wealthy families. This can create a bubble that prevents normal social development and understanding of how most people live.

Some billionaires actively fight against this isolation. Warren Buffett's decision to remain in Omaha rather than moving to New York or San Francisco was partly about staying grounded in a community where people knew him before he was wealthy. Bill Gates and Melinda French Gates tried to raise their children with relatively normal experiences despite their wealth.

But the isolation is fundamentally difficult to overcome. The differences in experience, concerns, and daily life between billionaires and ordinary people are so vast that bridging them requires conscious, sustained effort that many billionaires don't make or can't maintain.

Meaning, Purpose, and the Philanthropic Turn

Given the limits of what money can buy in terms of happiness, health, and relationships, it's perhaps not surprising that many billionaires turn to philanthropy as a source of meaning and purpose. When consumption no longer delivers satisfaction and relationship building is complicated by wealth, many turn to trying to improve the world.

Andrew Carnegie articulated this most explicitly in his essay "The Gospel of Wealth," arguing that the rich have a moral obligation to use their fortunes for public benefit. He believed that dying rich was dying disgraced. After selling Carnegie Steel for $480 million in 1901, he spent the remainder of his life giving away his fortune, funding libraries, universities, and peace initiatives.

John D. Rockefeller underwent a similar transformation. Early in his career, he was arguably the most hated man in America, a robber baron whose ruthless business practices crushed competitors and created a monopoly. But he became one of history's greatest philanthropists, giving away the equivalent of over $10 billion in today's money to medicine, education, and scientific research. His foundations helped eradicate hookworm, funded medical schools, and advanced scientific knowledge.

Bill Gates's transformation from ruthless monopolist to beloved philanthropist followed a similar arc. As Microsoft's CEO, he was widely criticized for aggressive competitive practices and was literally found guilty of monopolistic behavior. But through the Bill & Melinda Gates Foundation, he became a force for fighting disease, improving education, and addressing global poverty. The foundation has given away tens of billions of dollars and is credited with saving millions of lives through vaccination programs and disease eradication efforts.

Warren Buffett pledged to give away 99% of his wealth, primarily through the Gates Foundation and his children's foundations. He decided that accumulating wealth beyond what his family needed was only worthwhile if that wealth would eventually benefit society. His "giving while living" philosophy encouraged other billionaires to give away their fortunes during their lifetimes rather than waiting until death.

The Giving Pledge, created by Gates and Buffett, has gotten commitments from hundreds of billionaires to give away at least half their wealth to philanthropy. Mark Zuckerberg and Priscilla Chan pledged to give away 99% of their Facebook shares over their lifetimes. MacKenzie Scott, Jeff Bezos's ex-wife, has given away billions at an unprecedented pace, often donating to organizations without restrictions or lengthy application processes.

But philanthropy as a source of meaning raises complex questions. Is it genuine altruism or is it legacy management, reputation laundering, or ego gratification? Critics argue that billionaire philanthropy gives wealthy individuals outsized influence over public policy and social priorities. Why should Bill Gates decide global health priorities? Why should Mark Zuckerberg shape education policy through his donations?

The tax benefits of philanthropy also complicate the picture. Donations are tax-deductible, which means billionaires can direct how their wealth is used while reducing their tax burden. They maintain control while getting credit for generosity. Foundations can hold wealth indefinitely, providing employment for family members and allowing the billionaire's priorities to shape society long after their death.

Some billionaires describe their philanthropy as the most meaningful work of their lives. Gates has said he finds his foundation work more satisfying than his Microsoft career. The ability to tackle major problems, disease, poverty and climate change with significant resources provides a sense of purpose that consumption never could.

But others question whether philanthropy fills the void effectively. Does funding malaria prevention deliver the same deep satisfaction as intimate relationships, creative work, or spiritual practice? Can meaning be purchased through charitable giving or does it require something money can't buy?

The Burden of Deciding What to Do With Billions

There's a less-discussed challenge that faces billionaires: the cognitive and emotional burden of deciding what to do with more money than can be meaningfully spent.

MacKenzie Scott has written about the difficulty of giving away money responsibly. With tens of billions to distribute, how do you choose between worthy causes? How do you evaluate effectiveness? How do you avoid creating dependency or unintended consequences? She's addressed this partly by giving away money faster and with fewer restrictions than traditional philanthropy, but she's also acknowledged the weight of these decisions.

The responsibilities that come with extreme wealth can be crushing. Every decision about resource allocation becomes momentous. Choosing one cause means not choosing another. Funding one organization means not funding its competitors. And the scale of billionaire philanthropy means these choices have enormous consequences for real people and communities.

Some billionaires essentially give up on trying to spend or give away their wealth during their lifetimes. They accumulate it, manage it, and leave the problem to their heirs or to foundations that will exist after their death. This approach avoids the burden of decision-making but also means the wealth compounds faster than it's distributed, leaving the problem to future generations.

The question "what should I do with this money?" haunts many billionaires. Unlike the question "how do I earn enough to be comfortable?" which has clear answers, the question of what to do with billions has no obvious solution. Consumption stops being satisfying. Accumulation becomes meaningless. Philanthropy is complex and fraught. The burden of choice, ironically, becomes its own form of suffering.

What Money Actually Delivers

After examining what money can and cannot buy through the lives of billionaires, several patterns emerge about what extreme wealth actually delivers:

Freedom is perhaps money's greatest gift. Billionaires have complete freedom in how they spend their time. They never need to do anything for purely financial reasons. They can pursue interests, build companies, or give to causes without constraint. This freedom is genuinely valuable and might be the clearest benefit of extreme wealth.

Security is another real benefit. Billionaires never worry about medical bills, emergencies, or financial ruin. Their families are provided for. This peace of mind is psychologically valuable even if it doesn't guarantee happiness.

Power and influence come with great wealth. Billionaires can shape markets, influence politics, fund research, and affect the lives of millions. For those who value impact and legacy, this is meaningful.

Options and convenience improve quality of life in concrete ways. Private jets eliminate travel hassles. Staff handle tedious tasks. Problems that money can solve get solved immediately. These conveniences are real even if they don't dramatically increase happiness.

But money does not deliver:

Authentic relationships become harder, not easier, with extreme wealth. Trust, genuine affection, and equal partnership are complicated by wealth disparities.

Health and longevity improve with wealth but only up to a point. Billionaires get sick, suffer mental health problems, and die like everyone else.

Meaning and purpose cannot be purchased. They must be created through work, relationships, creativity, or service, and having more money doesn't necessarily make this easier.

Happiness increases with wealth up to a point, then plateaus. Additional billions beyond what's needed for security and freedom add little to life satisfaction.

Immunity from suffering doesn't exist at any price. Billionaires experience loss, grief, anxiety, and existential questions just like everyone else.

The lives of billionaires reveal that money is a powerful tool that solves specific problems brilliantly while leaving the deepest human challenges untouched. It can buy comfort but not contentment, security but not serenity, options but not answers. The tragedy of some billionaires' lives is that they spent decades accumulating wealth in the belief that it would solve problems it was never capable of addressing.

The wisest billionaires seem to be those who figured out early that money was not the point, it was a tool to enable freedom, security, and the ability to do meaningful work. They pursued wealth strategically but didn't confuse it with wellbeing. They maintained relationships formed before wealth, stayed connected to communities and activities they genuinely enjoyed, and used their resources to tackle problems they cared about.

The question "is it worth it?" haunts many billionaire stories. Was the sacrifice of time, relationships, and sometimes health worth the fortune accumulated? The answer seems to depend less on the size of the fortune and more on what was preserved or lost along the way. A billionaire who maintained loving relationships, good health, and a sense of purpose seems to have won the game. One who sacrificed everything for wealth and discovered too late that money couldn't buy what mattered most becomes a cautionary tale regardless of how many billions they accumulated.

In the end, money is like any other powerful tool. In the right hands, used for the right purposes, it can accomplish remarkable things and enable a good life. But it's not a substitute for the fundamental sources of human wellbeing: meaningful work, loving relationships, good health, and a sense of purpose. The billionaires who understood this distinction seem to have lived well. Those who didn't often discovered, too late, that they'd been climbing the wrong mountain all along.

Chapter 25

The Future of Billionaires

In 2021, Elon Musk's net worth briefly exceeded $300 billion, making him not just the richest person alive but potentially on a trajectory toward becoming the world's first trillionaire. The milestone seemed almost inevitable if current trends continued, if Tesla's stock maintained its momentum, if SpaceX achieved its ambitions, someone would eventually reach a trillion-dollar net worth. The question wasn't if, but when and who.

Yet by 2022, Musk's wealth had dropped by nearly $200 billion, the largest one-year decline in history, reminding everyone that paper wealth in volatile stocks is not the same as actual cash. The near-miss with the trillion-dollar threshold raised profound questions: Will we see trillionaires? Should they exist? What does the future hold for extreme wealth concentration? And what new frontiers might create the next generation of billionaires?

The answers to these questions will shape not just individual fortunes but the structure of our economies, the stability of our societies, and the future of humanity itself. We stand at a unique moment in history where the forces that create billionaires are accelerating while simultaneously facing political, social, and technological challenges that could fundamentally reshape how wealth is created and distributed.

The Path to a Trillion: Is It Inevitable?

The mathematics of reaching a trillion dollars in net worth are both simple and daunting. If Jeff Bezos's wealth grows at 10% annually from a base of $150 billion, he'd reach a trillion in about 20 years. If an AI or biotech company achieves the kind of monopolistic dominance that Google achieved in search, but in an even larger market, its founder could theoretically hit a trillion within a decade or two.

Several factors suggest trillionaires are possible, perhaps even likely:

Market concentration continues to increase. Winner-take-all dynamics driven by network effects show no signs of weakening. The companies dominating their sectors, Apple, Microsoft, Amazon, Google and Meta have achieved market power that would have been unthinkable a generation ago. If this trend continues, the founders and major shareholders of the next dominant platform could reach trillion-dollar valuations.

Global markets mean global scale. A successful product can now reach billions of customers almost instantaneously. When Facebook launched, it could only grow as fast as it could physically acquire servers and users. Today's platforms can scale faster, reaching global audiences in months rather than years. This compression of time-to-scale could compress time-to-trillion.

Asset inflation creates paper wealth rapidly. Tesla made Musk the richest person not because the company was the most profitable, but because investors bid up the stock price based on future expectations. In an environment where central banks have kept interest rates low and money supply growing, asset prices have inflated dramatically. This dynamic could push paper net worth to a trillion even without proportional real wealth creation.

Compound growth is exponential. For those already at $100-200 billion, the mathematics of compound returns mean that even modest annual growth rates produce astronomical absolute increases. A 10% return on $150 billion is $15 billion, more than most people's entire net worth in a single year.

However, several factors suggest trillionaires might never materialize:

Political limits will emerge. As wealth concentration increases, political pressure for redistribution through taxation, regulation, or even wealth caps grows. Already, wealth taxes, billionaire minimum taxes, and increased capital gains taxes are being seriously proposed in multiple countries. Before anyone reaches a trillion dollars, political systems might impose limits.

Market corrections are inevitable. Much billionaire wealth exists as stock in publicly traded companies, which means it's subject to market volatility. Musk's $200 billion wealth decline demonstrated how quickly paper fortunes can evaporate. A sustained bear market could prevent anyone from reaching a trillion on paper.

Antitrust enforcement may return. The lack of antitrust enforcement over the past decades enabled the extreme concentration we see today. If regulatory attitudes shift and there are signs they're shifting the monopolistic dynamics that create extreme wealth might be curtailed before producing trillionaires.

Technological disruption cuts both ways. The same forces that could create trillionaires, AI, biotech, space could also disrupt existing fortunes. The billionaires of today might see their wealth destroyed by technologies they didn't anticipate, just as the railroad barons were eventually displaced.

Reputational and social limits exist. At some level of wealth, the social backlash becomes untenable. Would society tolerate someone with a trillion dollars while others starve? The anger directed at current billionaires suggests there might be a social maximum that's less about law and more about legitimacy and public tolerance.

The most likely scenario is that we'll see individuals approach a trillion in net worth during market peaks, possibly even briefly cross the threshold on paper, but that sustained trillionaire status will prove elusive due to some combination of market corrections, political intervention, and social pressure.

Wealth Inequality and Social Stability

The trajectory of wealth concentration we've witnessed over the past half-century raises urgent questions about social stability. History suggests that extreme inequality eventually produces either reform or revolution, and we may be approaching a point where one or the other becomes inevitable.

The numbers are stark. In the United States, the wealthiest 1% now control more wealth than the bottom 90% combined. Three individuals, Jeff Bezos, Bill Gates, and Warren Buffett owned more wealth at one point than the bottom 50% of Americans combined. Globally, the 26 richest billionaires owned as much wealth as the poorest 3.8 billion people.

This level of concentration is historically unusual even compared to the Gilded Age. While robber barons like Rockefeller and Carnegie controlled enormous percentages of GDP, the global nature of today's inequality is unprecedented. A French peasant in the 18th century might never encounter the aristocracy. Today's poor can see billionaires on their phones, compare their lives directly, and feel the gap viscerally.

The social consequences are already visible. Populist movements across the political spectrum draw energy from anger at inequality. Trust in institutions has declined. Social mobility has stagnated. The sense that the system is rigged, that billionaires play by different rules has become mainstream rather than fringe.

From a historical perspective, this level of inequality has rarely been stable. The Gilded Age ended with Progressive Era reforms, antitrust enforcement, and eventually income taxation and the New Deal. The inequality of pre-revolutionary France ended with guillotines. The Russian Empire's inequality ended with the Bolshevik Revolution. While modern societies have more robust institutions than 18th-century monarchies, the basic dynamic that extreme inequality eventually produces political instability hasn't changed.

Several scenarios could play out:

Reform from above: Billionaires themselves, recognizing the danger, could support reforms that reduce inequality while preserving capitalism. The Giving Pledge represents one version of this, voluntary wealth redistribution. More aggressive proposals include wealth taxes, higher capital gains taxes, stronger labor protections, and reforms to make wealth creation more broadly shared. This scenario requires billionaires to act against their short-term interests for long-term stability.

Political revolution: Democratic processes could produce governments committed to dramatic wealth redistribution. This could involve confiscatory taxes, nationalization of key industries, or even wealth caps. This scenario is more likely if inequality continues to increase while living standards for ordinary people stagnate or decline.

Technological disruption: New technologies could dramatically increase productivity and reduce scarcity to the point where inequality matters less. If AI and automation produce such abundance that even the poorest live very comfortable lives, billionaire wealth might become politically tolerable. This is the optimistic techno-utopian scenario, but it requires both technological breakthroughs and political choices to distribute benefits broadly.

Continued concentration with control: Billionaires could use their wealth to shape political systems, media, and technology in ways that preserve their position despite public opposition. This dystopian scenario leads to a kind of neo-feudalism where a wealthy elite controls increasingly sophisticated tools of surveillance, persuasion, and control.

Collapse and chaos: If inequality becomes extreme enough without either reform or effective control, the result could be social breakdown, violence, and chaos. History shows this is a real possibility when institutions fail and desperation becomes widespread.

The most likely outcome is probably some combination of these scenarios, partial reforms, continued concentration in some areas, disruption in others, with different countries taking different paths. But the fundamental tension between extreme wealth concentration and social stability seems likely to define much of the 21st century.

Effective Altruism Versus Structural Change

The rise of effective altruism as a philosophy among tech billionaires has created a curious paradox. Many of the wealthiest people in the world are committed to doing good with their fortunes but they want to do so without changing the systems that allowed them to accumulate those fortunes in the first place.

The effective altruist approach, as exemplified by the Giving Pledge and foundations like those run by Gates and Zuckerberg, treats inequality as a problem to be solved through charity rather than through structural reform. Billionaires will earn vast fortunes, then give them away to worthy causes. The system that creates billionaires remains intact; only the distribution of their wealth changes.

Critics argue this approach is fundamentally inadequate. They point out that billionaire philanthropy is undemocratic, why should Bill Gates decide global health priorities rather than elected governments? That it's inefficient, billions spent on charity could be more effective as public investment with democratic oversight. And that it treats symptoms rather than causes, fighting malaria is good, but perhaps we should address the economic systems that keep billions in poverty while creating billionaires.

The alternative is structural reform: progressive taxation that prevents extreme wealth accumulation in the first place, stronger labor protections that ensure workers share more in productivity gains, antitrust enforcement that prevents monopolistic concentration, public investment in health and education rather than relying on philanthropy.

From this perspective, every dollar a billionaire gives away is a dollar that should have been taxed and spent democratically. The existence of billionaire philanthropists is evidence of system failure, not system success. As Anand Giridharadas argues in "Winners Take All," elite philanthropy can actually preserve the inequality that created it by making that inequality seem benevolent.

The tension between these approaches, charitable altruism versus structural reform will likely define debates about wealth and inequality for decades. Billionaires generally prefer the former, which preserves their wealth and autonomy while allowing them to feel virtuous. Democratic movements increasingly demand the latter, which would limit billionaire wealth creation but potentially distribute prosperity more broadly.

The question is whether philanthropy can scale fast enough and effectively enough to address global problems while maintaining popular legitimacy. If billionaire giving successfully tackles major challenges like disease, poverty, and climate change, the case for structural reform weakens. If it proves insufficient or undemocratic, pressure for systemic change will grow.

Sam Bankman-Fried's collapse illustrated the dangers of the effective altruist approach. He claimed to be earning to give, accumulating wealth to do maximum good. Instead, he committed fraud and destroyed billions in value. His downfall suggested that "ends justify means" reasoning, accumulate wealth however necessary, then use it for good can lead to moral catastrophe. Perhaps the means matter more than the ends, and how wealth is created cannot be separated from how it's used.

The Next Frontiers: Space, AI, Life Extension, and Climate

If history teaches us anything, it's that the next generation of billionaires will come from industries that don't yet dominate the economy. Just as the richest people of 1990 couldn't have predicted that search engines and social networks would create the richest people of 2020, we likely can't predict exactly where the next fortunes will come from. But several emerging frontiers seem particularly likely to produce billionaires:

Artificial Intelligence presents perhaps the largest wealth-creation opportunity in history. If AI truly transforms every industry as predicted, the companies and individuals who control foundational AI models could wield unprecedented power and wealth. Sam Altman at OpenAI, Demis Hassabis at DeepMind, and founders of AI startups could become household names or they could be displaced by larger companies like Microsoft, Google, and Amazon that have the resources to dominate AI through sheer scale.

The concentration dynamics in AI look troubling from a competition perspective. Training advanced AI models requires enormous computational resources that only a few companies can afford. The data needed to train models comes from platforms with billions of users, again only a few companies. If AI follows the pattern of previous platform technologies, we might see even more extreme concentration than in previous tech waves.

Space commercialization is creating new categories of billionaire. Elon Musk, Jeff Bezos, and Richard Branson have all invested heavily in space ventures. The potential markets, satellite internet, space tourism, asteroid mining, Mars colonization are vast enough that success could create trillionaires rather than mere billionaires. The question is whether these markets materialize quickly enough and whether first movers can defend their positions.

Space also represents a new frontier for inequality. If space resources become economically viable, who owns them? If Mars is colonized, what political and economic systems govern it? The billionaires investing in space today could be creating new realms where they and their descendants have foundational advantages, extending wealth concentration across planets.

Life extension and biotech could create health-span billionaires. If someone genuinely solves aging or develops cures for major diseases, the market is enormous. Every human wants to live longer and healthier. A company that dramatically extends healthy lifespan could be the most valuable company in history, and its founders would be proportionally wealthy.

The ethical implications are troubling. If life extension is expensive, we could see a future where the rich live decades or centuries longer than the poor, creating not just wealth inequality but longevity inequality. The poor might age and die while billionaires rejuvenate indefinitely. Few scenarios would be more socially destabilizing.

Climate technology presents both opportunities and moral complexities. The transition to renewable energy, carbon capture, sustainable agriculture, and climate adaptation will require trillions in investment. Entrepreneurs who successfully scale climate solutions could become very wealthy. But there's something uncomfortable about individuals getting rich from solving a crisis that their class partially created through fossil fuel investments and high-consumption lifestyles.

That said, if the only way to mobilize sufficient capital for climate solutions is through profit motives and wealth creation, perhaps climate billionaires are acceptable, even necessary. The question is whether we can design systems that solve climate change while distributing benefits broadly rather than concentrating them in a few hands.

Synthetic biology and genetic engineering could create billionaires through applications ranging from medicine to agriculture to materials science. The ability to engineer organisms or grow products in labs rather than farms could transform multiple industries. As with other technologies, the question is whether these advances reduce scarcity and improve lives broadly or whether they create new concentrations of power and wealth.

The pattern across these frontiers is consistent: technologies that create platform effects, that benefit from scale, that have winner-take-all dynamics, will likely produce billionaires. Technologies that are easily replicable, that operate in competitive markets, that distribute value broadly, will produce successful businesses but fewer extreme fortunes.

Should Billionaires Exist? The Political Debate

This question, once confined to leftist political circles, has entered mainstream discourse. Politicians from Bernie Sanders to Elizabeth Warren have questioned whether a society should permit individuals to accumulate billions while others lack basic necessities. The debate reveals fundamental disagreements about capitalism, property rights, and social organization.

Arguments against allowing billionaires:

Moral argument: No individual's contribution to society is worth thousands of times more than others'. The difference between a brilliant CEO and an average one might be significant, but not billions-of-dollars significant. Much billionaire wealth comes from market positions, timing, and network effects rather than proportional value creation.

Democratic argument: Extreme wealth translates to extreme political power. Billionaires can fund campaigns, lobby legislators, own media companies, and shape public opinion in ways that undermine democracy. One person, one vote becomes meaningless when some people can spend billions influencing elections.

Economic efficiency argument: Concentrated wealth sits idle or gets invested in financial assets rather than productive economic activity. Money in the hands of ordinary people gets spent on goods and services, driving economic growth. Billionaire wealth often sits in stocks, art, real estate, and other assets that don't drive economic activity.

Social stability argument: Extreme inequality breeds resentment, social division, and eventually instability. Societies function better when wealth is broadly distributed and people feel the system is fair. Billionaires create a sense that the game is rigged, undermining social cohesion.

Arguments for allowing billionaires:

Innovation argument: The possibility of extreme wealth motivates risk-taking and innovation. Would Elon Musk have poured his fortune into Tesla and SpaceX if he knew he'd be capped at $10 million? Would entrepreneurs take huge risks if the upside were limited? Extreme rewards motivate extreme effort.

Property rights argument: People have a right to the value they create. If Jeff Bezos built Amazon, why shouldn't he own the resulting wealth? Confiscating legally earned wealth, even through taxation, is a form of theft that undermines property rights and rule of law.

Practical argument: Wealth taxes and caps are difficult to implement and enforce. Billionaires will find ways around them through legal structures, offshore accounts, and creative accounting. The administrative costs and evasion might make such policies ineffective.

Philanthropy argument: Billionaires give away enormous sums to worthy causes. Government spending is inefficient and politically constrained; billionaire philanthropy can take risks and innovate in ways the government cannot. The Gates Foundation has saved millions of lives. Would that money have been better spent as tax revenue?

The debate ultimately reflects different values and empirical beliefs. Those who prioritize equality, democratic participation, and social solidarity tend to oppose billionaires. Those who prioritize innovation, property rights, and market efficiency tend to defend them.

Interestingly, the debate might become moot through technological or social change rather than policy. If AI and automation create such abundance that scarcity essentially ends, inequality might matter less. If social norms shift strongly against extreme wealth, billionaires might voluntarily give away their fortunes to maintain legitimacy. If economic growth slows globally, wealth concentration might naturally decline as new fortunes become harder to build.

A Future Without Billionaires? Alternative Scenarios

Imagining a future without billionaires requires imagining significant changes to current economic systems:

Social democratic model: High progressive taxation, strong labor protections, robust social welfare, and limits on wealth accumulation could keep the richest individuals at hundreds of millions rather than billions. Scandinavian countries approximate this model, though even there, some billionaires exist. Expanding this globally would require international coordination to prevent capital flight and tax evasion.

Stakeholder capitalism: Requiring companies to share ownership with workers, communities, and other stakeholders could distribute wealth more broadly. If Amazon employees owned significant equity from the beginning, Bezos would be wealthy but not $150-billion wealthy. Germany's co-determination model, where workers sit on corporate boards, points in this direction.

Technological abundance: If AI and automation dramatically reduce the cost of producing goods and services, scarcity might diminish to the point where wealth concentration matters less. Universal basic income, funded by taxes on automation and AI, could ensure everyone has comfortable lives even while some remain much wealthier. This is speculative but not impossible.

New economic paradigms: Concepts like degrowth, circular economies, and post-capitalist organization could produce systems that don't generate billionaires. These ideas remain marginal but climate change and resource constraints might make them more relevant. A steady-state economy focused on sustainability rather than growth would likely have less extreme wealth concentration.

Catastrophic collapse: Major crises, climate catastrophe, nuclear war, pandemic worse than COVID-19 could destroy enough wealth and disrupt systems enough that billionaires cease to exist, at least temporarily. This scenario is possible but obviously undesirable as a path to equality.

The most realistic future probably involves continued existence of billionaires but with changing constraints, norms, and distributions. Some countries might limit billionaire wealth while others allow it. Some industries might be regulated to prevent extreme concentration while others remain winner-take-all. Public opinion and political movements will create pressure for changes that modify but don't eliminate the dynamics that create extreme wealth.

Conclusion: The Unfinished Story

The story of billionaires is far from over. We're living through a period of unprecedented wealth creation and concentration, but we're also at a potential turning point where political, social, and technological forces could fundamentally reshape who becomes wealthy and how much wealth they can accumulate.

The billionaires of 2050 might look very different from those of 2025. They might work in industries that barely exist today. They might face regulations and tax rates that would seem inconceivable now. They might operate in a world of abundance created by AI and automation, or a world of scarcity created by climate change and resource depletion.

What seems certain is that the forces creating billionaires, technological innovation, market concentration, globalization and compound returns will continue to operate unless consciously constrained by policy or disrupted by unforeseen events. The question isn't whether great fortunes will be built, but whether societies will tolerate the level of concentration we've seen in recent decades or whether they'll impose limits.

The billionaires themselves will play a role in determining this outcome. Those who use their wealth thoughtfully, who support reforms that reduce inequality, who maintain connection to ordinary human concerns, might help preserve a system that allows for wealth creation. Those who flaunt their wealth, resist all redistribution, and use their resources to entrench their advantages might provoke the backlash that destroys the system that enriched them.

History suggests that extreme concentration rarely persists indefinitely. Either reform or revolution eventually redistributes wealth. But history also suggests that wealth creation continues across political systems and economic models, just with different people winning and different rules governing the game.

The future of billionaires is ultimately the future of capitalism itself, can it evolve to distribute prosperity more broadly while maintaining the innovation and dynamism that create wealth? Or will the contradictions between wealth concentration and social stability eventually force more fundamental changes?

We're watching this story unfold in real time, and unlike the historical billionaires we've examined, we don't yet know how it ends. What we do know is that the choices made in the coming decades about technology, taxation, regulation, and social organization will determine not just who becomes wealthy but what kind of society we become. The age of billionaires might be just beginning or it might be approaching its end. Only time will tell.